Ethnologia Europaea

Journal of European Ethnology

Volume 44:2
2014

Special issue editor: Marie Sandberg

MUSEUM TUSCULANUM PRESS · UNIVERSITY OF COPENHAGEN

Copyright © 2014 Ethnologia Europaea, Copenhagen
Printed in Sweden by Exakta, Malmö 2014
Cover and layout Pernille Sys Hansen
Cover photo A fieldworker joyfully jumping out of a window.
From the Sigurd Erixon collection at the Library of Linköping, undated.
ISBN 978 87 635 4263 0
ISSN 0425 4597

This journal is published with the support of the Nordic board for periodicals in the humanities and social sciences. This special issue has generously been supported by the Einar Hansen Foundation.

Museum Tusculanum Press
University of Copenhagen
Birketinget 6
DK-2300 Copenhagen S
Denmark
www.mtp.dk

CONTENTS

Marie Sandberg
Ethnologia Europaea Revisited: Launching Future Ethnologies. An Introduction   5

Tine Damsholt and Astrid Pernille Jespersen
Innovation, Resistance or Tinkering. Rearticulating Everyday Life in an Ethnological Perspective   17

Anders Kristian Munk and Torben Elgaard Jensen
Revisiting the Histories of Mapping. Is there a Future for a Cartographic Ethnology?   31

Frida Hastrup
Analogue Analysis. Ethnography as Inventive Conversation   48

Karin Gustavsson
Returning to the Archive in Search of Everyday Practices in Fieldwork   61

Fredrik Nilsson
Border Practices and Speed. Cultural Perspectives on Borders and Smuggling   76

Signe Mellemgaard
Rupture and Continuity. Reflections on the Relationship between Synchrony and Diachrony in Ethnology, in Memoriam Bjarne Stoklund   94

Comments   111

Valdimar Tr. Hafstein
Haunted Places   113

Orvar Löfgren
At the Ethnologists' Ball. Changing an Academic Habitus   116

Katharina Eisch-Angus
Fluid Classics. Ethnographic Challenges in Everyday Fields   123

Regina F. Bendix
Experiments in a Time of Overabundant Disciplinary History   130

ETHNOLOGIA EUROPAEA REVISITED: LAUNCHING FUTURE ETHNOLOGIES
An Introduction

Marie Sandberg

Arrival
Ethnographic accounts often include an arrival story, which is intended to set the scene and launch some of the main points of the analysis to come. Most importantly, it situates the researcher and builds the reader's trust in the recorded observations. As the newly-assigned editor of *Ethnologia Europaea*, I allow myself to use this age-old device, and tell the story of how I entered this lively journal of the European ethnological scholarly field. In doing so, I intend to signal the core themes and issues raised within this volume.

One of my first undertakings as soon-to-be editor was to set up an interview with the now late Professor Emeritus and editor of *Ethnologia Europaea* in 1984–2004, Bjarne Stoklund. The interview was held on a December afternoon in my office at the University of Copenhagen and, as it happens, only few months before Stoklund passed away in May 2013.

I was keen on knowing more about Stoklund's thoughts on the European dimension of the journal, and how he had experienced his twenty years as the journal editor. And, of course, I wanted to learn some tips and tricks of the trade. Our conversation addressed these themes and many more, and was accompanied by the tea and pastries I had brought to our meeting. I heard many interesting stories that afternoon and I paid particular attention to the fact that the word "persuasion" was used both in the case of Stoklund's stepping in as editor after Günther Wiegelmann in 1984, and later, when referring to Orvar Löfgren taking over the editorship in 2004.[1] I pondered whether the role of journal editor was ever accepted voluntarily.

Together we looked at one of the first calls for papers Stoklund had launched as the editor, a flyer from 1984, which included the following passage: "The new editor [i.e. Stoklund] (…) shall direct his efforts towards the creation of a journal of interest not only to European ethnologists but also to anthropologists, social historians and others studying the social and cultural forms of everyday life in recent and historical European societies." On the back of the flyer, Stoklund had listed the core research themes to be covered by the journal, on which he commented: "They [the research themes] are of course totally outdated by now and have long since been revised" (Interview 2012, translated from Danish by the author). The list was as follows: "[T]owards a history of everyday life: trends, methods and sources; aspects of 'the civilizing process'; social structures and cultural diversity; material culture; migrants and minorities; ethnicities and identities." Whereas my immediate response was to ask whether this list of themes really was all that outdated, Stoklund continued: "It's funny to see, when you get so old, how phenomena turn into something completely different when they reappear. That's how it goes" (ibid.).

That's how it goes. This last part of our conversation was the inspiration for the theme of this special issue of *Ethnologia Europaea*, in which the authors revisit concepts and approaches, which have long since been discarded or deemed completely outdated by our scholarly discipline. The question is: How *does* it go? Ethnologists tend to claim that the past is in the present, but how does this play out in our own research practices? Which patterns of continuity appear, and where can we identify instances of rupture?

The act of "revisiting" is the *leitmotif* of this volume, and this alludes to several different actions: to visit again, return, reexamine, revise, recycle, or even retire. To be sure, such visits can take many shapes and forms: they may counter-balance recent aspirations or provide inspiration; they may be a learning experience; or they may highlight or even discard previously-used approaches and concepts. A revisit can be a courtesy call from which one wishes to depart again as soon as possible. And past concepts can strike back and even haunt us, like "zombie-concepts" that refuse to remain buried.[2] At least two different yet related strategies seem feasible when undertaking this kind of endeavour: we can deliberately go backwards in time and pay past concepts and approaches a visit in order to examine how they may be reread and reappear again in new guises and types of dialogues, or the investigation can be prompted by challenges in our present work and research endeavours, which require us – whether we like it or not – to dive into the pool of knowledge and experience of our ethnological forebears.

This special issue is the result of a workshop series held at Lund University and the University of Copenhagen in 2013–2014. Swedish and Danish scholars of ethnology were invited to reflect upon and present innovative ways of rethinking past concepts, approaches, contributions or discussions within the scholarly field. The context for this special issue is therefore Scandinavian ethnology with particular emphasis on the Swedish and Danish ethnology developed within the Lund and Copenhagen milieus respectively. Furthermore, a range of commentators were invited to read about the revisits and contribute their own rethinking of them to this issue. We set out to explore different modes of revisiting European ethnology, as both reflected in the journal of *Ethnologia Europaea* and in the broader sense of the previous knowledge claims and research practices of our field.

Four Themes

Depicting the history and the current state of Swedish ethnology, Orvar Löfgren has suggested four lineages between the folklife researchers around the turn of the twentieth century and present-day ethnologists: a keen interest in the mundane activities of everyday life; doing fieldwork; the combination of historical and contemporary analysis; and the use of mobile research methods (Löfgren 2008). Whereas the first line of continuity relates to the ardent interest of folklife researchers and ethnologists alike in illuminating the importance of the otherwise overlooked and seemingly insignificant trivialities of our mundane activities and routines, the second points to the ever-present "fieldwork mentality" of ethnology and related disciplines. The third line of continuity stresses historical comparison and contrasting as ways to show that the present could have been organised differently. With the fourth lineage, Löfgren highlights the virtue of flexibility with regards to the researcher's choice of approach – when ethnologists use the "mobile search light method", they are not only mobile when it comes to conducting the fieldwork but also in terms of choosing analytical concepts and perspectives for further scrutiny.

Löfgren's list forms the perfect backdrop for the four main, interconnected themes in this special issue, which I designate: *reworking everyday life, fieldwork as craftsmanship, mapping connections* and *conversing with the past*. Our act of revisiting exposes solid patterns of continuity. However, readers of this volume might also find themselves straying from the customary path. Along with in-depth interrogations of the four themes, the contributions touch upon experiments and engagements with the past such as:

- a reintroduction of the diffusionist concept of "cultural elements" (Munk & Elgaard Jensen)
- a reawakening of long forgotten archives and how they can be reread by paying attention to the material-technological aspects of knowledge production (Gustavsson)

- a reinvention of fieldwork as conversation, and an answer to why ethnologists should start counting more (Hastrup)
- a relaunching of Braudel's *longue durée* as a marker of the inertness of everyday life cultures (Damsholt & Jespersen)
- a rereasoning for the importance of ecotypes (Mellemgaard)
- a rethinking of borders through the notion of speed (Nilsson).

Revisiting European Ethnology does not aim to create a representative history of the discipline. Rather, it offers selective approaches to rearticulating the ethnological scholarly field. The volume presents a handful of innovative contributions that twist and turn through well-known terrain by engaging with the past and with a thrust towards the future. In this sense, all the papers take part in creating a "history of the present", which takes a critical look at current strands and approaches and thereby suggests future contours for ethnological endeavours.

Importantly, this special issue aims to open up the "bonnet of the car", explicating dimensions of research that often remain tacit knowledge: how are inspirational sources activated, how do we work as ethnologists, and, not least, how do we learn from others before us? In other words, this volume presents the everyday life of research. The front cover encapsulates one such moment: it depicts a young man joyfully jumping out of the window of a peasant house. The man is an (unknown) student of folklife researcher Sigurd Erixon (1888–1968), who was collecting information on the vanishing peasant culture in the Swedish countryside in the early twentieth century (see Gustavsson's contribution). This is a "backstage" picture, which was probably shot at the end of a hard day's fieldwork – taking notes, photo documentation and drawing up sketches, all while carrying heavy photo gear. However, as Gustavsson shows in her paper, the laughter, jokes and feeling of being a part of a collective project are just as important dimensions of the research process as the actual research result in itself. Thus, we invite you to join the revisiting of European ethnology, and to engage with discussions and reflections which might not usually be in the foreground, but which are nonetheless intrinsic aspects of ethnological research practices.

This introduction is a tour around the four main themes and a contextualisation of the papers' chosen strategies for revisiting European ethnology.

Reworking Everyday Life

In the essay "On the Concept of Everyday Life" (1978), Norbert Elias stresses the salient elusiveness of this very concept.[3] Critically, Elias ponders why it appears to be so difficult for researchers of everyday life – especially etnomethodologists and phenomenologically inspired sociologists – to define this "anything but homogeneous concept" ([1978]1998: 167). The problem arises when it comes to defining the oppositional concept of "the everyday life" in terms of what it comprises, rather than what it is *not*. Elias points to the "almost complete absence of attempts to discern the unity underlying the multiplicity of shades of meaning in the contemporary use of the concept of the everyday" (ibid.: 170). In order to clarify this lack of consistency, Elias provides a selected overview of the concept's various meanings in which he includes the implied antitheses: everyday versus holiday, routine versus the extraordinary, the life of the masses versus the life of the privileged and powerful, to name a few. Despite his efforts, it remained unclear to Elias whether the everyday life is a particular sphere or region of human societies which is easy to distinguish from the "non-everyday".

Everyday life can rightly be characterised as an a priori object for European ethnologists. However, ethnologists may also find themselves estranged from Elias' definition exercise. Rather than attempting to establish a more precise concept of everyday life (what it is/what it is not), ethnologists tend to be interested in finding out what it *does*; how is everyday life practised in different yet related ways, and how can one study it? Everyday life is a highly dynamic term, which is continuously reconstructed and co-constituted, also by ethnological engagements in everyday worlds. It is in this engagement that a reworking of the concept of everyday life can take place.

One such conceptual reworking of everyday life practices unfolds in the contribution by Tine Damsholt and Astrid Pernille Jespersen (this volume). As a possible answer to Elias' question of whether everyday life has the quality of being a delimited sphere distinguishable from "non-everyday life", Damsholt and Jespersen assert that everyday life as an ethnological object of study has always been shaped within governmental practices; from the pastoral power of the late eighteenth century to the current versions of biopolitics of the twenty-first century. Following a Foucauldian genealogy, the authors are not in search of the "Ursprung" (origin) but rather the "Herkunft" (descent) of a careful selection of classic figures, which have been formative for their ethnological understanding of everyday life practices such as the ideology of "the good life" and the idea of *la longue durée* as an intrinsic element of cultural change.

When Elias published his essay in the 1970s, sociologists, European ethnologists, folklorists and scholars of history, cultural studies and cultural anthropology all over Europe were beginning to make everyday life cultures their pivotal object of study (Tschofen 2013). The same can be said of Scandinavian ethnology. During the late 1960s and throughout the 70s, everyday societies gained prominence as a research object, rather than folk culture. Ethnologists became "experts on everyday life" (Löfgren 2008: 125). Daily life, routines, habits and traditions came into focus, due to influences from British social anthropology and American qualitative sociology (Löfgren 1997). There was also an increased interest in everyday life as an arena for resistance. In Sweden, this mode of research was particularly prevalent within the study of everyday consumption in the 1980s, which stressed the creativity and counterstrategies of the "little" (wo)man in a world of mass consumption and globalisation (ibid.). Only a stone's throw away from each other, the ethnology departments in Lund and Copenhagen each developed rather different kinds of approaches to theory and analytical work. Whereas researchers at the former carried out cultural analyses in an analytical bricolage taking inspiration from theoretical strands such as phenomenology and micro-sociology, the Copenhagen milieu, in particular the structural lifemode analysis, was based on structural linguistics (such as Louis Hjelmslev) and conceptual logics, and was engaged in cumulative theory building (Højrup 1983, 1989, 2006).

Versions of Everyday Life: The Good, the Bad… and the Ugly

Within broader everyday life scholarship, some characteristic distinctions can be made: On the one hand, there is phenomenological inspiration from various micro-sociological strands such as Husserl, Simmel, Goffman, Schütz and others. On the other hand, there are the more critically-oriented Marxist inspired studies of everyday life culture, in which Lefebvre and to some extent also Habermas played a role. Reading through these traditions, Mike Michael (2006) differs between *the good* and *the bad* versions of everyday life: the approaches that underline the promise of everyday life as a site for resistance, critique and ultimately change, and those that warn that everyday life might stagnate in false ideology as a site of repetition, discipline or alienation.

Michael's versions of the everyday contribute to a timely discussion on the study of everyday practices. In recent years, we have witnessed an increasing demand for ethnographic depictions of mundane activities and routines, requested by private businesses, organisations and industry (Jespersen et al. 2012). If not handled with care, this recent popularity could easily turn into what could be called *the ugly* version of everyday life conceptualisations: the uncritical, consumer-oriented version, which uncovers users' needs under the auspices of neoliberal "soft capitalism" (Thrift 1997). Within soft capitalism logics, everyday life – including its most intimate private spheres – becomes the number one zone for improvement through which populations may be encouraged into healthy aging and lifestyles, better parenthood or further education, or even to reduce climate change. At the same time, everyday life is posited as site for innovative thinking where mundane solutions and the practical uses of things and technologies become the key to new and creative solutions, which are then exported into user-driven design schemes (Petersen & Munk 2013; Elgaard Jensen 2012).

Indeed, it is soft capitalism's growing demand for user-driven innovation insights into our mundane activities that prompts Damsholt and Jespersen to question and examine how we conceptualise notions of everyday life. Damsholt and Jespersen's revisit is of a triggered kind, prompted by the challenging and provocative claims they encountered in a collaborative project involving user-driven innovation and everyday life, in which the other participants highlighted everyday life as a problem and a barrier to change. The authors were continuously expected to think "out of the box" and sketch future "mega trend scenarios" based on of a notion of instant change. However, in this contribution, Damsholt and Jespersen choose to do quite the opposite. Emphasising performative approaches to everyday life, they illustrate how cultural change often takes place imperceptibly, through the repetitive tinkering and mending of everyday routines (cf. Ehn & Löfgren 2010). The genealogy they present of how ethnologists have conceptualised the everyday as a realm of inertness certainly destabilises the figuration of the innovative, flexible user that tends to be inherently inscribed into user-driven innovation projects.

Damsholt and Jespersen's study also contributes to an exploration of both differences and similarities in the ways in which the Lund and Copenhagen milieus study everyday life cultures: Both sides of the Sound have worked with everyday life in its "good" as well as its "bad" versions, but it is perhaps indicative of yet another "inert structure" that both milieus have retained a keen interest in the structuring of everyday life and its possible conditions of existence, including its material implications, despite the differences in their theoretical-analytical *modus operandi*.

Ethnographic Craftsmanship

In the *Ethnologia Europaea* special issue *Irregular Ethnographies*, Tom O'Dell and Robert Willim (2011) ponder why they cannot clearly recall attending classes on fieldwork methods as part of their own education. Rather than being a mystery, this previous lack of visible methods training illustrates that in our educational programmes, we see a shift from apprenticeship to more explicit teaching of methods. In recent years, ethnology has witnessed increased market demands; not only for everyday life accounts but also for ethnographic skills. Fieldwork methods have become a commodity in their own right. At the same time, methodology classes and ethnographic workshops are generously sprinkled throughout all sorts of educational programmes with the prefix culture-, anthro-, or ethno- in their titles, whereas previously, the teaching of methods was "learning by doing" without any explicitly stated "learning outcomes".

Karin Gustavsson examines material that documents peasant life and material culture in the Swedish countryside in the 1920s, collected through an initiative by *Nordiska museet* (the Nordic Museum) and maintained for several decades in their folk archives. By revisiting the everyday lives of the student fieldworkers and researchers, Gustavsson vividly shows the meticulous practices and routines of the people involved in Sigurd Erixon's great atlas collective. This is a profound example of an ethnographic apprenticeship in its early days.

Gustavsson's piece is akin to Bruno Latour's study of the researchers in the *Boa Vista* forest, in which he closely follows the researchers' practices, from the sampling of data to detailed examinations in the laboratory (Latour 1999). Gustavsson traces how the collection practices of the students were converted into scientific knowledge claims while their voluminous cameras were carefully strapped to the back of their bicycles – and while they were still wearing their students' caps! Gustavsson's revisit takes us into the everyday practices of research and shows us how these practices are part of a material set-up, as they also were for our colleagues in the past.

Frida Hastrup extends the notion of fieldwork from collecting data, which then will be represented in novel ways, to a generative conversational endeavour closely aligned with analysis and theory work. In this sense, reading our classics is also a part of ethnological fieldwork practices. Thus, Hastrup offers an alternative to methodology as a commodity that is easy to pick and choose. Proposing the notion of "analogue analysis", Hastrup enters into dialogue with the early writings of the Norwegian folklife researcher Eilert Sundt (1817–1875). What Hastrup finds particularly appealing about Sundt's work is his invitation for readers, interlocutors and other laymen to contribute to a collective knowledge production about peasant house building customs and house crafts.

Hastrup combines Sundt's writings into a montage with her own fieldwork insights from south India, which were generated through several years of engagement with people living in Tharangambadi in the coastal region of the Tamil Nadu state. Here, we are introduced to the counting practices of a Tamil woman, Renuga, who works part time to implement a governmental nutrition programme for school children. Renuga has to make precise calculations, not only at work while calculating nutrition per pupil but also in order to secure her own daughters' marital and educational futures: how much it will cost in gold to pay for their unfair but expected dowry, and how well they can succeed in creating alternative biographical paths via educational scholarships.

Transcending the insights gained in different places and across time, this montage is held together by a shared concern with world-making; Renuga strives for a better future for her daughters, and Sundt aims to improve housing conditions for Norwegians. Thus, according to Hastrup's analogue analysis, ethnological craftsmanship is not intended only for a limited number of individuals within a given scholarly field; rather, it encompasses the endeavour of generating common worlds. Ethnographic work is about trying out different ways of thinking and writing about the world – for both the fieldworker and the interlocutor. In this contribution, the counting practices are not only the object for Hastrup's field research, but also becomes part of her own analytical strategy and understanding of Renuga's world and beyond.

Hastrup's revisit shows that ethnographic apprenticeship is neither the exclusive domain of folklife students around the turn of the twentieth century, nor is it confined to the educational programmes of our more recent past. Rather, crafting ethnographic accounts is part of a shared endeavour within a field of interrelation.

Mapping Connections

Since the spatial turn of the 1990s, a tsunami of approaches to space, place and locality has hit scholarly disciplines ranging from human geography and sociology to anthropology and ethnology (for an overview see Massey 2005). The spatial turn embraces the idea that various places and locations only gain meaning via the way they are inhabited and generated through practices. In these practice-oriented approaches to space, there is a keen interest in cartography and mapping. For scholars of folklore and ethnology, this should ring a bell. Around one hundred years ago, in the decades after the turn of the twentieth century, the historic-geographic method, also known as diffusionism or "the carthographic method", was the order of the day among folklife researchers. The objective was to map the diffusion of cultural elements and to illustrate the regional distribution of material culture. As one of the most prominent examples of a transnational, pan-European research project, this endeavour must be admired. Stoklund (2003) has characterised the diffusionist era as the only point in the history of our discipline that could come close to being classified as a normal scientific paradigm (see Mellemgaard; Munk & Elgaard Jensen, this issue). However, rather than creating synthesis, the historic-geographic project is infamous for resulting in detailed data piling and heavily loaded archives (Löfgren 1997; Højrup 2002).

In recent years, the use of the cartographic methods has received new attention in ethnology. Novel methods involving digitisation and user-friendly software might make it easier to process data and develop maps, which may well be relevant in handling big sets of data (see Tangherlini 2010). This volume introduces another revamping of the ethno-cartographic method. Anders Kristian Munk and Torben Elgaard Jensen take the current turn to cartography within science and technology studies (STS) as their point of departure, specifically a Latourian project concerned with public knowledge controversies, also known as controversy mapping. This is an approach that basically studies techno-scientific disputes by charting traces left by actors online. The authors compare controversy mapping with the atlas works of the early and mid-twentieth century in order to explore the kinds of realities enacted and to discuss the implications of the different mapping techniques, both in terms of the restrictions and the demands that are implied when the cartographic method is employed, and in terms of prospective results.

The European Atlases

Although a normal scientific paradigm may appear to be an unquestionable rule or structure in the eyes of its adherents, it is shaped by a considerable amount of actors, means and materialities. Therefore, in the following, I present a glimpse of the diverse set of contributors, conferences, journals and collaborations which all took part in the historic-cartographic project, and which extended far beyond the Scandinavian borders. From 1928 onwards, the organisation Commission Internationale des Arts et Traditions Populaires (CIAP) was a global network of national commissions for conducting research of folk culture under the auspices of the League of Nations. In 1964, and due to a long process of changes in its relationship with the League of Nations, CIAP was transformed into SIEF (Société Internationale d'Ethnologie et de Folklore), which is the present international organisation for European ethnologists. This transformation took place at a conference in Athens, which became notorious not least because Sigurd Erixon chose to leave the SIEF organisation, presumably because he felt it was becoming too folklore oriented (Rogan 2008).

After Erixon's exit, a cartography commission was placed outside of any formal European associations and several conferences and series of ethnological handbooks were initiated.[4] In 1967, Erixon and the three European colleagues Branimir Bratanić (Zagreb), Jorge Dias (Lisbon) and Géza de Rohan-Csermak (Paris) launched the first issue of the scientific journal with the Latin name *Ethnologia Europaea*[5], with Rohan-Csermak as its first editor and, at that time, with the bi-lingual subtitle: *Revue internationale d'ethnologie européenne/A World Review of European Ethnology*. With *Current Anthropology* as a role model, *Ethnologia Europaea* soon became an important scientific journal within the European community, and also amassed a significant readership among American folklorists and cultural anthropologists/"culturologists" (Bringéus 1983). The historic-geographic method of cartography had also been a widely-applied approach among European folklorists, primarily led by the Finnish School, which had been represented by Antti Aarne and Julius and Kaarle Krohn since the late nineteenth century (Tangherlini 2010). Whereas the "Finnish method" mainly focused on mapping folktales, the historic-cartographic paradigm of ethnology focused on material culture.

This atlas work can be viewed as an exemplary European project, which had the potential to bind together the separate national ethnographies (interview with Stoklund 2012). However, several problems accompanied this potential. As early as 1920, one of the stated goals at the first Nordic meeting for folklife researchers in Stockholm was to establish a Nordic atlas, with Erixon and Åke Campbell (1891–1957) – who later became Professor in Ethnology at Uppsala University – as prime movers. On the Danish side, the director of the Danish Folk Museum (later the National Museum of Denmark), Jørgen Olrik (1875–1941), was a partner (Vasström 2013). The making of a European atlas was also a goal, and there was a strong interest in this from the German partners, who provided abundant financial support. During the 1930s, this Scandinavian-German project became more and more dubious. It became increasingly obvious that the results were intended to generate a scientific basis for an expansion and consolidation of the German "Raum" as a shared cultural-political sphere. During the early 1940s, the Scandinavian partners withdrew from the cooperation, but they did not set aside the ethno-cartographic method entirely (Vasström 2014, in preparation).

As highlighted by Thomas Højrup, one of the often unacknowledged strengths of the atlas work was its pertinent questioning of nation-state borders (Højrup 2002; see also Munk & Elgaard Jensen, this volume). The cultural diffusion of a material cultural element very rarely respected the national borders of say, Denmark and Sweden (Campbell et al. 1957). Instead, focus was on cultural borders or regional differences between eastern and western Denmark, for example, concerning the forms and types of harvesting implements.

Dr. Faustus

In both the Scandinavian and the European perspective, one of the key players associated with cartography is Sigurd Erixon. Indeed, in his aftermath, he appears more as a figure or phenomenon than an individual researcher.[6] Erixon was also (in)famous for his ambitious, almost imperialist ideas about how the international ethnological scholarly society should be organised (Rogan 2008). Adopting a repertoire of terms from American cultural anthropology such as culture areas and relic's areas, the dynamics and stagnation of the diffusion of cultural elements, and acculturation processes, Erixon's vision for ethnology encompassed historical and comparative studies of culture in space, time and social strata (Arntsberg 1989). Diffusionism was his theoretical foundation and cartography his methodology. Setting up a strict methodology for the atlas projects was one expression of the desire to turn ethnology into an exact rather than a speculative science (Löfgren 2008, 1997). Löfgren has therefore designated Erixon the "Dr. Faustus of Ethnology"; the "disciplining force (…) who worked hard to structure the discipline, inventing concepts and definitions, drawing up boundaries, organising archives and conferences, and writing handbooks" (Löfgren 2008: 121). In a manner comparable to the Linnean taxonomical systems, Erixon wanted to name and classify the material peasant culture. Instead of theoretical discussions, the emphasis was placed on collecting and organising empirical data.

In the late 1950s and increasingly throughout the student revolts of the 1960s, the atlas projects stranded like a beached whale. It should perhaps be noted that, in part, this was due to a lack of technological and financial means. The maps were expensive to produce and to publish. However, the perhaps most important reason for this was the confusion regarding whether making cartographies was a means to some other end or a goal in itself. Apart from being illustrative or pedagogical tools, the atlases proved very difficult to use when it came to interpretation and explanation. As described by Arntsberg (1989), when Erixon discussed the further analysis and implications of the maps,[7] he used other kinds of material such as archival material and memoir resources. The atlas endeavour also had an Achilles' heel: the maps provided static, still pictures and failed to grasp the dynamics of culture (Rooijakkers & Meurkens 2000). Only a few years after the publication of the Swedish folk atlas in 1957, Erixon himself claimed – here quoted by Arntsberg from a conference presentation in Denmark 1961 – that the atlases are "actually a pretty unrefined instrument and usually they only provide vague results and a pretty incomplete impression" (Arntsberg 1989: 92, translated from Swedish by the author).

It is truly daring of Munk and Elgaard Jensen to choose to return to the diffusionist paradigm *after* the smoke of the revolution is already long gone. In their search for similarities and grounds for possible dialogues between controversy mapping on the one hand and the atlases of material folk culture on the other hand, the authors find further inspiration along the way and reintroduce the idea of cultural elements, which adds to the experimental character of their endeavour. They base their contribution on a radical empiricism that can be discerned in several science and technology studies (STS) or actor-network theory (ANT) contributions, celebrating ontology over epistemology, observation over speculation, and multiplicity over "perspectivalism". Their relaunching of the idea of cultural elements is thus not to be seen as any functionalist understanding of searching for cohesions of "functional cultural wholes", but in the form of open-ended assemblages. Rather than an expressive notion of culture, the authors suggest culture as ever-changing compositions. "Is there a future for a cartographic ethnology?" Munk and Elgaard Jensen ask. Their bold adventure invites ethnologists to embrace not only controversy mapping but also new-old notions of culture, connections and wholes. So in future ethnologies, we had better mind the map!

The Slowness of Borders

Mapping is intrinsically linked to the drawing of borders and demarcation of territories. Inspired by Paul Virilio, Fredrik Nilsson suggests speed as an analytical approach that can add new dimensions to practice-oriented border studies. Using the liquor smugglers of the 1920s in Sweden as an empirical case, Nilsson draws us into a fantastic universe of smugglers versus customs guards in the Baltic Sea. Due to a lack of technological means and equipment, the customs guards always appeared to be one step behind the border trespassing smugglers, who used motor schooners. The fact that the customs guards' steam-driven tugboat – especially hired for the purpose – was named "Hurtig" (which means 'fast' in Swedish), certainly adds a certain portion of humour and irony to the story (see Nilsson, this volume). Nilsson rightly states that when it comes to borders, "speed produces problems". In the current EU border regime this point can be taken even further; the so-called "fourth freedom of mobility" implies that the free movement of persons (along with capital, services and goods) across borders must not be hindered in any way. This means that if any EU member state suddenly erects devices and border control barriers that impede the free mobility across EU's internal borders, the European Commission is allowed to intervene and is likely to do so. This was the case in 2011, for example, when permanent customs checkpoints were (temporarily, as it turned out) established on Denmark's borders with Germany and Sweden. According to the political parties who backed this arrangement (the government along with the Christian Democrats and the Danish People's Party), the reason for this was the "… increase in cross border crime in Denmark… not least crimes committed by foreign gangs, smuggling of narcotics, weapons, persons and large amounts of money,

as well as avoidance of Danish tax due to the use of foreign labour" (here quoted from Gammeltoft-Hansen & Christiansen 2011, transl. by the author). The Danish case fed into a general fear of "Schengen anarchy" among EU members and, as a result, the European Commission visited and inspected the border crossing point. They queried the barriers, which were eventually removed. However, while the speed of crossing the EU internal borders must not be slowed down, EU citizens travelling inside the EU will have noticed the inertness of border crossings at airport security controls: the long time spent standing still in the passport control queue has been transformed into an experience of being trapped in a tightly-packed dressing room, including feverish and sweat-provoking disrobing, the removal of wrist watches and belts, and the exposure of intimate body parts as well as the emptying of toiletry bags.

Nilsson revisits both ethnological border literature from the end of the twentieth century and the cultural borders of the diffusionist paradigm in early folklife research. Thus, we are presented with the conceptualisation of border across the centuries, as well as the potentials of a dialogue between past and present ethnological material.

Conversing with the Past

During the late 1960s and 1970s when the cartographic school receded, one of the crucial points of discussion that remained was the role of history in ethnology. Was the discipline supposed to move onto a path of regional social-anthropologically inspired ethnologies of contemporary societies, or should it remain a historically-oriented humanistic discipline? In 1969, Åke Daun published *Upp till kamp in Båtskärsnäs* (Taking up the fight in Båtskärsnäs), a fieldwork-based study of workers' protests during the shutdown of a saw-mill in northern Sweden, which was solely oriented towards the social dynamics of the present. Daun had been a doctoral student under the guidance of social anthropologist Fredrik Barth at the University of Bergen who, in a Scandinavian perspective, was the key figure to introduce "generative cultural analysis" to the scholarly field. The generative cultural analysis was inspired by British social anthropology and emphasised the making of cultures through interactionist exchanges among individuals and group actors, mostly focusing on contemporary Western societies. Whereas the work of Erixon and his students paid attention to the present with the goal of understanding the "Ursprung" of still-existing cultural forms, this way of engaging solely with contemporary culture had not previously been seen in ethnology (cf. Arntsberg 1989).

In Denmark, Bjarne Stoklund was a central figure in handling the aftermath of the diffusionist paradigm, as discussed in Signe Mellemgaard's contribution. Stoklund was trained as a historian, and Mellemgaard shows how following his inauguration in 1971 as Professor of European Ethnology at the University of Copenhagen, Stoklund chose to mediate between the diffusionist or historic-geographic paradigm and the "new ethnology" of the 1970s. In contrast to the process-oriented and contemporary cultural analysis conducted by Lund's ethnologists, Stoklund's impact on Danish ethnology highlighted the continuity of the historical dimension of material culture in particular, while still combining it with synchronic studies. As Mellemgaard demonstrates, Stoklund maintained a close dialogue with historical anthropology. Perhaps Stoklund's historically-oriented profile contributed to making the shift from "old" to "new" ethnology a less dramatic affair in Copenhagen than it was in Lund.

Mellemgaard's revisit has an interesting duality to it: Throughout his work, Stoklund meticulously revisited his early studies and materials; he re-evaluated them and formed them into new insights. Thus, Mellemgaard revisits Stoklund's practice of returning to his own ethnological material, parts of which were gathered within a historic-geographical context. First, Mellemgaard shows how Stoklund dealt with the so-called "micro-macro problem" by discussing small details within larger cultural historical developments. Second, Stoklund introduced an ecological perspective, including an elaboration of ecotypes, which contributed important insights into the peasant economy. Mellemgaard argues that the ecotypes facilitated a distancing from the diffusionist explanatory models. Finally, her contribution discusses how Stoklund departures from the idea of relic areas by using Immanuel Wallerstein's and Fernand Braudel's world-system theories.

Making a Leap

What kinds of dialogues with the past are presented in this volume? We encounter novel readings of, and conversations with a range of ethnological predecessors such as: Sigurd Erixon (Gustavsson, Munk & Elgaard Jensen, Nilsson), Eilert Sundt (Hastrup), Bjarne Stoklund (Mellemgaard), and Fernand Braudel (Damsholt & Jespersen). Various types of materials and genres from the past are revisited, such as scholarly archives (Gustavsson), journals (Hastrup), material folk culture atlases (Gustavsson, Munk & Elgaard Jensen), official Swedish customs archives (Nilsson) and the topographies of eighteenth-century rural Denmark (Damsholt & Jespersen). These listings are not intended to be exhaustive since rather than attempting a "full" picture it is the different modes of revisiting that are in focus here.

The collection presents revisits that are sparked into being by provocation as in Damsholt and Jespersen's piece, which is fashioned as a challenge to their own habitual thinking about classical "ethnological virtues". Another mode of revisiting is deliberate inquiries into research practices of the past and research methods that were otherwise thought long gone, as in Gustavsson's contribution.

This revisiting of European ethnology is not an attempt to induce a recursive ethnology, which repeats itself throughout time. Rather, we wish to open up opportunities wherein the act of revisiting is a means to engage with the urgent themes and challenges of contemporary ethnology. These themes and more are further discussed in the comments by Valdimar Hafstein, Orvar Löfgren, Katharina Eisch-Angus and Regina F. Bendix. To engage in dialogues with our very much alive (and kicking) European colleagues is just as important as having conversations with the past. Indeed, this was also Stoklund's aim in his flyer, where he stressed that *Ethnologia Europaea* met the need for a *European* journal of interest for ethnologists and others.

Finally, allow me to add one more revisit to this

volume and bring a previous special issue of *Ethnologia Europaea* to the table: *Off the Edge – Experiments in Cultural Analysis* (Löfgren & Wilk, eds. 2005). Emphasising the sensing, ageing, moving and mystifying qualities of ethnological analysis, this is a call for exploring new modes of doing cultural analysis. By digging into "the large and disorganised historical tool chest of social analysis" Löfgren and Wilk (2005, p. 8) inspire us to take a leap without fearing the abyss; a rich repertoire of metaphors can be employed to help us continue experimenting with cultural analysis. For example, we learn that "fossilisation" can be a useful metaphor for understanding the inertia of cultural processes (Shove & Pantzar 2005), and also how the metaphor of "cream effects" can depict various registers of sensory highs (Bendix 2005). To me, this playful way of launching new modes of doing cultural analysis is not only emblematic for the kind of *Ethnologia Europaea* profiled by Löfgren and Bendix since 2007, it is also highly *persuasive*.

Stoklund's list from 1984 of relevant research themes for *Ethnologia Europaea* is not outdated. Although studying the civilising process might have morphed into various kinds of governmentality studies, and material culture into studies of materialisations, the everyday life, together with cultural diversity, migration and identity processes, are still among the core research areas in the ethnological field. Together with Löfgren's lines of continuities, these themes, among others, constitute the backbone of our discipline; the field is constantly under reconstruction, but some common denominators remain intact. Keeping this in our pocket, we are ready for take-off into ethnological futures.

Notes

1. The former editors of *Ethnologia Europaea* are Géza de Rohan-Csermak 1967–1971, Günther Wiegelmann 1971–1984, Bjarne Stoklund 1984–2004, with Peter Niedermüller 1999–2004, Orvar Löfgren 2004–2012, with Regina F. Bendix 2007–present.
2. The "zombie-concept" was coined by Ulrich Beck (see Slater & Ritzer 2011).
3. Elias himself did not want to be labelled an "everyday life researcher", since he regarded everyday life transformations not as "peculiarities", which are "different to those of other areas of social life," but as a change in personality structures, which correlated changes in the social structure, the social code or the standards of emotion management ([1978]1998: 169).
4. It is beyond the scope of this introduction to go further into this transformation, in which a self-instantiated reform-committee, the infamous "Gang of four" – Robert Wildhaber (Basel), Roger Pinon (Liège), Karel C. Peeters (Antwerp/Leuwen), Roger Lecotté (Paris) – led by German folk narrative researcher and Professor in Kiel and Göttingen, Kurt Ranke, elected a new board and renamed CIAP (*Commission Internationale des Arts et Traditions Populaires*) SIEF (*Société Internationale d'Ethnologie et de Folklore*). For a detailed analysis of the events, see Rogan 2008.
5. The title of the journal *Ethnologia Europaea* is formulated in contemporary Latin and translates into "The European Ethnology" or "European Ethnology". There seems to be no particular reason for the choice of this Latin name for the journal *Ethnologia Europaea*. However, using the former lingua franca in Europe could, according to Bjarne Stoklund, signal the international approach of the journal. Furthermore, the Latin inspiration in naming journals seemed to be in fashion at the time, cf. *Ethnologia Scandinavica*, *Ethnologia Polona*, *Ethnologia Slavica*, to name a few (interview with Bjarne Stoklund 2012, see also Bringéus 1983). Thanks to Christian Troelsgård, Saxo Institute, University of Copenhagen, for insightful remarks on the naming of journals in contemporary Latin.
6. Throughout his career, Erixon conducted in-depth studies of larger cities, towns and unenclosed villages, as well as peasant house building customs. In his early years, Erixon published the first volume on *Skultuna Bruk* (1918) and later, in the 1940s, he published a volume on life in and around the harbour as part of his Stockholm-studies (for an in-depth discussion on Erixon's work as a whole, see Arntsberg 1989).
7. As discussed in Rooijakkers & Meurkens (2000) one of the Dutch ethnologist J.J. Voskuil's points of criticism towards the European Atlas Project, in which he himself took part and about which he later wrote the sarcastic roman à clef *Het Bureau*, was that the process' perspective entailed only a comparison between the pre-industrial period and information collected around 1900, "as if it would entangle a static period with a continuity going back to the early Middle Ages or even the Roman period" (2000: 80).

References

Arntsberg, K.O. 1989: *Utforskaren: Studier i Sigurd Erixons etnologi*. Stockholm: Carlssons Bokförlag.
Bendix, R. 2005: The Cream Effect. *Ethnologia Europaea* 35:1-2, 15–18.

Bringéus, N.A. 1983: The Predecessors of Ethnologia Europaea. *Ethnologia Europaea* XIII:2, 228–233.

Campbell, Å., S. Erixon, N. Lindqvist & J. Sahlgren (eds.) 1957: *Atlas över Svensk Folkkultur*. Vol.1. Kungl. Gustav Adolfs Akademien (Uppsala, Stockholm). Uddevalla: Bokförlaget Niloé.

Daun, Å. 1969: Upp till kamp i Båtskärsnäs: En etnologisk studie av ett samhälle inför industrinedläggelse. *Etnologiska samhällsundersökningar* 1. Verdandi-debatt 41. Stockholm: Prisma.

Ehn, B. & O. Löfgren (2001)2006: *Kulturanalyser*. Århus: Klim.

Ehn, B. & O. Löfgren 2010: *The Secret World of Doing Nothing*. Berkeley; Los Angeles: University of California Press.

Elgaard Jensen, T. 2012: Intervention by Invitation: New Concerns and New Versions of the User in STS. *Science Studies* 25:1, 13–36.

Elias, N. (1978)1998: On the Concept of Everyday Life. Translated from German by Edmund Jephcott of 'Zum Begriff des Alltags' (1978). In: Johan Goudsblom & Stephen Mennell (eds.), *The Norbert Elias Reader: A Biographical Selection*. Oxford: Blackwell, pp. 166–174.

Gammeltoft-Hansen, T. & J. Christiansen 2011: Danmarks dilemma: Grænsekontrol og Schengen. *DIIS policy brief 2011*. Copenhagen: Danish Institute for International Studies.

Højrup, T. 1983: *Det glemte folk*. Hørsholm: SBI.

Højrup, T. 1989: Strukturanalyse og samfundsanalyse. *Nord Nytt* 37, 108–128.

Højrup, T. 2002: *Dannelsens dialektik*. Copenhagen: Museum Tusculanum Press.

Højrup, T. 2006: Gennem negation og konstruktion: Den etnologiske stats- og livsformsteoris tilblivelse. In: A. Jespersen, M.R. Melchior & M. Sandberg (eds.), *Verden over: En introduktion til stats- og livsformsteorien og dens aktuelle anvendelse i etnologien*. Copenhagen: Museum Tusculanum Press, pp. 221–256.

Jespersen, A.P., M.K. Petersen, C. Ren & M. Sandberg 2012: Guest Editorial: Cultural Analysis as Intervention. *Science Studies* 25:1, 3–12.

Latour, B. 1999: *Pandoras Hope: Essays on the Reality of Science Studies*. Cambridge: Harvard University Press.

Löfgren, O. 1997: Scenes from a Troubled Marriage: Swedish Ethnology and Material Culture Studies. *Journal of Material Culture* 2:1, 95–114.

Löfgren, O. 2008: When is Small Beautiful? The Transformations of Swedish Ethnology. In: U. Kochel & R. Johler (eds.), *Everyday Culture in Europe*. Abingdon Oxon, GBR: Ashgate Publishing Group, pp. 119–132.

Löfgren, O. & R. Wilk 2005: Off the Edge: Experiments in Cultural Analysis. *Ethnologia Europaea* 35:1–2. Copenhagen: Museum Tusculanum Press.

Massey, D. 2005: *For Space*. The Open University, London; Thousand Oaks: SAGE Publications.

Michael, M. 2006: Versions of Everyday Life and Technoscience. In: M. Michael, *Technoscience and Everyday Life: The Complex Simplicities of the Mundane*. Maidenhead: Open University Press, pp. 16–40.

O'Dell, T. & R. Willim 2011: Composing Ethnography. *Ethnologia Europaea* 41:1, 27–39.

Petersen, M.K. & A.K. Munk 2013: I vælten: Kulturanalysens nye hverdag. *Kulturstudier* 1, 102–117.

Rogan, B. 2008: From CIAP to SIEF: Visions for a Discipline or Power Struggle? In: U. Kochel & R. Johler (eds.), *Everyday Culture in Europe*. Abingdon Oxon, GBR: Ashgate Publishing Group, pp. 20–63.

Rooijakkers, G. & P. Meurkens 2000: Struggling with the European Atlas: Voskuil's Portrait of European Ethnology. *Ethnologia Europaea* 30:1, 75–95.

Shove, E. & M. Pantzar 2005: Fossilization. *Ethnologia Europaea* 35:1-2, 59–62.

Slater, D. & G. Ritzer 2011: Interview with Ulrich Beck. *Journal of Consumer Research* 2011:1(2), 261–277.

Stoklund, B. 2003: *Tingenes kulturhistorie: Etnologiske studier af den materielle kultur*. Copenhagen: Museum Tusculanum Press.

Tangherlini, T. 2010: Legendary Performances: Folklore, Repertoire and Mapping. *Ethnologia Europaea* 40:2, 103–115.

Thrift, N. 1997: The Rise of Soft Capitalism. *Cultural Values* 1:1, 29–57.

Tschofen, B. 2013: On Everyday Life: Fates of the Obvious in European Ethnology. In: M. Scheer, T. Thiemeyer, R. Johler & B. Tschofen (eds.), *Out of the Tower: Essays on Culture and Everyday Life*. Tübingen: Tübinger Verein für Volkskunde E.V., pp. 72–83.

Vasström, A. 2013: Blutsverwandten. In: *Nationalmuseets Arbejdsmark*. Copenhagen: National Museum Denmark, pp. 236–247 (with English summary).

Vasström, A. (2014, in preparation): At sætte verden i system: Om udarbejdelsen af en saglig registrant for danske kulturhistoriske museer i en krydsild mellem faglige problemstillinger og politiske dagsordener. Copenhagen: National Museum Denmark.

Interview
Interview with Bjarne Stoklund, by Marie Sandberg, University of Copenhagen, December 12, 2012.

Marie Sandberg, Ph.D., is associate professor of ethnology at the Saxo Institute, University of Copenhagen. Her research focuses on labour migration within the EU, border practices and experiences of borders in everyday life Europe. Since 2013, she is the editor of *Ethnologia Europaea* together with Regina F. Bendix.
(sandberg@hum.ku.dk)

INNOVATION, RESISTANCE OR TINKERING
Rearticulating Everyday Life in an Ethnological Perspective

Tine Damsholt and Astrid Pernille Jespersen

In this paper, we investigate the background and history that ethnologists bring to bear on interdisciplinary innovation projects. We argue that although ethnology is well-equipped to contribute to innovation projects, our discipline also builds upon a series of conceptual configurations, and that these classic ethnological concepts and "taken for granted" understandings sit oddly with contemporary ideas about innovation as expressed in recent Danish innovation policy. These reflections were prompted by our participation in a joint innovation project funded by a Danish programme for user-driven innovation. By revisiting the discipline of ethnology as it has been conducted in southern Scandinavia, we identify three key points that explain our concerns regarding the way in which everyday life was analysed and configured in the innovation project.

Keywords: everyday life practices, user-driven innovation, tinkering, resistance

Since the beginning of this millennium, the idea of the user as an important figure and actor in different versions of innovation projects – such as product and service development – has been on the agenda in Danish innovation and research policy. The inclusion of user-studies in product and service development is believed to have an economical potential from which Danish businesses could and should benefit. In 2007, the Danish government launched two funding programmes focusing on user-driven innovation (UDI), which specifically urged social scientists to take on roles in various innovation projects. In the words of the Danish Minister for Economic and Business Affairs, "anthropologists and sociologists could contribute with a new understanding of users' unacknowledged needs and preferences" (Bentsen 2006, quoted in Elgaard Jensen 2012). With their apparently intimate understanding of users, the Minister envisioned social scientists as key players in innovation and product development, who could take on the task of ensuring growth in the private sector.

The Box of Everyday Life

In this paper, we describe an experience we had as ethnologists involved in a user-driven innovation project on "The interactive grocery shopping of the future", funded by one of the UDI-programmes. This experience led us to reflect on the premises for our involvement: How well did our disciplinary background in ethnology fit into the premises of innovation projects? What notions of everyday practices and change did we bring to the project? And how did our notions differ from those of the other scholars in the project, as articulated in our mutual discussions? Especially the way in which they configured everyday life – as a box that we could (and should) abandon or "think out of" in order to pursue innovative solutions – challenged some of our fundamental ethnological understandings.

The project we were part of was a collaboration between researchers of European Ethnology at the University of Copenhagen, a small private enterprise called Art of Crime, a division of a major supermarket chain called COOP-NETTORVET and the Copenhagen Institute for Future Studies. The project was initiated by the Institute for Future Studies, and was funded by the Danish Enterprise and Construction Authority's programme for user-driven innovation. The purpose of the project was twofold. One of its objectives was to formulate innovative models for future online grocery shopping. The other was to develop and experiment with new methods for user involvement in innovation processes. The project was led by the Institute for Future Studies, but was organised in a number of relatively independent phases, each headed by one of the involved partners. At the beginning of the project, our main contribution as ethnologists and researchers was to analyse existing grocery-shopping and related practices through ethnographic fieldwork combined with more experimental methods that involved the users. The material gathered during this phase was intended to provide extensive empirical knowledge about the everyday life practices of grocery shopping – from planning, buying, choosing, and bringing the groceries back home, to preparing the meal, eating and dealing with the leftovers[1] – which would be used in the subsequent phases of the project. In our ethnographic material, we identified seven factors of interest, which we termed *rationales*: economy, time, logistics, morality, social relations, health and experience/pleasure. These refer to "logics, strategies and arguments, as well as specific doings and material elements in shopping practice" (Jespersen et al. 2010: 6–7; see also Elgaard Jensen 2012).

In the main part of this paper, we delve back into our ethnological upbringing in search of ways of conceptualising everyday life practices, and the mechanisms by which they are changed. These conceptualisations, which are normally more or less implicit, were challenged and therefore also articulated through our participation in the project. We revisit our ethnographic backgrounds and history in order to more fully understand the contrast between our approach to innovation processes and the one articulated in the UDI programmes, especially by the scholars from Future Studies. But first we describe some of the main characteristics of UDI. In doing so, we hope to provide the reader with an insight into the types of understandings that we encountered, and with which we found ourselves at odds throughout the project.

User-Driven Innovation and Ethnology

One striking feature of the UDI agenda has been a request for a scientific expertise in unravelling and understanding the practices of users, and thus delivering methods for including users in innovation processes, as well as in turning the resulting insights into a competitive advantage for the businesses involved. In the wake of this commercial turn to the users, the skills of ethnologists and anthropologists have come into demand in relation to the associated challenges of including and stimulating the practices of users in innovation processes. This new interest in ethnology and similar disciplines should be understood in the context of the disciplines' long record of studying everyday life practices, which epitomises what the private enterprises seem to lack; namely, an intimacy with, and a profound understanding of, the lives of regular people – the future users/consumers of the new products (Halse 2008; for ethnological studies and involvements in innovation projects see: Holst Kjær 2011; Petersen & Munk 2013). In Denmark, this attention to users and user-research is reflected by a variety of concepts such as participatory design, user-centred design, business anthropology and so on. However, most recently, an interest in users has been put on the agenda by large national funding programmes for user-driven innovation. The term user-driven innovation was originally formulated by the American innovation theorist Eric von Hippel (1986) but in the case of Danish innovation policy, UDI is an umbrella term that refers to several different approaches (Rosted 2005; Elgaard Jensen 2012).

The key definition of UDI in the Danish programme was formulated by FORA, a research unit under the Ministry of Economic and Business Affairs. FORA argues that users have "unacknowledged needs", which may be discovered through ethnographic studies of the users' current use of products and services in their everyday life practices. Thus, the deployment of social science expertise with the aim of understanding users' unacknowledged needs may become a new and valuable source of innovation (Rosted 2005). The project we were a part of clearly referenced the UDI programme's ambition of uncovering users' unacknowledged needs (Elgaard Jensen 2012). Since this was one of the premises of the programme, we were obliged to work with it as our starting point. From an ethnological perspective, however, it is striking that the programme took its point of departure in an individualistic notion of the user; unacknowledged needs are the needs of individuals, not communities.

In the following, we describe three occurrences where we were at odds with the ways in which everyday life (including the concepts of the user, innovation and change) was conceived and articulated within the project group. These three situations raise questions about how we engaged in the project, the kind of ethnography we articulated, and the strikingly different perspectives brought to the project by the participants from future studies in particular.

The first situation occurred during the planning of the ethnographic fieldwork, where we found it very difficult to work with the individualistic idea of the "user with unacknowledged needs". In preparing for our fieldwork, we realised that grocery shopping may be carried out by an individual (the one doing the actual shopping). But we also soon realised that the shopping situation is packed with a whole range of crucial social relations, such as relationships to other members of the household, and this made it meaningless for us to regard the user as merely an individual. Accordingly, we chose to replace "the user with unacknowledged needs" with a focus on *heterogeneous practices* (Shove et al. 2007), understood as intertwined practices of eating, shopping and planning within the context of a household. In doing so, we moved away from an individualistic perception of users to a relational understanding.

The second occurrence of "being at odds" unfolded during the next phase of the project. At this point, we had finished our ethnographic account of the everyday practices, and the scholars from future studies took over. One of the methods they introduced into the project was a megatrend analysis. Megatrends are meant to illuminate future developments that are considered to be more or less inevitable. Within future studies, such analyses are used as reference points that facilitate discussions about future developments that affect all actors on all societal levels: "Megatrends are the great forces in societal development that will very likely affect the future in all areas the next 10–15 years … In other words, megatrends are our knowledge about the probable future" (Larsen 2006). It is argued that by analysing the social patterns and trends behind changes, megatrends provide an understanding of the possible future consequences for society and companies affected by these changes. From an ethnological point of view, this way of conceptualising societal changes resembles the perspective of "cultural diffusion" from cultural centres to peripheries (see the contribution by Munk and Elgaard Jensen in this volume). The idea of inevitable and universal megatrends was at odds with our classic ethnological understandings of changes in everyday life, and the inertness that characterises these transformations and reconfigurations.

During the course of the project, there was a third occurrence. Here, what can be seen as an initially underlying assumption – one which shaped the project's understanding of innovation and innovation processes – became increasingly evident, and this eventually led to an open disagreement between the partners. The assumption in question was that the innovation we were striving for in the project should abandon what we knew about the current practices of the users in order to produce something truly new and innovative for the future. The method of "future scenarios" was introduced at this stage as a way for the project to create alternative visions of the future. A core assumption in "future scenarios" is the importance of avoiding a prognostic flavour in the scenarios; that is, the scenarios should preferably not become mainstream because that would produce "an unfortunate attitude to the future, because they suggest that the future is something you know (if you're smart enough), i.e. the future is already determined" (Bjerre 2004).[2] At this point, the insights from the ethnographic fieldwork became "nice to know", but also something we were urged to think beyond in order to work truthfully with the different future scenarios. As one of the partners involved in the project stated, it was now time to "think out of the box"; that is, step out of the conceptual constraints of everyday life, which supposedly restricted our creative and innovative process. This talk of everyday life – as a box, which we could and should abandon in our efforts to pursue innovative solutions for an unknown future – seemed truly odd to us. It clearly contradicted our deeply-held ethnological assumptions about how to engage with people and their everyday practices in a professional and proper manner.

In the following, we focus on two aspects of the disagreement between the ethnological configuration of everyday life and the way everyday life was understood and used by our partners in the project. Firstly, we ask the question of why we were triggered to such an extent by the idea of thinking outside of the box – but also why our insights into everyday life were considered a box and a burden. What kind of box? Why a burden? Secondly, we discuss what we saw as a very specific configuration of the relationship between the future, innovation and everyday life as articulated by the other partners involved in the project, especially the scholars from future studies.

To pursue this task, and inspired by the genealogical approach, we revisit aspects of our classic ethnological understanding of everyday life and of practices as resistant and inert. A genealogy in the Foucauldian sense is not a search for "Ursprung" – origins, essence, or a linear development. Rather, it is an attempt to reveal the heterogeneous, contingent and even contradictory "Herkunft" – the past of phenomena we tend to think of as devoid of history (Foucault [1971]1977). In line with this version of genealogy, we revisit some of the classic Scandinavian[3] ethnological studies that formed the backbone of our education. Through a couple of cases in point, we revisit studies of habits and routines, as well as notions that deal with the adaptation of new lifestyles, such as "longue durée" and neoculturation, and the ideology of "the good life". On the basis of this, we qualify and rearticulate our understanding of the "resistance and inertness" of transformations to everyday life, and the conditions under which everyday life can be reconfigured. This brings forth an alternative vision of innovation in the realm of everyday life practices; one which lies closer to the ethnological body of knowledge.

The relationship between past, present and future everyday life practices has been one of the pivotal focuses of the ethnological disciplines. However, everyday life is not to be perceived as an entity or an object in and of itself. Rather, as an object of study, it is configured and shaped in specific types of agendas, problematisations and concerns. The ethnological understanding of everyday life is not just a body of knowledge compiled through disciplined investigation at different times. Instead, everyday life, as a concept and a body of knowledge, has become intelligible and authoritative in various and specific historical contexts and situated fields of knowledge.

Based on our return visit to the ethnological classics, we suggest three key points that also have the potential to answer our initial question of why we were so concerned by the way everyday life was configured in the project. Accordingly, we present the response we came up with based on our ethnological body of knowledge. Our first point relates to the shift from a focus on an individualistic user to a focus on households and heterogeneous practices. The second point is concerned with a shift from the idea of abrupt movements between distinctly different scenarios to an emphasis on innovation as an ongoing tinkering, and as changes in and of an established order. The third point deals with the role that ethnologists are called upon to play, and points to the difference between, on the one hand, the role of an agent of radical change or reformist and, on the other hand, the more traditional (curatorial) role which often is played by ethnologists.

The Shaping of Everyday Life as an Object of Study

It has often been argued that the discipline of European ethnology has two separate yet intertwined "roots"; one is the political sciences of the eighteenth-century Enlightenment, the other is the national-romantic "Golden Age" of folk culture studies in the nineteenth century (Stoklund 1979; Damsholt 1995). Folk culture, which includes objects of study such as costumes, habits and the everyday life of common people, has been the shared and permanent focus of both of these configurations of the discipline of ethnology. However, there are some important differences regarding how these configurations relate to the inherent inertness of everyday practices and their ability to resist transformation.

Scholars of folklore in the late nineteenth century conducted what they considered to be a "last-minute rescue operation", saving old traditions and crafts from the grinding mill of modernity. Folk life and habits were worth saving because they were regarded as pathways to the true national culture, and therefore not only as educational tools for museums but also as sources of inspiration for artists and designers evolving national styles to compete in international fairs and exhibitions. The traditional ways of life were to be preserved from the contemporary decay and dissolution, even though it often was the "Sunday best" side of peasant culture and its most colourful features that were preferred in these collection practices (Stoklund 1999). As such, laborious and painstaking efforts were made to purify the contemporary habits of the rural population into what was considered to be the past – and therefore original, authentic and "true" – traditions and customs worthy of being saved, protected, and to form an ideal for future practices. Even in this quest for an authentic national culture, everyday life and habits had to be selected, purified and cultivated in the interest of academic practices.

The "rescue operation" approach of the late nineteenth century is, however, qualitatively different from earlier approaches of a more interventionist kind, in which the everyday life of the common population had long been a realm for government attention. This can be illustrated with the official Danish ordinances from the seventeenth and eighteenth century against the excess regulation of consummation and festivity in detail – as many habits were considered harmful not only to people's health and souls but also to the state economy. However, the everyday life of the peasantry came into existence as an object of scrutiny in a new way in the late eighteenth century, shaped by what Foucault has termed biopolitics, pastoral power and the reason of the state (Foucault [1994]2000b). Through these endeavours, the problems presented to governmental practices by the phenomena that are characteristic of a group of living human beings were rationalised and configured as questions concerning governing a "population" ([1994]2000a: 67). The population was framed as a problem in a new way; not as a sum of individuals inhabiting a territory, but as an entity with its own 'nature', which could be rationally analysed and governed in accordance with that inherent nature, and which could enhance the state's strength ([1994]2000b: 315–317). The new pastoral form of power stirred a flood of political concerns regarding the everyday life of the population, and took charge of a whole series of questions and problems related to material culture, property, productivity, education, health, meals etc. A pivotal dogma within the reason of state was that any object of governing should be governed in accordance with its own nature (Foucault [1994]2000a). Thus, an interest in and knowledge of the population's everyday life, its nature and possibilities for change were shaped within the broader field of governmental technologies "peculiar to the state; domains, techniques, targets where the state intervened" (Foucault [1994]2000b).

The new and "ethnographically" based investigations into the everyday life of the rural population in late eighteenth-century Denmark-Norway, whereby vicars[4] described the everyday habits of their congregations, was also entangled with concerns about how the state should and could manage its population, which was regarded as a resource that could strengthen the state. Often, the vicars' accounts stemmed from the idea that knowledge about the facts relating to the conditions and nature of the population was an important precondition for improving the economy of the country (Damsholt 1995). Thus, investigation and intervention were part of the same practice. In this perspective, everyday habits were by no means considered valuable or worth preserving; on the contrary, they were considered barriers to progress. The superstition and "backward irrationality" of the peasants and their everyday life was viewed as something to be overcome, and change was expected to come through enlightenment. Spreading informative material, education, and setting a good example became technologies in this biopolitical project to improve the health, civilisation and productivity of the common people.

If the peasantry as a central resource of the state was to be fully exploited, barriers had to be eliminated. In the biopolitical perspective, everyday life and its resistance to (or possibility for) change thus became central objects of study. Could peasant culture and everyday life be changed? And if so, how? The vicars involved in mapping life and habits in their parishes had different ideas about the causes of resistance. Some believed the backwardness was a matter of "character" (e.g. Junge 1798), while others believed that it was a question of living conditions (e.g. Blicher 1795). Different beliefs also led to different solutions for changing habits. Despite all of these differences, the vicars agreed that everyday life and routines seemed to have inherent reasons or logics that made them difficult to change from the outside (for more on this topic, see Damsholt 1995). In this way, one could argue that everyday life as an object of study and body of knowledge was (and is) shaped within governmental practices with specific agendas of improvement and change. As mentioned earlier, the change and improvement projects of the twenty-first century are often discursively articulated as innovation (Godin 2012, 2013).

A similar entanglement of investigation and intervention (and thus a "war against habits") was the mainstay of studies of everyday life among common people from the start of the twentieth century, where reformers in the Scandinavian welfare states set out to improve the everyday life of the working class and petty bourgeoisie. Practices which were seen to be "bad habits" had to be replaced with good ones, but the common people "surprisingly" resisted the well-meant recommendations of the superior "know-it-alls" and their scientifically-based arguments. From the perspective of the reformers, common people were "slaves of habit" and ruled by a conceptual world of prejudices, dogmas and tradition without reflections upon and insights into the "true nature of things" (Frykman & Löfgren 1996). Everyday life had to be intervened in, and scientifically-based information should be disseminated via home visits from health visitors and caregivers, and a combination of investigation and education programmes became new technologies for installing new and better habits.

In the light of this history of often insensitive social reformers, it is easy to understand why ethnologists in the 1960s and onwards abandoned the concepts of "customs" and "habits" and, when studying cultural groups and phenomena of the modern society, engaged with new technical terms borrowed from British and American anthropology and sociology. "Terms such as patterns of interaction, role-play, forms of communication, transactions, and ritual life now colonised the field of study" (Frykman & Löfgren 1996: 6). Often, ethnologists ended up as defenders or curators of local cultures or logics of culture. However, everyday life has turned out to be a recurring theme in ethnology, if not *the* object of study that has defined the discipline at least since the 1980s (Stoklund 1994; Tschofen 2013: 73). As Frykman and Löfgren state in the Festschrift to the former professor Bringeus: "The strength of ethnology is often the concreteness and the link between the seeming insignificance of everyday life and its consequences in a broader context" (1996: 7). Understanding everyday life from within – its routines, practices and organisation – and exposing its inherent logics and thereby the conditions for change and sustainability, have become the approaches ethnologists most often employ when studying culture.

Thus, ethnologists have become interpreters of

habits and everyday life, explaining why seemingly irrational practices have their own logics, and why well-meaning reformers are met with resistance, as well as why new social or material innovations tend not to succeed. Even if they are not necessarily curators of every form of everyday life, many ethnologists at least consider everyday life to be something that should be taken seriously; not as a barrier to change, but as one of the key preconditions for change. From this perspective, change is only thought to be possible if it can be integrated with the constitutive logics of everyday life.

The genealogy that we outline here suggests that the ethnological idea of everyday life's inherent inertness is a legacy of the ways in which everyday life was shaped as an object of study within political practices of improvement. Whether habits were seen as problematic or as something to be preserved, refined or defended, they are configured within these practices of improvement or innovation. Furthermore, it seems that there is an inherent dilemma or paradox entangled with the ethnological study of everyday life: ethnologists are caught between being interpreters who understand and explain the inertness and resistance of everyday life to the practices of intervention on one hand, and being part of these intervening practices or at least having their agenda of investigation set by them on the other hand. This entanglement of investigation and intervention could be considered integral to the biopolitical "Herkunft" and descent of ethnology.

In the following, we turn our attention to three more recent ethnological studies of habits and routines, as well as notions dealing with the adaptation of new lifestyles. These studies have been important in the formation of our "taken for granted" ethnological concept of everyday life and its adaptability. In revisiting them we qualify and articulate our understanding of everyday life and the conditions under which it can be transformed.

Cultural Adaptation and Neoculturation

At least two pivotal concepts regarding changes to everyday practices and culture have permeated Danish ethnology as it has been taught at the University of Copenhagen since the late 1970s. The first is the concept of "enduring, even obstinate structures", which is a translation (with some degree of interpretation) of the concept of "longue durée". This concept was used by the French Annales School of historical writing to designate their approach, which prioritised long-term historical structures over events. The longue durée designates old attitudes of thought and action, resistant frameworks which die hard, at times defying all logic. In relation to the inertness of everyday practices, this concept is used by the French historian Fernand Braudel to characterise how structures of everyday life underlie and are sustained beyond political events and structural crises ([1979]1981). The second concept is that of "the good life", as articulated by the American anthropologist Robert Redfield. Referring to one of the oldest books about peasant life – *Work and Days* by Greek Hesiod – and contemporary American Indian peasants of Yucatan, he describes "the (peasant) view of the good life" to be an "integrated pattern of dominant attitudes or ideas about as to how life ought to be lived". And, as Redfield argues, such fundamental orientations of life remain unchanged, and peasants are likely to try to find compromises between ideas about how life should be lived and their current way of life (Redfield 1956: 60–63).

Braudel and Redfield's concepts have been translated and transformed within Danish ethnology. However, with regards to understanding changes to culture and everyday practices, they themselves became a kind of longue durée for the discipline. Danish ethnologist Palle Ove Christiansen illustrates this understanding of change in the paper "Peasant Adaptation to Bourgeois Culture? Class Formation and Cultural Redefinition in the Danish Countryside" (1978), in which he uses historical source material from a village in southern Denmark. Christiansen's main argument is that the changes of lifestyle among the rich segment of the peasants, who became "farmers" in the late nineteenth century, were not merely an adaptation of urban middle class culture or an "embourgeoisement", as it often has been interpreted. Instead, he argues that this cultural redefinition was a much more complex process and that it did not take place overnight. The new "farmer sub-culture" was integral to the way in which the owners of medium sized farms reformulated a new social position between the townspeople and the small cottagers. This cultural reformulation consisted of the strategic selection of certain (but not all) traits from urban culture. The new social position was translated into "cultural language" (1978: 148).

Thus, to understand such cultural change and "innovations in material culture", ethnologists must study "the necessary preconditions for the acceptance and integration of new cultural elements" (1978: 101). With reference to Swedish ethnologist Börje Hanssen, Christiansen points to the "tricky complex of social, economic, political, and cultural phenomena" as a prerequisite for understanding processes of change (1978: 106). With reference to the Danish ethnologist Ole Højrup, he emphasises that the necessary preconditions for change in material culture can partly be found within new ways of organising daily work within a household. However, the way "the good life" was perceived did not change, but rather continued in the form of old norms in a new guise. As such, the idea of the good life was an obstinate structure that was resistant to changes to the economy and social organisation.

Furthermore, cultural change was not a matter of "calm reasoned decision-making in order to satisfy new needs" (1978: 148), but was instead a gradually emerging outcome of social and economic change. Thus, rather than being a sudden or manipulated breaking of habits, cultural change is described as follows: "Slowly and unconsciously new features sneaked into and became part of the 'natural' order of living" (1978: 148).

From Christiansen's work, we learned to consider processes of cultural change as much more complex than a simple diffusion of megatrends (from upper classes to lower, or from centres to periphery). Instead, changes to the everyday life of the household occur slowly and as a result of complex processes that lie beyond calm, reasoned decision making. To understand how innovations in (material) culture become integrated and unquestioned components of everyday life, we must analyse the necessary preconditions for the acceptance and integration of such new cultural elements. The structures of everyday life are "obstinate structures", resistant to change. To understand potentials and barriers to innovation, we must investigate how the subjects of everyday innovations perceive "the good life".

Another important conceptual translation of the longue durée and the "view of the good life", which is relevant when analysing the complex adaptation of new lifestyles or routines, is the notion of neoculturation as developed by the Danish ethnologist Thomas Højrup in the context of his theory of life-mode analysis (1983, 2003). Here, the point of departure is the understanding of a population as culturally heterogeneous. However, rather than dividing the population into classes or an infinite number of subcultures, Højrup argues for an (analytical) division into a number of life-modes; fundamentally different forms of practice, ideology, social organisation and ways of structuring everyday life. The empirical examples that are used to illustrate the different life-modes are seldom concerned with individuals, but rather focus on families and households. These collective subjects (with the same or aligned life-modes) do not necessarily pursue the same universal goals. Even if they use the same words, their understandings of the central aspects of everyday life are culturally diverse; each life-mode corresponds to a specific ideology, teleology or version of "the good life" that people try to practice.[5] The central point here is that the bearers of a certain life-mode will attempt to live their version of "the good life" as well as possible under their given living conditions. In that sense, "the good life" is like an obstinate structure of everyday life.

Being inherently distinct, the life-modes each define the specific, necessary preconditions for their reproduction. If these preconditions are threatened, they must be defended (2003: 15), as life-modes are always striving for the necessary conditions. Every bearer constantly struggles to maintain, re-establish or create in new forms the conditions of possibility for their own life-mode. This process is called neoculturation (2003: 28). As conditions of living change over time, transitions of a life-mode may take place. However, an important insight here is that the specific ideology or version of what "the good life" is will not change following a change in conditions, as the ideology of the life-mode is not determined by its conditions. Instead, Højrup argues that life-modes are flexible, and that the bearers of a life-mode reorganise themselves when conditions change.[6] The concept of neoculturation implies "that the societal transformation process in the problematique of the particular life-mode is viewed as a change in the conditions of possibility. One then tries to manipulate these changes in order to defend or improve one's existential foundation" (2003: 153): A family can reorganise its resources; a fishing-unit can reallocate its components or develop new tools for surviving. Thus, any adaptation to societal change or the integration of new cultural inputs, products or services depends on the conditions that correspond with the basic features and logics of the specific ideology of "the good life".[7]

What we emphasise here from Christensen and Højrup's respective work is their common understanding of how adaptations or transformation to everyday life come about. In this understanding, the image of "tinkering" – understood as the meticulous and ongoing process of adapting, meddling with or adjusting something in order to make repairs or improvements – is far more relevant than the idea of a sudden break, as the former highlights the flexibility and selectivity of a household or family. The ideology of the good life as practised, and hence the logics and structures of everyday life, are what form and constitute the very core of inertness and resistance to qualitative change. New elements, tools, products, technologies and even individuals can be integrated into everyday life if they correspond with and are culturally meaningful to, and within, the underlying logics and rationales of this everyday practice. In this sense, "the good life" is not just a mental discourse or ideology, but something that is practised and thus reproduced every day. Change is either "superficial" (as a new product or technology is domesticated within the rationales of the practice) or slow and gradual (as resistance is manifested before a necessary neoculturation takes place).

In both of these analyses, the point of departure is neither an individualistic user nor universal cultural needs or trends. Instead, social organisations and, often, the family or the household serve as pivotal contexts in which everyday practices and their involved ideologies are enacted and eventually transformed. Thus, processes of cultural change are much more complex than a simple diffusion of megatrends (from upper classes to lower, or from centres to peripheries). Changes to everyday life and the social organisation of work within the household come about slowly and as a result of complex processes beyond calm, reasoned decision-making. To understand how innovations in culture become integrated and unquestioned parts of everyday life, we must analyse the necessary preconditions for the acceptance and integration of such new cultural elements. Thus, in order to understand potentials for and barriers to innovation, we must investigate how the subjects of the everyday innovations view "the good life". Since perceptions of the good life are integral to the structures of everyday life, everyday practices often seem to be "obstinate structures", resistant to change.

Everyday *practices* and their basic logics and rationales are, then, core concepts in the (often somewhat taken for granted) ethnological understanding of the conditions for change. However, the inertness of everyday life is not a question of stasis. On the contrary, it is something that comes about through a constant reproduction of practices. It simply takes a lot of work to stabilise and maintain. Thus, our ethnological understanding of everyday practices not only involves an ideological and teleological dimension, but also an understanding of practices as tacit and embodied – as routines. We revisit this perspective on everyday practices through another formative tradition in our training as ethnologists, namely: cultural analysis conducted by ethnologists at the University of Lund, Sweden.

Everyday Life as Routines

Billy Ehn and Orvar Löfgren's recent study *The Secret World of Doing Nothing* (2010) sums up a plethora of insights into the resistances and adaptabilities of everyday life. In their definition, routines are the performance of mundane or repetitive tasks to which one does not give much thought, but which organise and support everyday life and draw invisible maps that make the everyday run smoothly. Routines are linked to order, predictability and control. They are rhythms and patterns that sequence and synchronise time. Routines are routes or cultural paths in one's life, created through repetitions. Thus, they become invisible to the individual or the household in which they are performed. Once established, they work as "silent agreements" or "the way things are (or have to be) done here." These are only apparent to visitors and sometimes become problematic, as though the visitor is breaking a secret rule.

However, the routines that make up the stuff of everyday life also require flexibility, so that people can figure out what to do when the order is interrupted. Mornings are used as a recurring example of the "humdrum minutiae" of everyday existence in which we collectively, silently and inarticulately coordinate our everyday activities (2010: 86). Thus, routines or everyday practices are created through repetitions of an almost unconscious, silent and mutual choreography. This is a way to deal with all of the necessary actions of everyday life, as well as all the materiality that has to be handled, without having to think about it. This also emphasises that everyday practices are enacted in a social setting; in a family and a household. Even if a person is single and lives alone, their everyday life is socially and culturally organised rather than defined by individual needs.

While routines make up everyday life and bring us safely through the day, they can also become a battleground precisely because they are not individually enacted. The period when they are being settled is a period of tension and negotiation: "The coming together of a couple is one of those situations where routines all of a sudden become visible arenas of social and cultural conflicts" (2010: 99). This case opens up a laboratory in which routines are created or shaped: Two individuals with diverse sets of ingrained habits have to negotiate a shared household (2010: 100). As a new couple builds a daily life, they create a shared choreography of working together in the kitchen, and what may become a lifelong division of labour. They synchronise their individual habits into a common routine and, once settled, routines are not easily changed. Nevertheless, new technologies often make people aware of how naturalised and invisible their routines are. Radio, telephone, TV, computers etc. are examples of the necessity of not only learning how to handle these gadgets, but how to integrate them with other activities. Ehn and Löfgren conclude that some technologies and routines have the capacity to blend rather easily with other activities, whereas others do not and may fail to become part of everyday family life. These processes and negotiations that take place within the family and household highlight how everyday practices are social and heterogeneous, and make relevant the concept of innovation as tinkering when it comes to understanding slow, ambiguous, and even selective changes to an established order. The processes by which societal change occur are much more complex than a mere diffusion of megatrends. Ehn and Löfgren describe how everyday life may change as follows:

> In everyday life small transformations smoulder without becoming conscious until some later stage when they become obvious in a dramatic way that overshadows the slow, preceding change. ... Tension between recurring repetition and the more or less surprising deviations from the rehearsed program creates confrontation between routine and change. (2010: 121)

Löfgren and Ehn emphasise that repetition is also a way of hiding change. "Small gradual dislocations are hidden by well-known retakes; the same procedure as yesterday, but not quite" (2010: 121). A free zone is created within mundane and seemingly unimportant alterations. Small improvisations or gradual domestications of new technologies may be welcome. As such, most people seem to prefer their everyday to transform through slow, non-dramatic and even silent changes. In this perspective, everyday life is practised as routines and patterns, shaped by negotiations or even battles, and maintained but also transformed through constant repetition. As such, the structure of everyday life is not a superstructure, but rather resembles a performative approach, where the matrix only exists qua the constant citation of it (as argued by Judith Butler 1993) and by being practised.

Towards a Performative Understanding of Everyday Life

It is, then, possible to argue that such a performative understanding of everyday life – as configured and maintained by its repetition, by being practised and performed – highlights precisely the inertness, which is thought to characterise its transformation and reconfiguration. Practices, understood as repeated (and enduring, or even obstinate) structures and logics of action, are not easily changed. Changes must make sense within the already established "view of the good life" – that is, the logics of everyday life – though not in the specific way it is enacted and materialised. But when understood and analysed as practices, everyday lives are neither unchangeable nor do they exist in themselves; rather, they are matters of practical tinkering and attentive experimentation (Mol, Moser & Pols 2010). They only exist if and as they are practised and enacted every day. How, then, can such a performative understanding contribute to innovation projects?

If we return to the project about the interactive grocery shopping of the future, then this paper's genealogical expedition into our formative ethnological classics frames the disciplinary background for the way we configured everyday life in the UDI project. In practical terms, the specific ethnological configuration of everyday life was an "intermediary product", which we, as ethnologists, had to pass on to the other participants when the phase of the project directed by us was about to end, and when the subsequent project phase directed by others was about to begin.

On the basis of the ethnographic material and our disciplinary understanding of everyday life practices and cultural changes, we developed our configuration in opposition to entirely different ideas about singular users' needs, and the future as a hidden unknown. The configuration we passed on was also an experiment on how to render genuinely ethnological knowledge into a form that could be accessible and usable to the subsequent phases of the innovation project, and which would eventually have a recognisable impact on the resulting innovation. Our argument for a performative "tinkering" approach to everyday life was not based on the idea that everyday life does not change. Nor did we, as ethnologists, want everyday life to be fixed or remain the same; on the contrary. As we have mentioned, we identified seven *rationales* in the ethnographic material. A rationale should be understood as a relatively stable pattern of practice that households and individuals enact and to which they relate. A rationale never exists alone; there is always more than one rationale in play and, in practice, they align or clash in multiple ways. Furthermore, we argue that the described rationales are not only stable patterns of practice in specific households, but that they are also longue durée in the sense that they will probably also exist in ten years. They may well be articulated, materialised and combined in slightly new ways, but they are not likely to evaporate or change radically. Thus, we dispense with the idea of abrupt movements towards future scenarios and instead point to an understanding of innovation as an ongoing tinkering with and within an established order. Thus, any innovation in the field of grocery shopping should take these rationales into consideration in order to create sustainable innovations.

In the process of handing over the ethnographic findings, we chose to "package" our material in quite a specific way. For each of the rationalities, we created a portfolio containing both a conceptual description of the rationale and a collection of quotations, observations and images, which illustrated the rationality. The portfolios were meant to serve as a source of inspiration and point to new potentials, which could bring the everyday practices and diverse ideas of "the good life" into the innovation project. Conceptualised and packaged in this manner, the rationales became a distinct ethnological contribution that drew upon classical notions such as households, routines, and habits as well as inertness and "longue durée". It also drew upon ideas of everyday practices as social and heterogeneous – and thus configured an alternative understanding of everyday life.

Nevertheless, this attempt to stabilise some of the logics and practices of everyday life in the UDI project also rearticulated the classic dilemma between ethnologists' role as curators of everyday life practices and their role as reformers. With our contribution to the project, we aimed to be innovators and reformers but, faced with the method of "future scenarios", we ended up becoming curators. When everyday life (especially the complex understanding of it that we had established) was configured as a box that we should abandon and "think outside of" in an effort to pursue innovative solutions for an unknown future, then the role of curator became the obvious choice.

Thus, the innovation project triggered the inherent dilemma of the ethnological study of everyday life: We are caught between being the interpreters who analyse the inertness and resistance of everyday life to the practices of intervention on the one hand, and are a part of these intervening practices on the other hand, or, at least, our agenda of investigation is set by them. In this paper, we argue that this entanglement of investigation and intervention could be considered part of the biopolitical descent of ethnology. If everyday life as an object of study and body of knowledge is shaped within governmental practices with specific agendas for improvement and change, then discourses of innovation in the twenty-first century configure everyday life as answers to individual and superficial needs, which are bound to change sooner or later and should be easily overcome. And, faced with such a configuration of everyday life, we as ethnologists must either end up as "grumpy old curators" or rearticulate and qualify our understanding of the "resistance and inertness" of transformations to everyday life and the conditions under which it can be reconfigured.

The contribution of ethnology to innovation projects may, then, be an understanding of everyday life and its resistance to change; not as something to be overcome, but as a potential for change and growth, as long as the longue durée and its preconditions for change are taken into consideration. This understanding implies that one moves from an understanding of users as individual consumers to an understanding of socially and culturally organised and performed use-practices, often within households and families, and to an understanding of changes in everyday life as gradual tinkering processes rather than as sudden, abrupt and complete shifts between scenarios. Thus, the productive challenge for an ethnologist is not to think outside of the box, but rather to think about what can be absorbed by the practices that unfold inside the box.

Notes

1 We visited a total of 36 households over a period of three months, using methods such as participant observations, qualitative interviews, visual ethnography, walk and talks, "surfing conversations" and design games (see also Jespersen et al. 2010; Jespersen & Breddam 2010).
2 Our translation of the following statement in Danish: "en uheldig holdning til fremtiden, fordi de antyder, at fremtiden er noget, man kan kende (hvis man er klog nok), dvs. at fremtiden for så vidt er fastlagt."
3 The sample is highly subjective and selective, and consists mainly of some of the Danish and Swedish ethnological studies that formed the backbone of our education in the 1980s and 90s at the Ethnology Section, University of Copenhagen. Thus, although questions of change and everyday life have been thoroughly discussed outside Scandinavia (e.g. by Bausinger and Schütz), our focus remains the Scandinavian perspective on the discipline in our "revisit".
4 The description of the peasantry was mostly undertaken by the clergy, partly in the format of parish-topographies. Vicars and curates were familiar with the outlook and everyday life of the peasants, and the priestly call also involved popular education in both religion and the agrarian economy (Hortsbøll 1983).
5 Højrup does not refer to Redfield's understanding of the concept of "the good life". However, in spite of the differences in their theoretical background, the inspiration may very well stem from Redfield and his significance in Danish ethnology of the 1970s.
6 The aim of this analysis of societal change is to "explore, calculate, and specify the conditions for adding new features in a given social formation and excluding others" (2003: 153).
7 Eventually, individual subjects work to maintain their mode of existence, and the necessary innovations in-

volved may transform the particular life-mode in a longer historical perspective. In this analysis, Højrup differentiates between the particular "object level" and the "meta-level", where cultural historical transformation is constituted. We find that this emphasis on how particular practices and more general cultural changes are related in complex processes and even co-configured is important, even if we do not pursue this line of investigation further in this article.

References

Bjerre, A. 2004: Dialogbaserede scenarieprocesser – et innovationsværktøj. *Fremtidsorientering* 6.
Blicher, N. 1795: *Topographie over Vium Præstekald*. Reprinted in Blicher-Selskabets festskrift til Poul Skadhauge 1978. Herning: Blicher-Selskabet.
Braudel, F. (1979)1981: *Civilization and Capitalism, 15th–18th Century. Vol. I: The Structure of Everyday Life*. New York: Harper and Row.
Butler, J. 1993: *Bodies that Matter: On the Discursive Limits of 'Sex'*. New York; London: Routledge.
Christiansen, P.O. 1978: Peasant Adaptation to Bourgeois Culture? Class Formation and Cultural Redefinition in the Danish Countryside. *Ethnologia Scandinavica* 1978, 98–152.
Damsholt, T. 1995: On the Concept of the 'Folk'. *Ethnologia Scandinavica* 25, 5–24.
Ehn, B. & O. Löfgren 2010: *The Secret World of Doing Nothing*. Berkeley: University of California Press.
Elgaard Jensen, T. 2012: Intervention by Invitations: New Concerns and New Versions of the User in STS. *Science Studies* 25:1, 13–36.
Foucault, M. (1971)1977: Nietzsche, Genealogy, History. In: D.F. Bouchard (ed.), *Language, Counter-Memory, Practice: Selected Essays and Interviews*. Ithaca: Cornell University Press.
Foucault, M. (1994)2000a: "Security, Territory, and Population". In: P. Rabinow (ed.), *Ethics: Essential Works of Foucault 1954–1984, Vol. 1*. London: Penguin.
Foucault, M. (1994)2000b: "Omnes et Singulatim: Towards a Criticism of 'Political Reason'". In: J.D. Faubion (ed.), *Power: Essential Works of Foucault 1954–1984, Vol. 3*. London: Penguin.
Frykman, J. & O. Löfgren (eds.) 1996: *Force of Habit: Exploring Everyday Culture*. Lund: Lund University Press.
Godin, B. 2012: Innovation Studies: The Invention of a Specialty. *Minerva* 50, 397–421.
Godin, B. 2013: The Unintended Consequences of Innovation Studies. Paper prepared for a communication presented at "Policy Implications due to Unintended Consequences of Innovation", Special Track at EU-SPRI, Madrid, April 10–12, 2013.
Halse, J. 2008: *Design Anthropology: Borderland Experiments with Participation*. Copenhagen: IT University of Copenhagen, Ph.D. dissertation.
von Hippel, Eric 1986: Lead Users: A Source of Novel Product Concepts. *Management Science* 32:7, 791–805.
Holst Kjær, S. 2011: Designing a Waterworld: Culture-Based Innovation and Ethnography in Regional Experience. *Ethnologia Europaea* 41:1, 81–96.
Højrup, T. (1983): *Det glemte folk: Livsformer og centraldirigering*. Copenhagen: Statens Byggeforsknings Institut.
Højrup, T. (2003): *State, Culture and Life-modes: The Foundations of Life-mode Analysis*. Aldershot, England; Burlington, USA: Ashgate.
Horstbøll, H. 1983: "Nedsivningsteori", kultursammenstød og kulturhistorie: Kampen mod bondesamfundets husholdningshorisont i Danmark i det 18. århundrede. *Den Jyske Historiker* 26, 76–98.
Jespersen, A.P. & M.D. Breddam 2010: Surfing Conversations: The Development of a Methodological Approach to the Internet as Practice. *Nätverket – etnologisk tidskrift*, Uppsala University, pp. 8–16.
Jespersen, A.P., M.D. Breddam, J. Bønnelycke & T. Damsholt 2010: *Fremtidens interaktive dagligvarehandel*. Copenhagen: Center for Cultural Analysis, University of Copenhagen.
Junge, J. 1798: *Den nordsiellandske Landalmues Charakter, Skikke, Meninger og Sprog*. Copenhagen: Danmarks Folkeminder 1915.
Larsen, G. 2006: Why Megatrends Matter. *Futureorientation* 5.
Mol, A., I. Moser & J. Pols 2010: Care: Putting Practice into Theory. *Care in Practice: On Tinkering in Clinics, Homes and Farms*. Bielefeld: Transcript Verlag.
Petersen, M.K. & A.K. Munk 2013: I vælten: Kulturanalysens nye hverdag. *Kulturstudier* 2013:1, 102–117.
Redfield, R. 1956: *The Little Community and Peasant Society and Culture*. Chicago: The University of Chicago Press.
Rosted, J. 2005: *Brugerdreven Innovation – Resultater og anbefalinger*. FORA, Økonomi- og Erhvervsministeriets enhed for erhvervsøkonomisk forskning og analyse.
Shove, E., M. Watson, M. Hand & J. Ingram 2007: *The Design of Everyday Life*. Oxford: Berg Publishers.
Stoklund, B. 1979: Europæisk Etnologi. In: *Københavns Universitet 1479–1979*. Copenhagen: University of Copenhagen.
Stoklund, B. 1994: Europæisk Etnologi. In: *Den Store Danske Encyclopædi*. Copenhagen: Gyldendal.
Stoklund, B. 1999: *Kulturens nationalisering: Et etnologisk perspektiv på det nationale*. Copenhagen: Museum Tusculanum Press.
Tschofen, B. 2013: On Everyday Life: Fates of the Obvious in European Ethnology. In: M. Scheer, T. Thiemeyer, R. Johler & B. Tschofen (eds.), *Out of the Tower: Essays on Culture and Everyday Life*. Tübingen: Tübinger Vereinigung für Volkskunde e.V.

Tine Damsholt is professor in ethnology at the University of Copenhagen. Her primary field of research is political culture, that is, national and patriotic material-discursive practices in early modern Denmark and in contemporary Western countries, based on cultural history and ethnographic fieldwork. Materiality, emotions, landscape, body and gender are recurrent themes in her research and publications. Further, she has been involved in several research projects on everyday life in contemporary Denmark.
(tinedam@hum.ku.dk)

Astrid Pernille Jespersen is associate professor in ethnology at the University of Copenhagen. Her main scientific expertise is on cultural analysis and humanistic health research with special attention to health in everyday life, lifestyle changes, obesity, ageing, physical activity and interdisciplinary collaboration. A recent publication is Careful Science? Bodywork and Care Practices in Randomised Clinical Trials (together with Bønnelycke & Eriksen, 2013, in *Sociology of Health and Illness* 35:8).
(apj@hum.ku.dk)

REVISITING THE HISTORIES OF MAPPING
Is there a Future for a Cartographic Ethnology?

Anders Kristian Munk and Torben Elgaard Jensen

This paper revisits the cartography of material folk culture from the point of view of a current cartographic project in science and technology studies (STS) known as controversy mapping. Considering the mutual learning that has already taken place between ethnological engagements with material culture and material semiotic strands of STS, we ask, what kind of cross-fruition could be gained from expanding the dialogue to cartography and mapmaking? We suggest that a shared focus on open-ended assemblages of cultural elements, rather than functional cultural wholes, provides a good basis for such a conversation. We argue that the capacity of the atlases of material folk culture to draw their own theoretical assumptions into doubt could serve as a useful prototype for controversy mappers. Vice versa we suggest that recent innovations in controversy mapping might overcome some of the problems that have troubled earlier ethnological mapmaking projects.

Keywords: historical-geographical paradigm, diffusionism, actor-network theory, cartography, controversy mapping

A Return to Cartography?

Like so many of its fellow cultural sciences, the ethnology of material folk culture boasts a rich cartographic past.[1] The adoption of the historical-geographical paradigm within this discipline covers an era in twentieth-century ethnology where the spatiotemporal charting of material folk culture became a joint project for several generations of scholars in institutions across Europe. Tracing its origins to the late nineteenth century when German historians first began categorising and mapping the geographical distribution of agricultural implements and house types (e.g. Baumgart 1881; Rhamm 1905), the historical-geographical paradigm is sometimes seen as the closest thing ethnology has ever come to a period of Kuhnian normal science (see especially Stoklund 2003). It nonetheless still figures as a curiosity that has little or no relevance for today's research practices in the field. With very few exceptions (see e.g. Frykman et al. 2009), cartography remains a thing of the past. At its height, however, the cartographic method saw ethnologists across Europe and Scandinavia undertake a series of national atlas projects (e.g. Lithberg 1919; Erixon 1957), eventually culminating in the European atlas collaboration in the decades following the Second World War (Rooijakkers & Meurkens 2000). In its aftermath, the cartographic method has been dismissed for its lack of proper theoretical foundation, its naïve empiricism and atomistic notion of culture, its lack of qualitative depth and its inability to get beyond synchronic snapshots of something essentially processual.[2]

In this paper we revisit those histories from the perspective of a contemporary cartographic project in science and technology studies (STS). Controversy mapping traces its origin to the actor-network theoretical branches of STS where it was developed by Bruno Latour in the 1990s as a method for studying techno-scientific disputes and their consequences for democratic deliberation (Venturini 2010). Our errand is precisely a revisit from this particular point of view. Rather than providing a comprehensive account of the historical-geographical paradigm, we want to launch a discussion about the legacy of the atlas projects in contemporary studies of material culture and perhaps re-energise an ethnological appetite for maps and mapmaking.

Controversy mapping is a cross-disciplinary enterprise that brings together ethnography, media studies, data mining, information design and scientometrics to exploit the potentials of digital mediation and follow the various traces left by actors online. The method is developed both for didactical purposes in a coordinated course program taught at a range of European institutions,[3] as well as for research purposes in a series of ongoing mapping projects (Rogers & Marres 2000; Marres 2004; Venturini 2010, 2012; Beck & Kropp 2011; Yaneva 2012).[4] It is, in our view, particularly interesting to revisit the cartography of material folk culture from the point of view of a mapping project that has strong actor-network theoretical roots. Actor-network theory (ANT) and material semiotics have been important inspirations in many of the recent ethnological returns to material culture studies (Damsholt, Simonsen & Mordhorst 2009), much like the ethnographic method has been one of the major inspirations for the actor-network theoretical approach to the study of science and technology (Law 1994; Latour 2005). The two fields are not unfamiliar to one another and there has been significant mutual learning and cross-fruition over the past decades. This cross-fruition, however, has never been extended to cartography and experiences with mapmaking. This is a shame. From the point of view of controversy mapping – and, we would argue, from the point of view of a material-semiotic ethnology as well – the alleged atomism and naïve empiricism of the historical-geographical paradigm does not appear off-putting and cluelessly deprived of theory. In fact one can argue that controversy mappers would look upon the historical-geographical paradigm and its insistence on tracing cultural patterns composed of traceable elements, as an early example of good social cartography. Where others would see primitive atomism, a controversy mapper would see the compositionism of Latour or the monadology of Gabriel Tarde realised in practice (Latour et al. 2012).

Ethnology and STS have already learned a great deal from each other, and more mutual learning may lie ahead if we consider the two disciplines' vastly different, but also strangely cognate, experiences with mapping. The purpose of this paper is to explore what might be learned from a closer dialogue between the cartography of material folk culture that dominated European ethnology at the apex of the twentieth century and the cartography of controversies that is currently emerging as a way of doing digitally assisted ANT. The critical point for us is to show how mapmaking in the context of a material semiotic analysis that risks being side-lined as theoretically clueless and naïve can, if pursued in the right way, be an experimental device that puts knowledge claims at risk and slow down existing forms of theoretically informed reasoning.

What Is Controversy Mapping, and Why Does It Matter to Ethnology?

A typical controversy mapping begins with a list. It will be sparse and preliminary at first, containing the main points of contestation, a few names of prominent actors, perhaps some references to relevant academic publications, reports from government agencies or NGOs, and probably some more specific technologies, events, places, or pieces of legislation that are known to be, in one way or another, significant to the discussion. The point of the list is to provide the mappers with a set of *traceable elements* that they can follow across different datasets to determine who is talking about what, when they are doing so, and in which contexts. If the topic is a new immunisation scheme, then the list might contain the names of the pharmaceutical companies supplying the vaccine, the spectrum of reported side effects, the names of known anti-vaccination activists, or the most frequently cited studies on the safety of the vaccine.

The mappers will attempt to chart the presence and absence of these elements across web-pages and blog posts, across the scientific literature, in the news media, on the various social media platforms, in the search history of Google, in the editing history of a set of Wikipedia articles, or in more issue-specific datasets such as the reports submitted to the Vaccine Adverse Event Reporting System (VAERS). The goal is to enable a *visual exploration* of the controversy as it unfolds in *space and time*: Where are the important groupings? Who are the important actors? What are their respective matters of concern? Where are the defining faultlines and the relevant axes of difference? And when do these shift, dissolve, or become entrenched? Since actors in a controversy tend to promote their own specific view of the issue, the goal of the mapping is to assemble, element by element, a more hybrid overview of how actor worlds overlap, coalesce, or diverge to create a space of conflict. The goal is a cosmogram of the *controversy* rather than of one specific actor world within it.

As the project progresses and the mappers develop a sensitivity to the complexity of what they are dealing with, the list of elements expands and acquires detail. The mappers may learn that the use of adjuvants such as mercury or aluminium have been a contested issue in relation to other vaccines where interest groups have attempted to link them to a rise in the cases of autism. Indeed, they may have to extend the scope of their mapping in the realisation that the controversy is really about immunisation in general and not a particular kind of vaccine. They may discover that an argument like herd immunity is not only advanced by "pro-vaxers", but also attacked by "anti-vaxers" (two issue terms used by the actors) in support of their differing agendas, or they may begin to distinguish between those fractions of the anti-vaccination campaign that are committed to homeopathic alternatives, and those who make no mention of alternative medicine at all.

What is crucially important about the multifarious items on this expanding list is precisely that they are *traceable*, which means that the mappers will be able to identify them (for example in a Twitter stream or in a large batch of scientific papers), and that they are viewed as *elements*, which means that they are in one way or another part of the changing composition of the controversy, but that the question of how and in which situations this is the case remains open and empirical. There is a list of things that are known to generate concern (mercury, aluminium, herd immunity, homeopathy, etc.), but it is understood that it is an open list, and that it might be necessary to add to it as we move into other contexts or as the controversy develops over time. Below (illustration 1) is an example of a map of the pro-vax and anti-vax online communities produced in collaboration with our students. It traces the issue of homeopathic alternatives across the two actor worlds. It was made by first producing a base map of websites that are engaged in the discussion for or against immunisation. It can be said to be a map because the hyperlinks between the websites are used to create a networked space where stronger interlinked websites appear closer to each other than weaker interlinked ones. So there are "regions" in this map, namely a pro-vax and an anti-vax one, and it makes a difference where (i.e. in which region) one finds certain keywords.

To an ethnologist who is versed in the historical-geographical paradigm and the various atlas projects that defined ethnological research on material folk culture through much of the early- to mid-twentieth century, this account of a controversy mapping project will probably sound familiar. Although the elements traced in controversy mapping are not hay rakes, flail types, or folk costumes (at least not in most contemporary controversies), and although the spatial ordering of these elements does not have to be geographical (it might be equally interesting to locate them, for example, in a network of websites, see

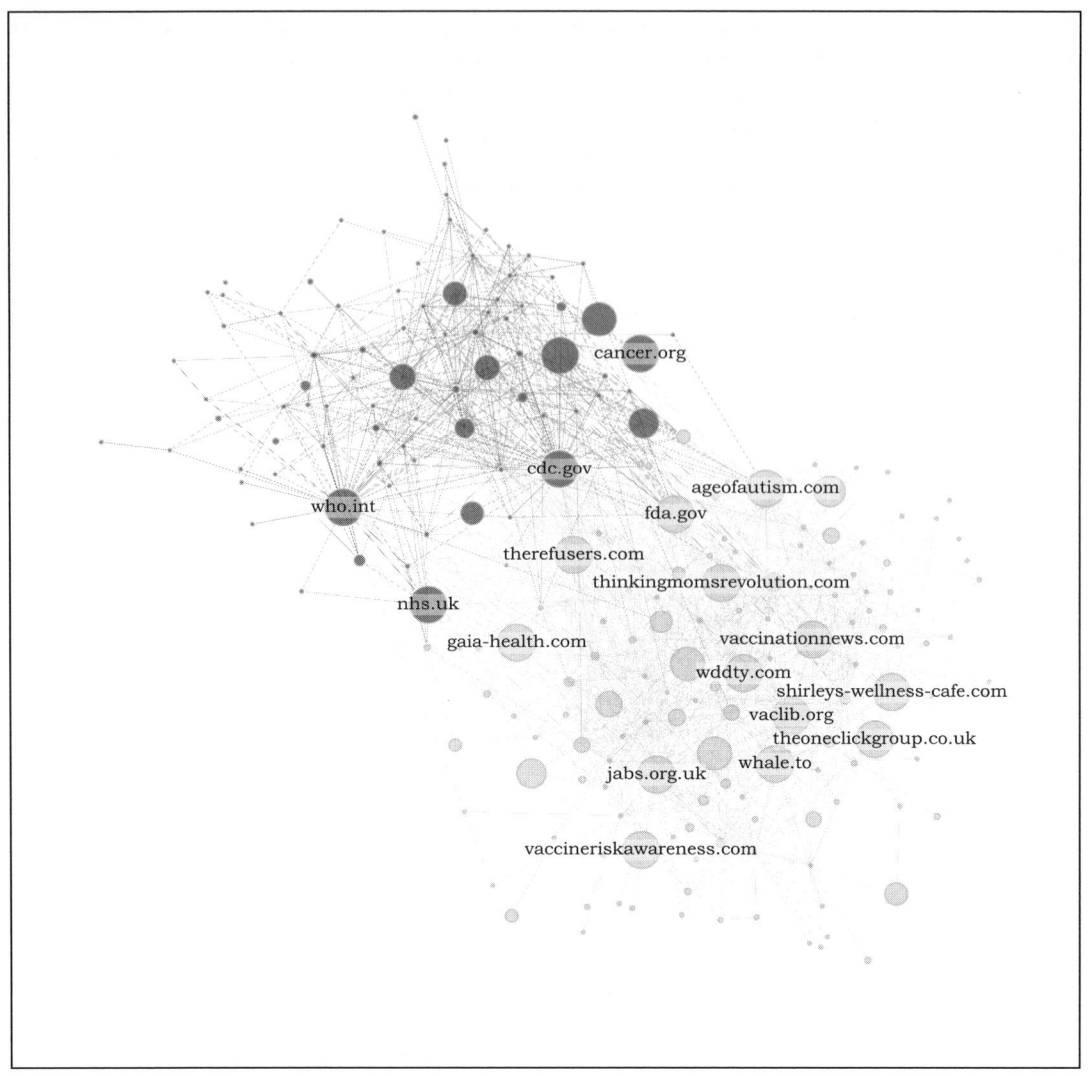

Ill. 1: Network of websites engaged in the vaccination controversy and the degree to which they talk about homeopathy. Websites that were specifically concerned with immunisation were scraped for hyperlinks using a tool called the Navicrawler. A network graph of websites connected by hyperlinks was then spatialised using the spring based ForceAtlas2 algorithm. We used the Google Scraper to query each website for a series of issue-relevant keywords that we could plot on the spatialised graph to examine their distribution (represented by the size of the nodes). Here we see the distribution of the words "homeopathy" and "homeopathic". Notice that 1) the network has an anti-vax (light grey) and a pro-vax (dark grey) pole. 2) That there are many links between the two poles. This indicates that pro-vaxers and anti-vaxers are aware of each other's existence and point to each other in their discussions. We could say that they take each other into account. 3) That it is only some of the websites that talk about homeopathy (bigger nodes indicate more mentions). It tells us not only that it is an issue that divides the anti-vaxers (not all mention them), but also that it is a point of contestation that gets the pro-vaxers' attention (albeit primarily the institutional actors). The map was produced collectively by students in a controversy mapping class at the Danish Technical University in December 2013.

illustration 1), the similarities are still noteworthy. One could certainly say that early twentieth-century ethnologists also began with a list, namely the typology of artifacts that enabled them to ask their evolutionary and diffusionist questions about cultural origins and developments. And one could equally say that as the ethnological mappers developed a sensitivity to the complexity of what they were dealing with, that list rapidly became more detailed.

The hay rake, for example, was initially divided into a few basic types, but as the subtler variations in how one attaches the handle to the head turned out to be more interesting than first assumed, more types were added to the list and traced on the maps (see e.g. Stoklund 1990 and his comparison of Erixon 1931 and Erixon 1957). The result of this increasing complexity is well known: as more variations crowded the maps, and as the spreading patterns diversified and became more ambiguous, the theoretical assumptions that had originally provided the impetus for the big cartographic projects (diffusionist or evolutionary alike) became increasingly untenable, at least in their purest of forms. Illustration 2 shows a map from Oskar Moser's monograph on rake types in Kärnten, Austria. It is an early example of a complex map leading to new theoretical ideas. In this case it is the proposition that the appropriateness of certain rake types for hard work on the mountain slopes is dependent on differing cultural classifications of what is a man's and a woman's rake, rather than functional criteria (Moser 1952, see also Stoklund 2003).

Moser's map in illustration 2 essentially asks a question, namely: why can the distribution of rake types not be explained by functional criteria alone? The answer to that question then had to be found through other means of inquiry, resulting eventually in the idea of a cultural classification based on gender. This capacity of maps to do what the Belgian philosopher of science Isabelle Stengers would call to slow down reasoning and put knowledge claims at risk (Stengers 2000, 2005) is in fact at the heart of what controversy mapping is meant to achieve. Originally developed as a way of teaching engineering students some basic intuitions from social studies of science and technology, the idea behind con-

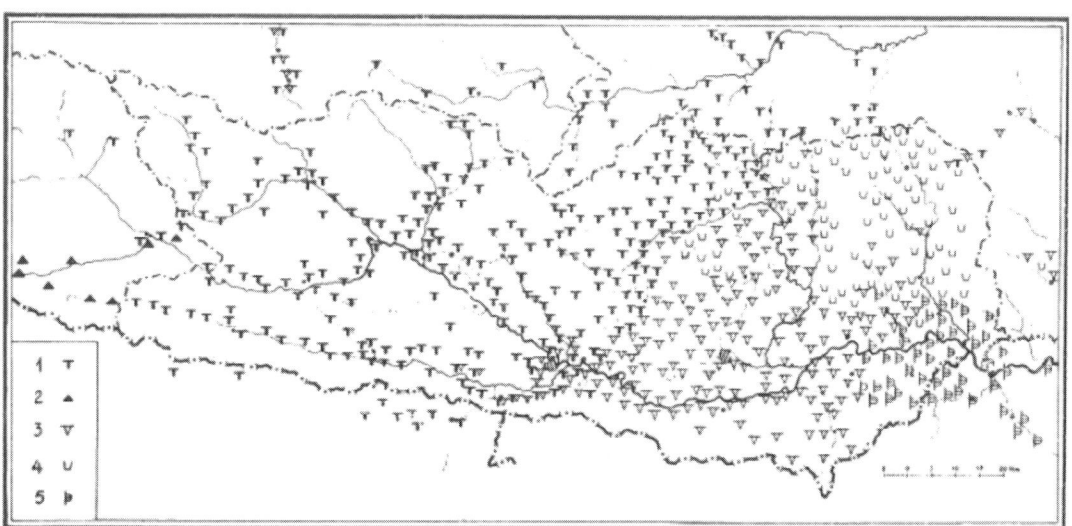

Ill. 2: Oskar Moser's map of rake types in Kärnten. The map shows five rake types (1: Blade handled rake. 2: Blade handled rake with short diagonal braces. 3: Simple split-handled rake. 4: Forked rake with natural handle. 5: Simple bow rake). The map does not show male and female rakes, but the distribution of rake types prompted the question that led to that conclusion. (Moser 1952, in Stoklund 1990: 13)

troversy mapping is essentially pedagogical: faced with the practical task of charting the claims made by different actors in a controversy over time (as well as the conflicting types of evidence and arguments deployed in support of these claims), students are prompted to reconsider any overly simplistic understandings that they might otherwise have been able to maintain about the role and place of scientific expertise in contemporary democracy. From this perspective, controversy mappers anno 2014 and the cartographers of material folk culture of the mid-twentieth century have a lot to talk about.

It must be acknowledged, however, that this is not always how the contentious story of the historical-geographical paradigm is being told. One of the more critical versions is summed up in the urban legend that as the mappers added ever more transparent overlays charting ever more formal variations to their base maps, what emerged was not the neat diffusion routes and well defined cultural zones that they had been hoping for, but a progressively overdrawn hairball that eventually went black with complexity. The story of a failure, in other words, and a failure that eventually lead to a paradigmatic shift. Another version is epitomised by the Dutch ethnologist J.J. Voskuil in his autobiographic novel *Het Bureau* (Voskuil 2000) about the capsised Great Atlas of European Folk Culture. Voskuil spent most of his career working on the atlas project and bitterly lamented the project leaders' increasingly dogmatic insistence on a methodology that produced very few results compared to the effort it required and, through its grandiose continental ambitions, systematically failed to take into account all the interesting problems that were emerging from mapping projects at the local and national scales. In their review of *Het Bureau* Gerard Rooijakkers and Peter Meurkens quotes a scene where, right towards the last convulsions of the European atlas project in the early 1980s, some of the first finished maps arrive for commentary in Amsterdam. Voskuil is addressing some of his assistants (Seiner is the alias for the leader of the German atlas project in Bonn, Matthias Zender):

He put the opened edition showing the Dutch map on top of the European one and pulled back a little in order to let Lien take a look at it. "That makes much more subtle distinctions." "Then who simplified it?" Lien asked. "Seiner." He looked at a distance at the European map. "In a way it is very German, isn't it? – such a European map. You see those signs march from the center of Europe towards the edges." "Do you think that this European Atlas initially is a German project?" Ad asked with unbelief. "Definitely! Just like the European Community. They are both a product of the national-socialism." (J.J. Voskuil, alias Marten Konig, in *Het Bureau*, translated and quoted in Rooijakkers and Meurkens 2000: 84)

The rather more positive legacy of the historical-geographical paradigm emphasises the maps' ability to enact a world of material folk culture that was both more complex than first thought, impossible to ignore once mapped, and thus something of an experimental device that prompted ethnologists to develop more sophisticated theoretical ideas, engage with new kinds of empirical material and acquire a broader suite of methodological approaches to do so (see for example Stoklund 2003). Along such lines, Thomas Højrup has made the case that maps were a powerful source of argumentation against political attempts to conflate nationality, ethnicity and culture. He thus writes about the European atlas collaboration that Voskuil and others so vehemently loathed:

It was not least within the study of building practices, which used to play a major role for the discussion about ethnic demarcations, that ethnologists torpedoed the basic presumption that folk culture develops according to national principles. (…) The European atlas collaboration, the study of diffusion paths, innovation centres and local forms of adaptation (…) heralded a modern European Ethnology (…) that trespassed not only the cultural nation states but also the iron curtain separating East from West. Part of the disciplinary ethos seemed to be that when the self-dependant folk culture could not be deterred or confined by "random" political demarcations, then neither would the European ethnologist. The historical-geographical method and the strong focus on things and customs could be turned to a quiet but bitingly effective bastion for a critique of nationalism. (Højrup 2002: 650, our translation)

Our ambition in this paper is not to reconcile these differences between positive and negative legacies, or to reach a verdict on what would be a "right" or "fair" representation of how folklife cartography has figured in the disciplinary history of European ethnology. We see no reason, for instance, why a project like the Great Atlas of European Folk Culture could not simultaneously have been a badly managed systemic monster that left its participant researchers rather disillusioned, and a manifestation of a methodological approach that proved highly productive in other respects (Karin Gustavsson's contribution in this volume certainly supports the idea that cartography could also be a great source of enthusiasm and inspiration). What we will do, however, is to revisit the historical-geographical paradigm from the vantage point of controversy mapping in order to explore two closely related lines of inquiry that are, to our minds, of relevance to contemporary research practices in both ethnology and STS.

First, considering that many ethnologists have taken inspiration from STS, and in particular from ANT and material semiotics, during the past decade (see Ren & Krogh Petersen 2013 for an overview), we ask what else could be learned from extending the conversation between the two fields of study to also include their common experiences with cartography. What would happen if we considered mapping to be more than an heirloom, but as a potential research strategy? And *second*, considering that STS, and in particular ANT and material semiotics, have taken much of their key inspiration, if not explicitly from European ethnology, then at least from related ethnographic traditions, what could be learned if controversy mappers acquainted themselves with the historical-geographical paradigm?

What Ethnologists Might Learn from Controversy Mapping

Like several other disciplines concerned with the study of culture, ethnology has, over the past couple of decades, rekindled its interest in the materiality of its subject matter. One notable way of doing so has been to draw inspiration from STS and in particular its material semiotic branch sometimes known as ANT. Several examples of how to do cultural analysis with such a revamped focus on materiality have come out of this dialogue (see for example Nilsson 2000; Jespersen 2008; Sandberg 2009; Ren 2009; Munk 2010; Boll 2011; Krogh Petersen 2011; Beck, Niewöhner & Sørensen 2012, or the papers collected in Damsholt, Simonsen & Mordhorst 2009) and are now prompting a more theoretical meta-reflection over their possible place in the ethnological repertoire (e.g. Ren & Krogh Petersen 2013).

On the one hand it seems straightforward that ethnologists should be susceptible to the claim that things (non-humans) are important, that they play an active role, and that the social fabric is thus composed not just of mental structures, language or texts, but of technologies, ecologies and bodies as well. After all, this is well-known terrain for a discipline dedicated from birth to the study of material culture. Neither is it perhaps so essentially different to think in terms of "modes of ordering" (Law 1994) or "modes of existence" (Latour 2013) when one is already used to, and well versed in, notions such as discourses or life forms. There have in other words been some clear affinities between established ethnological approaches to cultural analysis and the newer inspirations drawn from ANT and material semiotics.

On the other hand there is something about the radical empiricism and the relational ontology, on which ANT and material semiotics rely that can appear incomprehensibly naïve to an ethnologist. How is it possible to claim that something is multiple and enacted, when anybody who has observed cultural phenomena such as ideas about "the good life" or people's morning routines will have noticed that they are frequently both extremely enduring, uncompromisingly singular and taken absolutely for granted by their practitioners (Damsholt & Jespersen, this issue)? A critique to which those who find a material semiotic approach productive would habitually reply that such durations are indeed all the more interesting, since one would naturally have to wonder what kind of work and what kind of material devices achieve the amazing feat of keeping cultural phenomena so stable and enduring. The question is not so much what these phenomena are or what they do, but how they are being *done* (see especially Mol 2002 and her praxiography). The main concern for the cultural analyst may thus be to keep open the possibility of cultural phenomena being done differently, or even to actively contribute to their re-enactment (see Damsholt & Jespersen for a discussion of approaches to endurance vs. radical change, or see the papers collected in Jespersen et al. 2012 for a discussion of interventionist approaches to cultural analysis).

This problem of how to handle materiality as a part of cultural analysis is arguably predicated on what kind of concept of culture one adheres to. If culture is taken to be a unit of analysis with explanatory powers of its own, then the durability and particularity of cultural phenomena must be understood as the *consequences* of a culture. That, however, is not an option in a material semiotic analysis. What gets to count as "a culture" or "cultural" here is in itself the important research question, and thus something that must be answered empirically each time anew. The standard way of providing such an answer is to proceed ethnographically and "follow the actors themselves" (Latour 2005: 12), association by association, carefully assembling the phenomenon at hand. It is a radically empiricist approach that stubbornly adheres to "the prescription to be non-prescriptive" (Law 2009: 6), and it is slow and painstaking work.

To a certain extent, controversy mappers are in a similar kind of predicament. A frequently voiced reason for mapping controversies, and not some other phenomena, is precisely that they display most strikingly the social in its making (Venturini 2010). As we stressed in the beginning, the question of what belongs to a controversy, and in what way it does so, always remains open and empirical – it is an inquiry into the assemblage of the social in that specific situation. But contrary to material semiotic ethnographers, controversy mappers have an additional set of options at their disposal when they have to deal with these open and empirical questions. *First*, although the slow ethnographic footwork of following the actors themselves is arguably preferable in terms of quality and depth of the account, it has some tangible and practical limits that are given by the time, manpower and field access of the project. By following a series of traceable elements through online datasets instead, using digital methods such as web cartography or text mining (whenever these are applicable and make sense), controversy mappers can significantly speed up the assembly process without defaulting on the relational ontology (phenomena are still emergent and given by the actors).[5] ANT has been experimenting since the early 1980s with various computer assisted methods, not least with inspiration from scientometrics, and it has always been with this capacity problem in mind (Callon et al. 1983; Latour, Mauguin & Teil 1992; Teil & Latour 1995). *Second*, the ability to easily render these mapped assemblages visually explorable arguably provides a different kind of presence to whatever is the object of analysis. What should be particularly interesting to contemporary ethnologists with a material semiotic inclination is of course that they have such potentials readily available in their own disciplinary annals.

In the introduction to his book from 2003 on the cultural history of artifacts (*Tingenes Kulturhistorie*), Bjarne Stoklund offered his reflections on the material turn that was brewing across the spectrum of cultural sciences at the time (Stoklund 2003). Spurred by the publication of the new transdisciplinary *Journal of Material Culture* in 1996 the now late professor of Danish ethnology expressed his hopes that artifacts could once again arouse the appetite of European ethnologists. After being dethroned by social relations as the preferred object of study during the spree of community studies in the 1970s, and later somewhat half-heartedly reintroduced as "signs" and "language" by the consumption research program in the 1980s, artifacts, Stoklund argued, deserved to be taken seriously beyond the limits of textual analogy. They deserved to be recognised for their concrete and formative role in the human struggle for existence, and they deserved to be considered both as physical form and practical function, and not "just" as bearers of meaning, in a world where such things were understood to be of consequence to the development of human culture and society.

Stoklund was clearly contributing to a debate about the future direction of ethnological research, although his instrument was retrospective. By revisiting some of the seminal moments in the disciplinary history where the form and function of artifacts had figured prominently he struck up a distinction between artifacts as cultural elements and artifacts as cultural products that is particularly interesting from the point of view of material semiotics and controversy mapping alike. The notion of cultural *element*, argued Stoklund, belongs to a concept of culture that traces its origins to Edward Bernard Tyler and is essentially additional insofar as it considers culture to be the sum of its multifarious constituent parts, whatever they may be at that point in space and time (see illustration 3). This allows artifacts to have a real say in a cultural assemblage. The notion of cultural *product*, on the other hand, presumes the pre-existence of a culture, Durkheimian and *sui generis* in nature, from which the artifacts passively receive their meaning.

If we accept that distinction, then it is perhaps not so far-fetched to consider the historical-geographical paradigm as a kind of precursor to the current

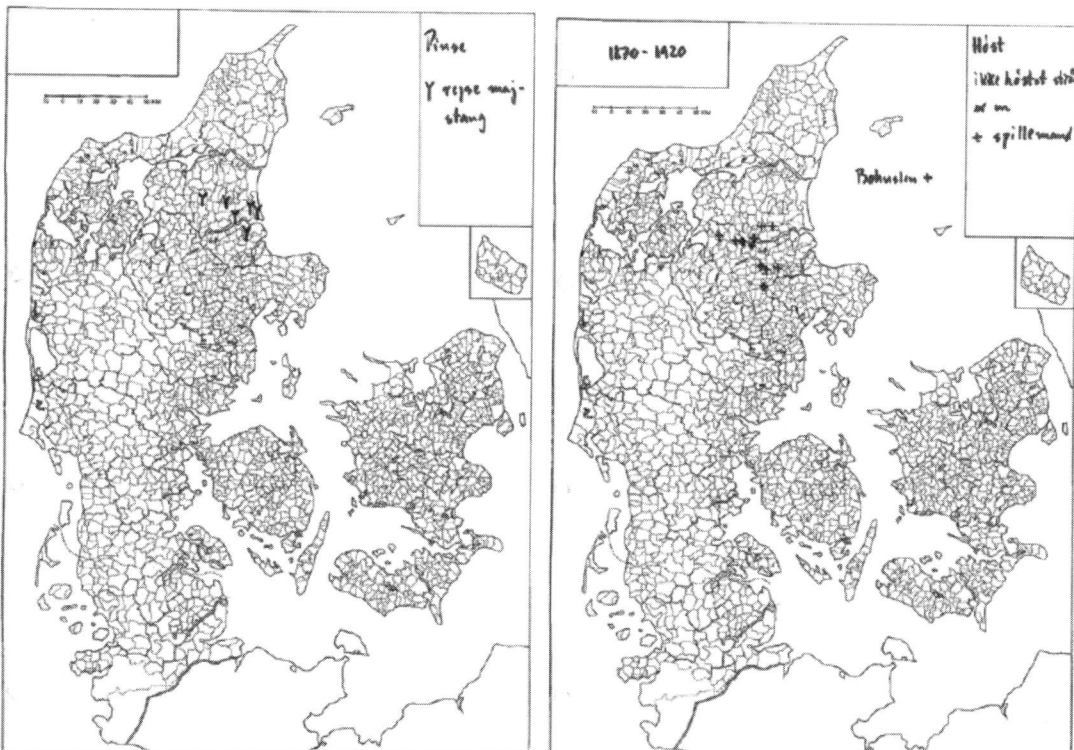

Ill. 3: Two examples of transparent overlays used to plot cultural elements from the archives of Ole Højrup (section on Eastern Jutland). To the left it is the practice of erecting Pentecostal May poles, to the right is the use of fiddlers for a particular part of the harvest. Here culture is in a very practical sense never more than the sum of its parts: it is by moving the transparent overlays on top of one another that a composition takes shape.

material semiotic types of analysis. At least they share the insistence on not deciding in advance what elements will be composed together, but devising instead a way of letting their changing composition be deployed and examined empirically. "The whole", in controversy mapping, is explicitly considered to be *less* than the sum of its parts (Latour et al. 2012). The same, we would argue, is true for the mapping of material folk culture (although not always for the theoretical agendas associated with it) and for material semiotic analysis in contemporary ethnology.

In this way one could say that ethnologists are currently going back to analysing open assemblages of cultural elements, but with a toolbox that was only later imported from British social anthropology to analyse self-contained cultural wholes and their various derivatives, namely the toolbox of ethnographic field methods like participant observation and semi-structured interviewing. Why not supplement this toolbox with some of the cartographic instruments that were originally available? There should be all the more reason to do so now, given the rapidly expanding array of topics that are considered suitable for ethnological analysis (indeed, the immunisation controversy itself has recently been subjected to such an analysis using participatory, ethnographic methods, see Cunha & Durand 2013). Whereas the historical realm of material folk culture could in principle be mapped and made available for analysis once and for all, contemporary ethnologists are faced with the challenge of having to enact a new object of study almost every time they engage in a new project. If mapping is a way of speeding up part of that assembly process, then it has a tangible and immediate application in contemporary ethnological research projects.

It has been suggested that cultural analysis should be particularly interested in computational methods because of the distributed nature of cultural phenomena (Abello, Broadwell & Tangherlini 2012). It is always desirable to be empirically as broad as possible when dealing with the everyday. Whereas we agree with this contention in general, we also want to make the more specific point about cultural analysis of the material-semiotic variety, that it champions its ability to situate complex problems in everyday life situations as one of its important contributions. Crudely put, this means that ethnologists are no longer working on a well-defined, common object of study, but are constantly cultivating new areas of cultural analysis. This analytical "promiscuity", that has been so valuable in terms of making ethnology relevant to a broad range of societal problems, makes it necessary to find new ways of quite literally putting the ever changing objects of study on the map.

On top of that, with the possibilities offered by the advent of digital mediation, some of the problems that originally tarnished the reputation of the historical-geographical method have now become solvable in ways that would have been unimaginable to folklife cartographers half a century ago. One of those is the problem of diachronicity. Both Sigurd Erixon in Stockholm and J.J. Voskuil in Amsterdam eventually became more interested in the ethnohistorical study of local communities where the sources (peasant diaries, among other things) permitted a proper diachronic understanding of the cultural processes at play. It was one of the most insurmountable problems of the atlas projects that they had to lump together in one synchronic snapshot all reported pre-industrial findings of an artifact in a particular area, sometimes covering a time span from Medieval times to the twentieth century (Stoklund 1990: 11). The maps therefore conveyed static, condensed images of relatively long time spans, and the reader would have to consult the often very voluminous commentaries to get the cartographers' account of the developments over time (see for example Erixon 1957). Notice the missing time indication on the left overlay in illustration 3: these inconsistencies in temporal data were notorious in the atlas projects, especially the ones dealing with material folk culture (folk-tale cartography came somewhat closer to a solution [Tangherlini 2013]). The difficulties of registering and presenting diachronic data does not arise with the same gravity when mapping is based on digital traces. Digital traces are often either time-stamped themselves (like a tweet or a status update), or left in a context where a time stamp can easily be associated with them (like in a blog post or a scien-

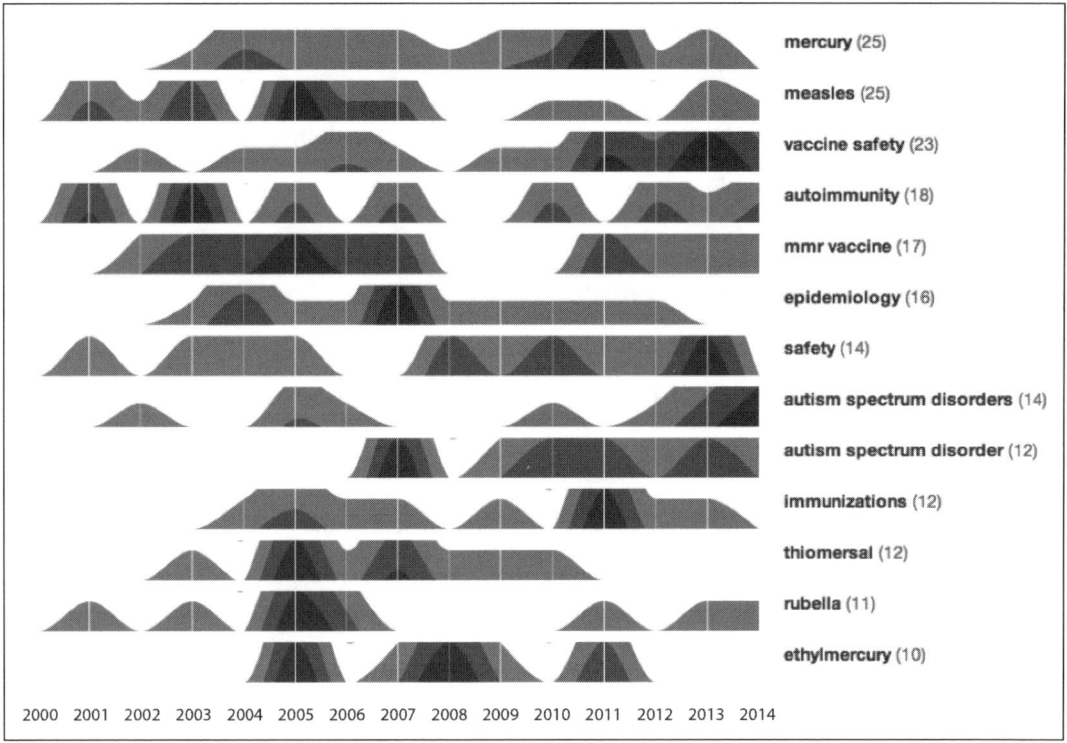

Ill. 4: Relative variations in author keywords in the scientific literature on immunization and autism over a time period from 2000 to 2014 on the horizontal axis. The data set was produced using the search query "(immuniz* OR vaccin*) AND autism" on Scopus and visualised using Sciencescape. The numbers on the right indicate the total number of papers on immunization and autism tagged by its authors with a specific keyword. The flowcharts indicate the publication of these papers over time. Mercury seems to have been particularly interesting to this literature in 2011, for example, whereas thiomersal or rubella topped in 2005.

tific publication). With time-stamped data, the plotting of variables against a timescale becomes readily accessible. As an example, illustration 4 shows the variations in keywords associated with immunisation and autism in the scientific literature over time.

Another of the notorious incapacities of the atlas projects that allegedly drove researchers like Erixon and Voskuil towards community studies, were their limitations with respect to local cultural processes. Such processes could effectively only be studied through a more in-depth qualitative approach. Looking at a map like the hyperlink network shown in illustration 1, very little seems to have changed in relation to this problem. The map itself is still equally incapable of qualitative engagements at the local level. What has to be taken into account, however, is that the previously insurmountable differences between the macro and the micro level of analysis is now only a click or a scroll away from one another. In fact, they are just different scalings of the same empirical material rather than two different analytical levels. Illustration 5 shows the content of a page on an anti-vaccination website that talks about homeopathy. It has been accessed directly from the network in illustration 1 and gives the researcher an immediate opportunity to explore qualitatively how a component like homeopathy becomes a matter of concern in this specific context. One can see the hyperlinks that give illustration 1 its structure and map-like qualities (herbalhealer.com, e.g.), and

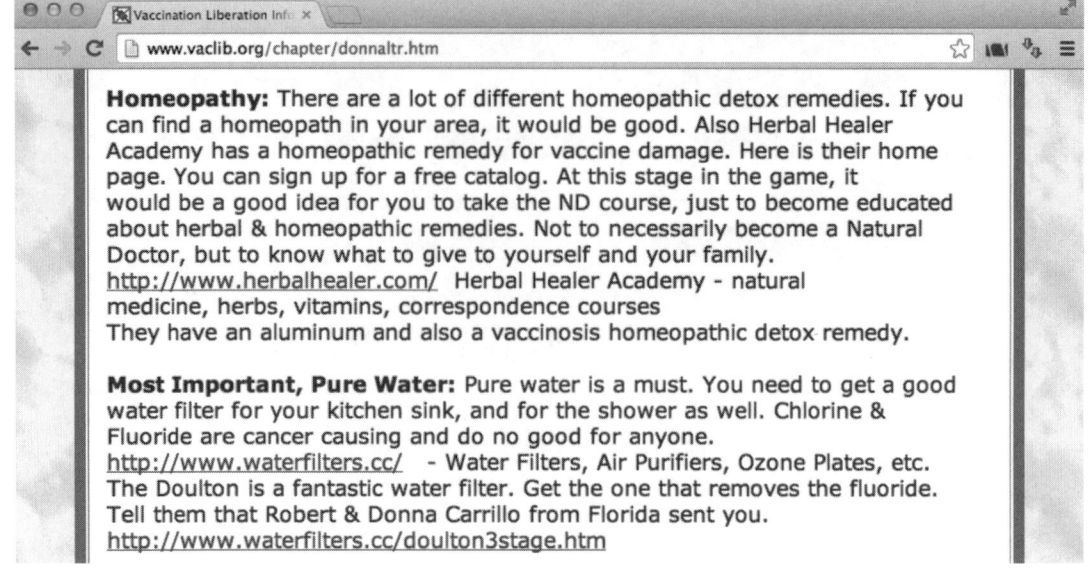

Ill. 5: Screenshot from an anti-vax website discussing homeopathy. The website has been accessed directly from the network in illustration 1.

one can explore the precise context in which they are used. There is also the possibility to situate the elements that we have traced, namely words like "homeopathy" or "homeopathic", in the text from which they were extracted.

These analytical moves were more or less impossible, or at least extremely laborious, for the cartographers of material folk culture. Although attempts were made to provide context in the elaborate comments to the atlas maps, it was always the mappers' interpretation of the maps. The flexibility that allows the same empirical material to be simultaneously explored through a map and through a qualitative analysis of the full record has only recently become available.

What Controversy Mappers Could Learn from Ethnology

But what if we were to turn the question on its head? What if we were to ask instead what controversy mappers could learn from their distant cousins in folklife cartography? To answer that question we should probably first try to establish what STS has already learned from ethnology. And strictly speaking, if one looks into classic works of the STS literature (Latour & Woolgar 1979; Knorr-Cetina 1981; Lynch 1985; Shapin & Schaffer 1985; Pinch & Bijker 1987), the answer to that question would be a resounding nothing. STS seems to have established itself in a world, or a part of social science, that has been completely unaware of the existence of European ethnology. STS researchers refer to sociologists, anthropologists, historians and philosophers – in particular French, British and American ones – but never to European ethnologists. Judging from literature references the conclusion is therefore clear: STS has learned nothing from European ethnology.

It is, however, possible to reach almost the opposite conclusion if we broaden the perspective a bit. A leading historian of science, Peter Galison, recently introduced a book chapter with the following remark: "Behind the most significant accomplishments of the last thirty years of science and technology studies – behind laboratory studies and actor network theory, at the centre of our ventures into scientific intellectual property, authorship, historical epistemology, media studies, book history, discourse analysis, participant-observation and the philosophy of experimentation – in back of all this is a turn toward locality" (Galison 2014: 197). If Galison is right that the turn to locality is the key intellectual source from which STS springs, then one could point out that this source was not of STS's own making. When STS established itself in the late 1970s it imported the turn to locality from other disciplines where this turn had been underway for several decades. In particular, STS drew on ethnography and pragmatist micro sociologies (e.g. symbolic interactionism and ethnomethodology). If we grant that the turn to locality, to "situatedness", to micro histories, to case studies and to field studies emerged on a broad front generated by exchanges within and between a number of cultural sciences, then it is not too far a stretch to give some of the credit for this localising turn to European ethnology. As a relatively new field, STS has had to find its inspiration elsewhere. One of them was in ethnography. Indeed, one of the founding moments can be said to have occurred when anthropologically trained scholars proposed to study science in its everyday practice (e.g. Latour & Woolgar 1979; Knorr-Cetina 1981; Lynch 1985; Suchman 1987; Traweek 1988). The conclusion then, is that STS has learned almost everything from the localising move that European ethnology was a part of and helped bring about.

What STS has not quite learned, however, is how to get comfortable with cartography, not as the object of a critical analysis (that has gone just fine, see e.g. Turnbull 1996 or Harley 1989), but as a methodological move that produces different and not always localising effects. While ANT and material semiotics have been helpful in prompting ethnologists to think through the material return of their discipline and establish new roles for themselves and their cultural analysis, ANT itself has been busy searching for a history to call its own. Born, as it were, in the late 1970s, scholars like Bruno Latour in particular have spent the past two decades substantiating the possible inspirations and forerunners that might define ANT as part of a specific tradition in the humanities and social sciences.

The gallery of forefathers now spans from American pragmatists like William James (whatever makes a difference is an actor) or John Dewey (a public is sparked into being by its matters of concern) to French philosophers such as Gilles Deleuze (the notion of rhizome and the notion of network) or Michel Serres (anti-correspondence theory), but what is perhaps most relevant here is the rediscovery of the pre-Durkheimian French sociologist Gabriel Tarde (Toews 2003; Latour 2005; Barry & Thrift 2007). In his day (the late nineteenth century) Tarde was considered to be the founding father of a burgeoning French sociology that was based around the study of associations. For him, the social had nothing to do with the *sui generis* existence that could explain collective behaviour that his predecessor Durkheim would later become famous for claiming. On the contrary, Tarde believed that the social was the very thing that had to be explained through what he called a monadological social science (Tarde 2011). The main feat of such a monadology would be the meticulous mapping of the basic components (monads) that made up the social fabric.

We can safely read "cultural elements" instead of "monads" here. Tarde explicitly stated his methodological ambitions for a corps of sociologists that would travel the French countryside and "write out with the greatest care and in the greatest possible detail, the succession of minute transformations in the political or economic world" (Tarde 1999: 130–131), and that this would include charting the spread and variation of both dialects, artifacts, habits and rituals, much like the various atlas projects over folk culture that would later be launched by ethnological departments across Europe. While we tend to think about the historical-geographical paradigm in the study of material folk culture as originating in German *Volkskunde* (e.g. Baumgart 1881; Rhamm 1905), a simultaneous experiment with diffusion maps was going on in France.[6]

Contrary to this Tardean vision, which was never realised, most likely due to a practical lack of hands, the historical-geographical paradigm in ethnology actually came to fruition, and not only that: it stayed within the mainstream of ethnological research for well over half a century. That is particularly interesting in the landscape of cultural scientific disciplines from which STS has otherwise drawn its inspiration. Atlas projects were also carried out in anthropology, leading for example to the "Standard Cross-Cultural Sample" (Murdock & White 1969), the *Ethnographic Atlas* (Murdock 1969) and the *Atlas of World Cultures* (Murdock 1981). The approach here was very different, taking as a given the existence of well-defined cultural wholes (mainly tribes) to which habits and rituals could be ascribed. In stark contrast to this, the ethnological atlas projects were truly monadological, which is arguably why they succeeded in putting the knowledge claims of their diffusionist, evolutionist and nationalist forefathers at risk. They might serve as a positive role model for controversy mappers in a world where cartography is far too often associated with imperial power and colonial dominance. They show us that maps can work on material semiotic terms.

Conclusion: Mapping as an Experimental Device

Revisiting the historical-geographical paradigm, as we have done in this paper, and bringing it into dialogue with the current mapping controversies efforts in STS may not seem the most obvious thing to do. After all, many contemporary ethnologists consider the historical-geographical paradigm to be something of an epic failure that one would be ill advised to spend more time on. In this paper we have attempted to argue the contrary: We argue that a reconsideration of the historical-geographical paradigm in a dialogue with STS might provide contemporary ethnology with a cartographic future.

To set the stage for our argument, we have pointed out the dialogues that are already taking place between ethnology and STS. Briefly put, ethnologists have recently drawn on STS to rekindle their interest in materiality. And, again briefly put, STS is essentially based on the turn to locality that ethnology along with other social sciences brought about in the mid-twentieth century. But the shared interest in materiality, everyday practices and locality are not the only possible objects of dialogue between ethnology and STS. There is also mapping.

It is all too easy to suggest that the current mapping controversies projects in STS and the ethnological atlas projects of the twentieth century are worlds apart: Search engines vs. bicycles, databases vs. notebooks, Twitter streams vs. hay rakes, digital data vs. physical objects. But as we have pointed out, the mapping projects in STS and ethnology share some fundamental features that set them apart from other mapping projects, such as Murdock's anthropological atlases. To identify these shared features, we have focused attention on the role played by, for example, lists of traceable elements. Cartographic ethnologists of the past and controversy mappers of the present began and begin their endeavours with a simple list of elements that they set out to trace. As the collection of elements proceeds, the list is expanded and revised. The cartographic projects that grow from this starting point entail a commitment to the idea that "a culture" or "a controversy" is an assemblage, which is composed out of a constantly evolving multitude of bits and pieces. In Stoklund's terms the collected objects are seen as *cultural elements*, that is elements that collectively produce an assemblage. This approach is directly opposed to the functionalist view that the collected objects must be seen as *cultural products*, that is material expressions of an underlying culture *sui generis*. With Stoklund's distinction between cultural elements and cultural products, it becomes clear that the mapping projects in STS and ethnology are quite similar in their fundamental "monadological" strategies, and quite different from "functionalist" mapping projects that build their mapping projects from the assumption that a number of distinct underlying cultures exist and express themselves through material artifacts.

If the shared commitment to a monadological mapping strategy becomes a part of the ongoing dialogue between STS and ethnology, then one might ask what the two participants could learn from each other? We have no final answer to this question, but we have suggested that controversy mapping might provide some valuable resources that were not available to the cartography of material folk culture: The time stamps available in much online material could alleviate some of the problems of diacronicity. The scalability of digital maps could do away with the insurmountable difference between micro- and macro-level analysis. Controversy mappers, on the other hand, might learn important lessons from the historical-geographical paradigm, in particular on how successfully the truly monadological atlas projects succeeded in putting the knowledge claims of their diffusionist, evolutionist and nationalist forefathers at risk.

Our conclusion then is that a combination of the productive experiences from the cartography of material folk culture and the cartography of controversies in material semiotic STS holds promises for the future. We will make more of the resources and flexibility of digital mapping if we constantly bear in mind that we are mapping cultural elements rather than cultural products. Mapping may then become an experimental device that will constantly refresh our ideas about what "a culture" or "a controversy" consists of. Our theoretical baggage makes it all too easy to claim that the things we observe are the expressions of "a cultural pattern", "a type of person" or "a dominating discourse". Resourceful, flexible and well-crafted monadological mapping projects might challenge such quick certainties in productive ways.

Notes

1 The neighbouring discipline of folkloristics also has a rich cartographic tradition, often referred to as the Finnish School (Tangherlini 2010). In this article, we specifically revisit the historical-geographical paradigm in the study of *material* folk culture. We have chosen this focus because the ethnologists that currently see themselves as descendants of the studies of material folk culture also are the ones that currently engage actively with science and technology studies.
2 We are grateful to Bjarne Stoklund, the late professor of Danish ethnology, who agreed to be interviewed as part of our research for this paper before he passed away. We want to thank Thomas Højrup, who kindly answered our questions and lent us some volumes from his father's archives (Ole Højrup worked on the Danish atlas project). We also want to thank Orvar Löfgren for his elaborate and encouraging comments on a previous draft of this paper, the editor of the special issue, and our two anonymous reviewers.
3 A collection of student projects can be found at http://controverses.sciences-po.fr/archiveindex/. In Denmark, where we have been involved in establishing the course, controversy mapping is taught to designers at the Danish Technical University, to techno-anthropologists at the University of Aalborg and to sociologists, ethnologists and anthropologists at the University of Copenhagen.
4 See for example the E-Maps project (http://www.emapsproject.com/), the Digital Methods Initiative (https://digitalmethods.net/), or the Macospol project (http://www.mappingcontroversies.net/).
5 It is true that digital mapping projects require a lot of manpower and hard work as well, especially if one includes the time and resources spent writing the necessary code. What is encouraging, however, is the increasing availability of free and ready to use online applications that allow the researcher to harvest or analyse data with relative ease. The tools used to trace keywords in illustration 1 (the Google Scraper) and visualise scientometric data in illustration 4 (Sciencescape) are both freely accessible online.
6 It is an interesting story in itself how diffusionist Scandinavian ethnology forged ties with the remainders of Tardean French sociology and folkloristics. We know that Sigurd Erixon worked tirelessly to promote a dialogue between the different schools of thought separating ethnology and folkloristics in Germany, Scandinavia and the Slavic countries from France and the rest of Latin-speaking Europe. Erixon participated, among other things, in the founding of the Commission Internationale des Arts Populaires (CIAP), the Congrés Internationale de Folklore (CIFL) and the Société Internationale de l'Ethnologie et de Folklore (SIEF) and he befriended the French museologist Georges Henri Rivière as early as the 1930s (Rogan 2008). Rivière was an interesting character and a good friend of Arnold van Gennep (Zumwalt 1982), which places him right in the company of intellectual outcasts that had been effectively marginalised by the reigning Durkheimeans of interwar French sociology.

References

Abello, James, Peter Broadwell & Timothy R. Tangherlini 2012: Computational Folkloristics. *Communications of the ACM* 55:7, 60–70.
Barry, Adrew & Nigel Thrift 2007: Gabriel Tarde: Imitation, Invention and Economy. *Economy and Society* 36:4, 509–525.
Baumgart, R. 1881: *Die Ackerbaugeräthe in ihren praktischen Beziehungen wie nach ihrer urgeschichtlichen und ethnographischen Bedeutung.* Heidelberg.
Beck, Gerald & Cordula Kropp 2011: Infrastructures of Risk: A Mapping Approach towards Controversies on Risks. *Journal of Risk Research* 14:1, 1–16.
Beck, Stefan, Jörg Niewöhner & Estrid Sørensen 2012: *Science and Technology Studies: Eine sozialanthropologische Einführung.* Bielefeld: Transcript Verlag.

Boll, Karen 2011: *Taxing Assemblages: Laborious and Meticulous Achievements of Tax Compliance.* Copenhagen: IT University, Ph.D. dissertation.

Callon, Michel, Jean-Pierre Courtial, William A. Turner & Serge Bauin 1983: From Translations to Problematic Networks: An Introduction to Co-Word Analysis. *Social Science Information* 22:2, 191–235.

Cunha, Manuela Ivone P. Da & Jean-Yves Durand 2013: Anti-Bodies: The Production of Dissent. *Ethnologia Europea* 43:1, 35–54.

Damsholt, Tine, Dorte G. Simonsen & Camilla Mordhorst 2009: *Materialiseringer: Nye perspektiver på materialitet og kulturanalyse.* Århus: Aarhus Universitetsforlag.

Erixon, Sigurd 1931: *Lantmannens lätta redskap.* Svenska Kulturbilder 5.

Erixon, Sigurd 1957: *Atlas över svensk folkkultur* (Atlas of Swedish Folk Culture). Stockholm: Kungliga Gustav Adolphs Akademien.

Frykman, Jonas, Mia-Marie Hammarlin, Kjell Hansen, Bo Rothstein, Helena Olofsdotter Stenstöta & Isabell Schierenbeck 2009: Sense of Community: Trust, Hope and Worries in the Welfare State. *Ethnologia Europaea* 39:1, 7–46.

Galison, P. 2014: Visual STS. In: Annamaria Carusi, Aud Sissel Hoel, Timothy Weboor & Steve Woolgar, *Visualization in the Age of Computerization.* London: Routledge.

Harley, John Brian 1989: Deconstructing the Map. *Cartographica: The International Journal for Geographic Information and Geovisualization* 26:2, 1–20.

Højrup, Thomas 2002: *Dannelsens dialektik.* Copenhagen: Museum Tusculanum Press.

Jespersen, Astrid Pernille 2008: *Engagement i arbejdet? Konsultationsprocesser hos danske praktiserende læger.* Copenhagen: Ph.D. dissertation, Faculty of the Humanities, University of Copenhagen.

Jespersen, Astrid Pernille, Morten Krogh Petersen, Carina Ren & Marie Sandberg 2012: Cultural Analysis as Intervention. *Science Studies* 25:1, 3–12.

Knorr-Cetina, Karin 1981: *The Manufacture of Knowledge.* Oxford: Pergamon Press.

Krogh Petersen, Morten 2011: *'Good' Outcomes: Handling Multiplicity in Government Communication.* Copenhagen: Copenhagen Business School, Department of Intercultural Communication and Management.

Latour, Bruno 1991: Technology is Society Made Durable. In: John Law (ed.), *A Sociology of Monsters.* Sociological Review Monograph, pp. 103–131. London: Routledge.

Latour, Bruno 2005: *Reassembling the Social: An Introduction to Actor-Network-Theory.* Oxford: The University Press.

Latour, Bruno 2013: *An Inquiry into Modes of Existence.* Cambridge MA: Harvard University Press.

Latour, Bruno, Pablo Jensen, Tommaso Venturini, Sébastien Grauwin & Dominique Boullier 2012: The Whole is Always Smaller than its Parts – a Digital Test of Gabriel Tardes' Monads. *The British Journal of Sociology* 63:4, 590–615.

Latour, Bruno, Philippe Mauguin & Geneviève Teil 1992: A Note on Socio-Technical Graphs. *Social Studies of Science* 22:1, 33–57.

Latour, Bruno & Woolgar, Steve 1979: *Laboratory Life: The Social Construction of Scientific Facts.* Princeton: Princeton University Press.

Law, John 1994: *Organizing Modernity.* Oxford: Blackwell.

Law, John 2009: The Greer-Bush Test: On Politics in STS. Draft paper, version of December 23.

Lithberg, Nils 1919: Till allmogekulturens geografi. *Rig.*

Lynch, Mike 1985: *Art and Artifact in Laboratory Science: A Study of Shop Work and Shop Talk in a Research Laboratory.* London: Routledge & Kegan Paul.

Marres, Noortje 2004: Tracing the Trajectories of Issues, and their Democratic Deficits, on the Web: The Case of the Development Gateway and its Doubles. *Information Technology & People* 17:2, 124–149.

Mol, Annemarie 2002: *The Body Multiple: Ontology in Medical Practice.* Durham (NC): Duke University Press.

Moser, Oskar 1952: Der Heurechen: Versuch einer volkskundlichen Bestandsaufnahme des Arbeitsgerätes in Kärnten. *Carinthia I: Mitteilungen des Geschichtsvereins für Kärnten.* Klagenfurt.

Munk, Anders Kristian 2010: *Risking the Flood: Cartographies of Things to Come.* Oxford: Ph.D. dissertation, Oxford University.

Murdock, George Peter 1969: *Ethnographic Atlas.* Pittsburgh: University of Pittsburgh Press.

Murdock, George Peter 1981: *Atlas of World Cultures.* Pittsburgh: University of Pittsburgh Press.

Murdock, George Peter & Douglas R. White 1969: Standard Cross-Cultural Sample. *Ethnology* 8:4, 329–369.

Nilsson, Fredrik 2000: *I rörelse: Politisk handling under 1800-talets första hälft.* Ph.D. dissertation. Lund: Nordic Academic Press.

Pinch, Trevor J. & Wiebe E. Bijker 1987: The Social Construction of Facts and Artifacts: Or How the Sociology of Science and the Sociology of Technology Might Benefit from Each Other. In: Wiebe Bijker, Thomas Hughes & Trevor Pinch (eds.), *The Social Construction of Technological Systems: New Directions in the Sociology and History of Technology.* Cambridge, MA: MIT Press, pp. 17–50.

Ren, Carina 2009: *Constructing the Tourist Destination: A Socio-Material Description.* Ph.D. dissertation, SDU, Faculty of Humanities, Department of History, Centre for Maritime and Regional Studies, Esbjerg.

Ren, Carina & Morten Krogh Petersen 2013: The Study of Culture at the Intersection of Actor-Network Theory and Ethnology. *Ethnologia Europaea* 43:1, 98–111.

Rhamm, Karl 1905: *Ethnographische Beiträge zur germanisch-slawischen Altertumskunde I–II.* Braunschweig.

Rogan, Bjarne 2008: From Rivals to Partners on the Inter-

War European Scene – Sigurd Erixon, Georges Henri Rivière and the International Debate on European Ethnology in the 1930s. *Arv* 64, 61–100.

Rogers, Richard & Noortje Marres 2000: Landscaping Climate Change: A Mapping Technique for Understanding Science and Technology Debates on the World Wide Web. *Public Understanding of Science* 9:2, 141–163.

Rooijakkers, Gerard W.J. & Peter Meurkens 2000: Struggling with the European Atlas: Voskuil's Portrait of European Ethnology. *Ethnologia Europaea* 30:1, 75–95.

Sandberg, Marie 2009: *Grænsens nærvær og fravær: Europæiseringsprocesser i en tvillingeby på den polsk-tyske grænse*. Copenhagen: Ph.D. dissertation, University of Copenhagen.

Shapin, Steve, Simon Schaffer & Thomas Hobbes 1985: *Leviathan and the Air-Pump*. Princeton: Princeton University Press.

Stengers, Isabelle 2000: *The Invention of Modern Science*. Minneapolis: University of Minnesota Press.

Stengers, Isabelle 2005: The Cosmopolitical Proposal. In: Bruno Latour & Peter Weibel (eds.), *Making Things Public: Atmospheres of Democracy*. Cambridge, MA: MIT Press, pp. 994–1003.

Stoklund, Bjarne 1990: Ethnological Interpretations of Implements: The Hayrake as an Example. *Ethnologia Europaea* 10:1, 5–14.

Stoklund, Bjarne 2003: Tingenes kulturhistorie. *Etnologiske studier af den materielle kultur*. Copenhagen: Museum Tusculanum Press.

Suchman, Lucy A. 1987: *Plans and Situated Actions: The Problem of Human-Machine Communication*. Cambridge: The University Press.

Tangherlini, Timothy R. 2010: Legendary Performances: Folklore, Repertoire and Mapping. *Ethnologia Europaea* 40:2, 103–115.

Tangherlini, Timothy R. 2013: *Danish Folktales, Legends and Other Stories*. Seattle: University of Washington Press.

Tarde, Gabriel 1999: *Les lois sociales*. Paris: Les empêcheurs de penser en rond.

Tarde, Gabriel 2011: *Monadology and Sociology*. Melbourne: Re-Press.

Teil, Geneviève & Bruno Latour 1995: The Hume Machine: Can Association Networks do more than Formal Rules. *Stanford Humanities Review* 4:2, 47–65.

Toews, David 2003: The New Tarde: Sociology after the End of the Social. *Theory, Culture & Society* 20:5, 81–98.

Traweek, Sharon 1988: *Beamtimes and Lifetimes: The World of High Energy Physicists*. Cambridge, MA: Harvard University Press.

Turnbull, David 1996: Cartography and Science in Early Modern Europe: Mapping the Construction of Knowledge Spaces. *Imago Mundi* 48:1, 5–24.

Venturini, Tommaso 2010: Diving in Magma: How to Explore Controversies with Actor-Network Theory. *Public Understanding of Science* 19:3, 258–273.

Venturini, Tommaso 2012: Building on Faults: How to Represent Controversies with Digital Methods. *Public Understanding of Science* 21:7, 796–812.

Voskuil, Johannes Jacobus 2000: *Het bureau: Meneer Beerta*. Vol. 6 of 7. GA van Oorschot.

Yaneva, Albena 2012: *Mapping Controversies in Architecture*. Farnham: Ashgate Publishing.

Zumwalt, Rosemary 1982: Arnold van Gennep: The Hermit of Bourgla Reine. *American Anthropologist* 84:2, 299–313.

Anders Kristian Munk is associate professor in techno-anthropology at Aalborg University Copenhagen, and visiting researcher at the Sciences Po Medialab in Paris. His research focuses on knowledge controversies, risk issues, digital methods and data visualisation.
(akm@learning.aau.dk)

Torben Elgaard Jensen is professor in techno-anthropology and science & technology studies at Aalborg University Copenhagen. He is co-author of *Bruno Latour: Hybrid Thoughts in a Hybrid World* (Routledge 2011, with Anders Blok).
(tej@learning.aau.dk)

ANALOGUE ANALYSIS
Ethnography as Inventive Conversation

Frida Hastrup

This article explores ethnographic work as an inventive conversational practice, through which fieldworker and interlocutors continuously process the world. Rather than a summary description, ethnography emerges as an analytical product by which people generate a world to live in, think and write about. Ethnography, then, is not about representation of an empirical setting, but a generative practice of analytically relating some features of the world to others. My ambition is to suggest the notion of analogue analysis to articulate this relational and inventive nature of ethnography, and further to explore the implications of this for revisits to work of founding figures in ethnology. As a way of engaging ethnography in analogue terms, the article combines work of Eilert Sundt with contemporary material from south India.

Keywords: ethnography, fieldwork, Eilert Sundt, quantifications, Tamil Nadu

Fieldwork as Inventive Conversation
What if ethnographic fieldwork, for long providing the basis of much ethnological work, were seen not primarily as a systematic method of description learned and then applied by the ethnographer with the aim of representing worlds, but as a kind of inventive sociality built on unsettled particulars? What if ethnography were seen first and foremost as a conversational product – brought about by fieldworkers as well as interlocutors – that continuously generates worlds through discussion of concerns and crisscrossing of perspectives? These are the questions that I focus on in this contribution, by engaging and bringing together some of the work of folk-life researcher Eilert Sundt (1817–1875), appearing here primarily as a pioneer of fieldwork-based ethnology, interested in the lives and knowledge of common people in Norway, and pieces of my own contemporary ethnography among villagers in rural south India.

My point in making the seemingly improbable connection between work by Eilert Sundt and present-day fieldwork from an Indian fishing village and have them both speak to the nature of ethnography is just that: that the connection is seemingly improbable – and thereby enables me to argue that ethnography is always about crafting and articulating different ideas, perspectives and practices in order to craft and articulate more ideas, perspectives and practices. Ethnography, in this sense, is thus not about scholarly representations of empirical settings nor about deciding what belongs in the context, but can instead be seen as a series of world-making conversations and juxtapositions – between analysts, interlocutors and anyone else who cares to join. Put differently, I suggest that the field of ethnographic fieldwork is not constituted by one or more given empirical sites, say, Norway and/or south India, but is created in an ongoing and principally unending dialogue between different people and perspectives, as they encounter one another across time and space. In the following, I will show how this might play out.

My overall ambition is to propose the notion of *analogue analysis* as a way of articulating the continuous inventive character of ethnographic work and of capturing that ethnography is constituted by selective combinations of different features and experiences rather than summation. I borrow the word analogue from electronics and take it to imply signals or features that occur, are processed and work on one another within one uninterrupted domain, that is, within a non-dualistic register of sustained interrelation. As such the analogue is implicitly contrasted with the digital, the foundational principle of which is based on discrete entities and binary relations. Essentially, what I want to propose is an ethnographic practice undertaken as a deliberately analogue endeavour understood and performed in non-dualistic terms, and to suggest that in ethnography thus conceived dichotomies of here/there, now/then, self/other, observation/analysis and the like no longer hold. This poses a challenge to scholarship that allegedly works by separating entities such as theory and data, empirical and analytical objects, expert knowledge versus local knowledge and other such binaries, including possibly a too clear-cut distinction between classical ethnology and more recent work. In other words, what I am after in suggesting the notion of analogue analysis is a way to qualify the fundamentally unlimited and inventive nature of ethnography – underlining that it emerges as a creative feat in whatever occasional analytical domain the ethnographer (so-called interlocutors included) engages.

To me, the apparently simple proposition of analogue analysis has an important bearing on how we might think about theory and productively explore the rich fund of already existing work within ethnology and related disciplines. The practice of analogue analysis thus speaks directly to the idea of revisiting previous scholarly work in ethnology. If, indeed, ethnography is not about mapping a place for purposes of representation, but about talking and bringing worlds to life along with others and on the basis of particular perspectives and combinatory interests, why not extend the field to also include long since published ethnological works and let them be part of the always composite, unfinished and non-singular unit of analysis? To thus perceive of prior scholarly work as open to ethnographic inquiry paves the way for a dynamic dialogue with classical ethnological studies and for a revisit to the discipline's history without being burdened by an ambition to represent, however loyally or critically, this or that established school of thought.

To put it differently, as I see it, a revisit to the work of predecessors is interesting to the extent that I can come up with a partial reading (as opposed to a representational one), akin to the kind of analytical choices I would make when talking with people during contemporary fieldwork and writing about it, or indeed the analytical choices they would make as they process their world. The point here is that I revisit Eilert Sundt, not because he is uniquely important to ethnology as a whole, nor because I want to offer a well-resembling portrait by looking back at his work, but because I can bring some of his ideas into the conversation I am presently engaging in about how to generate ethnography as an inventive conversational practice that features unsettled and sometimes contradictory practices and ideas about life. The criterion for revisiting Sundt – and indeed for revisiting rural south India – is not one of objective relevance, because I would not know how to identify any fixed scale against which to assess that, but one of ethnographic (and thus analytical) mileage in the field that matters to me in this particular article – to discuss ethnography as generative and sustained conversation about world-making.

The notion of analogue analysis also suggests that we might do well to consider a deliberate conflation of what academics do and what the people we work with in the field do, and think of these activities as in a sense equally ethnographic and theoretical, quite simply because they are undertaken in an always current field of concern that cannot be seen as a totality or from the outside, even if it encompasses long gone historical features or facts of life on distant shores. All these heterogeneous features, I suggest, can be seen as analogically connected; because ethnographic fields offer open-endedness rather than settlement it takes theoretical work to even see them and live them, let alone write about them – for all involved. The field implied in ethnographic fieldwork, then, is doubly located as a particular place and time and as a shared and continual analytical domain, features of which are realized to the extent that they happen to concern people, whether fieldworker or host (cf. Strathern 1999; Hastrup 2011b). Importantly, this is not meant as a contribution to discussions about the limits to scholarly authority or about the problems inherent in attempts to represent others in writing. Influential work on these issues has long been available (see e.g. Clifford & Marcus 1986). Instead, and perhaps put somewhat radically, what I mean to suggest here is that in principle in ethnographic writings any feature of the field can be combined with any other feature, provided that some insight or other emerges from this encounter and selective comparison (cf. Brichet & Hastrup in press). Might the non-committal nature of a field observation be what makes it ethnographic?

With these ideas in mind, I want to look first at the work of Eilert Sundt, with special attention to the ways in which he discusses the necessity, problems and indeed pleasure of actively engaging readers and interlocutors primarily in his ethnographic work on house building and house crafts. I then move on to discuss complex and more recent discussions about lives and futures as they appeared during my fieldwork in south India. Finally, in an attempt to perform analogue analysis all the way through, I weave together these strands across time and space to reflect on the implications of seeing ethnography as an inventive conversation that resists fixed scales of living. If ethnography thus produces complexity through the very practice of discussing features of life with people we meet or with founding mothers and fathers of scholarly disciplines, might we then identify an overall impulse of ethnography – including revisits to previous work – as that of acknowledging and nurturing social life as contingent?

Inviting Ethnography: Working with Shared Concerns

In the epilogue of Sundt's work on building customs in the Norwegian countryside, he explains why he was pleased to have published his work in a series of articles in the popular educational journal *Folkevennen* ("Friend of the People"), of which Sundt was the editor in the years 1857–1866, in addition to presenting it as a scientific thesis that in Sundt's own words is long and elaborate (Sundt 1862: § 50). The continuous publication of portions of his work in a journal reaching readers with a shared concern for the advancement of popular education ("folkeoplysning") seems for Sundt to serve as a kind of invitation. Based on the assumption that people share his opinion that the well-being and potential improvement of conditions of the Norwegians is enfolded into the house building customs, Sundt uses the periodical to ideally summon those interested and capable of contributing to his findings on the matter.

If we look for a minute to the incipient Danish archaeology in the early nineteenth century, for instance as it gradually equipped what was to become the National Museum, farmers from around the country were encouraged to search and hand over (pre-)historic artefacts, as these were gradually uncovered from the lands increasingly put under the plough. In acknowledgement of the importance of engaging the public in the ambition to salvage ancient artefacts, Christian Jürgensen Thomsen, the founder of the museum, took great care to express his gratitude for lay people's vital contributions (Jensen 1992: 50–51). Looking at the meeting minutes of the so-called Antiquities Commission, a precursor of the museum proper, which collected both artefacts and information about these, we learn of a school teacher chipping in the Commission's collection in 1821:

School master Holger Njelsen of Asminderup in Odsherred had sent a beautiful and ornamented metal plate, presumed to have been attached to a shield, found along with many others in a bog near Høiby. The school master is thanked in a letter and asked to be attentive whenever peat is dug out of this bog, and according to circumstances the Commission will bestow an appropriate reward upon the finder, should something remarkable turn up. (Cited in Jakobsen & Adamsen 2007: 268)[1]

What is interesting here is the call for continued attention towards peculiar findings in the peat bogs. Quite obviously, it was perceived as a collective task to recover the nation's past.

Further north, Sundt worked in an equally inviting way and called for assistance in his ethnographic project. Look at this passage from the final sections of his work on house building, which I need to quote at some length here:

To present the country's or the villages' building customs is a matter I view as having no little national significance, and my work could in no way rise to the task; but I thought that if I dared publish it in "Friend of the People", I would be granted assistance to in due course make a new and better attempt. Every lettered man can assist me. A school teacher or a farmer for instance in Vegusdal's parish can send me information as to whether, in his district, I have been right about the presence of the Mandal living room, if it can be found, or if it is recalled to have been in use in the said parish (…) Any herdsman who might know of a firehouse still inhabited or left unchanged as from a time when it was, would bring me much joy by informing me thereof (…) People who can draw, carpenters and others, would make me truly grateful by sending sketches of houses, equipment etc. (Sundt 1862: § 50)[2]

As I see it, what he proposes is a kind of public and distributed ethnographic project, the ambition of which is to present a complete picture of housing customs around the country, but which is only incompletely realized so far. As I imagine would be the case for any present-day ethnographer, Sundt is pleased to learn from the experts about whose lives he writes. In this regard, Sundt makes an explicit comment about the ingenuity of common rural people and their ability to overcome challenges. In his work on "house crafts" he states the following:

One gathers, then, that my work has come about in opposition to the oppressive opinion and gloomy claim that the peasantry is little capable and industrious. In Søndfjord it would please me to see even a bit of wood chip outside of the house, reminding me of the assiduous work on herring barrels inside. And even if the bulletins from the villages were ever so lengthy, it still amused me line by line to see the multifarious effort and inventiveness reported. The more I explored and stared, the more I saw of victorious industriousness and of external obstacles and challenges that have had to be overcome, and which still remain to be won over. (Sundt 1867–1868: preface)[3]

What I want to highlight here is the acknowledgement of the significance of public engagement and what one might call lay expertise in early archaeology and ethnology. The sense that people near and far can actually be trusted to contribute to projects of apparently great national and educational significance is clearly expressed in Sundt's work. People's customs, as Sundt discovered, might actually make sense when explored locally by those who are the practitioners (cf. Berggreen 1989: 60–64). Even more important, perhaps, is the shared curiosity that must drive a fieldwork of this kind – for both expert ethnographers and others. In addition to whatever insights from previous times that Sundt can find in a range of written sources, knowledge to support or indeed correct his account can surely be found among people inhabiting the very buildings that feature in his writings on housing customs – people who understand the need to dig deeper, as it were:

Many of these are members of the Association to the Advancement of Popular Education, and so they could both detect and correct omissions in my presentation, and they would not regret if "Friend of the People" takes it upon itself to shed light on issues that are as closely tied to the history of common life and the well-being of people as the building customs across the country. (Sundt 1862: § 50)[4]

What I find particularly interesting in these quotes is the implicit discussion in the way Sundt describes his project. Berggreen describes Sundt as both a statistician searching for definite numbers and percentages, and as a researcher willing to adjust his findings in the course of learning still more about people's living conditions and views (Berggreen 1989: 61). On the one hand, and perhaps as a result of the inspiration from the natural sciences, Sundt seems to believe that a complete and not least correct account of for instance the Norwegian housing customs is within reach, provided that people around the country join him in his descriptive efforts and that he employs systematic scientific methodology (cf. Stoklund 2003: 51). On the other hand, Sundt highlights the processual and dialogic nature of ethnographic writing and articulates a distinct and perhaps surprising humility, knowing well that his findings are in some sense preliminary and would benefit from further refinement and more discussion. Consider this passage:

> Those who have ventured into writing must know how it is: one often uses many words, when one is not really in control of the subject matter. Booklet by booklet, I came to understand this or that differently than I had in the beginning (…) and I was incessantly dealing with matters regarding which I had to waver my way forward by way of my incomplete observations and recollections. (Sundt 1862: § 50)[5]

Overview and closure, it would seem, are rare treats in Sundt's trade. However, this inadequacy appears to be a motor for new attempts at understanding the customs under investigation and for inviting a wide constituency of readers and potential informants into the conversation. To me, the periodical "Friend of the People" with its gradual publication of results is in a sense a perfect illustration of the continuous nature of ethnography. Even if Sundt did believe in the ability of (social) science to eventually map and classify the life and customs of the peasantry ("almuen"), what I find striking in these quotes is the way Sundt describes his work as provisional, acknowledging that more things to take into account abound.

The experience of having seen and heard stuff in the field that does not seem to add up and the not uncommon sense that one has missed important insights, I would argue, are in the nature of fieldwork itself where confusion is often the defining sentiment. Much has been written about fieldwork as a method and about the particular positioning of the researcher as enabling or inhibiting particular findings of various kinds. These discussions, important as they are, are not my focus here. Rather, what I want to focus on here is the nature of ethnography as an ongoing inventive practice, in which Sundt combines what he, aided by informants, sees as a series of distinct features that jointly make, say, the Norwegian house building customs. This is to say that Sundt's keen interest in traditional building methods and designs is what continuously generates ethnography about these. In consequence, for the kind of analogue analysis I envision to be productive and thoughtful, fieldworkers should not work to identify bias or subjective positions in order to try to eliminate these, as if they could be sieved from raw data. Rather the "biases" of all, understood as particular concerns and intersecting analyses emerging out of conversations and encounters in a domain of sustained interrelation (e.g. between houses from different parts of the country, between Sundt and his interlocutors, or between people and buildings, to name but some), are vital in even generating ethnography and as such valuable sources. In all the quotes from Sundt that I have presented so far, I would not be able to sort the features into his personal interests, empirical facts or analytical findings. All of these elements come together to constitute an analogue field of concern – house building and handicraft customs

– generated along the way as a result of that concern.

One way to go about grappling with such analogically related different observations and analyses working one another is to explore the confusion often articulated by the people among whom ethnographers work. To further explore and nurture the notion of analogue analysis occurring in the field conceived as a continuous domain that produces ethnography out of encounters and conversation, I will now turn to some of the ways in which villagers I worked with in south India struggle with and debate some often troubling local customs. If Sundt requested the assistance of (other) house building experts from near and far to correct him and ideally make a coherent picture that adds up to a neat whole, villagers in the coastal town of Tharangambadi do their bit of mathematics to make things – and ends – meet.

Ethnographic Quantifications: Discussing what Counts

Numbers abound in my ethnography from the south Indian coastal village of Tharangambadi, where I have worked intermittently since 2005 (see e.g. Hastrup 2011a). Sometimes they serve as at least momentarily convincing and acceptable attempts to describe and order the world, sometimes they register as confusing or colonizing and call for alternative orderings as countermeasures. To move on with my discussion of ethnography as an inventive conversation that generates a world by combining different features and selecting focal points, in this section I look at quantification as a complex local analytical practice of world-making. As I will show, for people of Tharangambadi quantifying practices work to resist fixed scales of living and to articulate a way to engage with contradictions. Numbers and measurements, in this light, are generative and social devices, rather than straightforward representations of that which is quantified; they can serve as materialized relations (Verran 2010). I take a cue from philosopher of science Helen Verran who states that thinking about numbers in this way "takes them as inseparable from the practices in which enumerated material entities come to life, and as semiotically agential" (Verran 2012: 112). The issue here is to explore the different practices and discussions of quantifying that appear in the social life of Tharangambadi, by which entities – whether persons, government, voters, gold, village, sugar, state, nature, fish, cyclones or what have you – of the coastal world come to be in light of one another. This relational take makes the quantifications, although perhaps seemingly abstract and transparent, appear as thoroughly ethnographic phenomena occurring in a continuous but complex field – in situ (Verran 2010: 172).

Dwindling fish catches and overexploitation of the marine resources are an immediate concern on the coast of Tamil Nadu, the state where the village of Tharangambadi is located. The issue emerged time and again in my talks with the fishermen, who complain that the sea's yield has decreased drastically in recent years, most of them blaming the introduction of more efficient fishing equipment and lack of government control mechanisms. The Tamil Nadu state government on its part has implemented schemes to encourage people to do other things than inshore fishing, inciting people to educate themselves or at least diversify their fishing to deep ocean activities, of which tuna fishing is launched and subsidized as a viable option. From a policy note from the Tamil Nadu Fisheries Department, I sense a ring of both alarm and optimism in the face of ever more distressing numbers in the fishing trade. The Fisheries Department states that:

> The vast fishery resources of both marine and inland waters have not yet been fully brought under production. The fishery resources in the inshore areas have been overexploited, whereas the offshore resources and deep sea resources are yet to be tapped to the optimum level. The prime responsibility of the Department is to judiciously balance enhanced fish production with sustained conservation of resources as well as to improve the socio-economic standards of the fishing community. (Policy note 2011–2012)

The act of judiciously balancing how to make the most of the stock of the sea for both fish and people is important here. As a policy note the statement is official, self-confident and sober; yet it articulates a necessity of balancing concerns that might pull in opposite directions. The open question is of course how to enhance life for the fishing communities while not overexploiting the marine resources. This problem leads other numbers to emerge as important. Thus, boys and girls from fishing communities such as that of Tharangambadi who complete 10 and 12 years of schooling, respectively, are rewarded with cash grants, provided that they finish school in the "top rank". Furthermore, subsidies are provided for fishermen who are willing to shift to offshore fishing, where apparently the resources are yet to be tapped, as expressed in the quote above. All of these government schemes, of which the fishermen often talked, use quantifications of marine resources, water depths, exam marks, financial incitements and the like to intervene into the coastal nature and to create it as a sustainable world in which both fishermen and environment survive. The future of both people and nature is at stake, and accordingly the quantifications are launched with prescriptive authority, as well as invested with a much less assertive measure of hope, aided by calls for collaboration.

The idea of Tamil Nadu being a welfare state is recurrent in the government documents from the various departments and is mirrored in the range of protection projects and services that people in and around Tharangambadi clearly expect the authorities to provide. Along with my field assistant Renuga, a native to Tharangambadi with whom I have worked closely since my first stay in the village and whose company has guided my view of Tharangambadi perhaps more than anything and much to my joy, I went to visit the so-called Government Fair Price Shop on Queen's Street in Tharangambadi. The shop provides household items for 1,250 registered fishing families, and I learn that according to the state-sanctioned subsidy ration system every fishing family is allowed to buy 500 grams of sugar every month per member of the household at a reduced price; specific quantities of rice, dhal, flour and salt are also offered as subsidized goods from the shop. Even though the rice and other of the goods on offer in the shop are only "third quality", as the shop manager expresses it, he and Renuga only thinks it right that the government takes on itself the responsibility for ensuring that even very poor villagers have enough to eat. The shop manager explains to me how he fills in the customers' state-issued ration cards by noting down the dates and quantities of any purchase. In the ration shop numbers in the guise of measures of foods, dates and costs of purchases are invoked to bring about a world in which the difference between rich and poor is ideally levelled. Different quantifications, it seems, are invoked to bring about equality in a community otherwise haunted by wildly unequal opportunities. When I ask about it, to Renuga and the shop manager this is clearly the obligation of the state, which must ascribe equal worth to all citizens. Standards of living are at stake, as they tell me. In Renuga's eyes, however, the success of such levelling exercises is threatened by their very practice. The more well-off fishermen, she suspects, will soon turn to what she terms the open market to buy food there at much higher prices, "just because they can. It's a prestige issue," as she says, reminding me again that I must remember that Tharangambadi is a very small town. This, she and the shop manager agrees, will humiliate and ultimately discriminate the poor people who will still have to count on the government shops to eat. In Renuga's and the shopkeeper's words, for all their interventionist objectives of equating differences, the subsidized quantities of basic foods might further exacerbate inequalities in the (inescapably) interrelated continuous domain of Tharangambadi.

People in the village cannot always rely on the state to intervene to muster hope or to try to ensure equal opportunities and protection of people under its authority. In the state elections in March 2011, formal democratic procedure had proved a threat to Renuga's family and other households in the village; the clear majority of the fishing families voted for the party that eventually won the election, but after the counting of votes a list was issued by the fisherman village council, naming 32 households including Renuga's where people had voted for the largest opposition party. For a short while, and obviously much to their distress, these listed families became fair game around the village, harassed by rowdy young fishermen who threw rocks, intimidated Renuga's daughters, and assaulted her husband. For a time, the list of the 32 named households, compiled on the basis of an alleged count of votes given in the otherwise secret ballot, created a menacing world causing Renuga's twin daughters to miss out on important classes at their college, because they were too frightened to leave the house. At one point there was even talk of excluding the families from the community; a rare sanction seen as appropriate only for the most severe violations of community customs. Little by little the anger and fear subsided, in part I suspect due to Renuga's ability, which I have witnessed many times, to smooth things over and her skilful navigation among her neighbours. Though still a little shaken when we discussed the election, things seem to have returned to normal. Reflecting on the experience, Renuga explained that the right to vote freely had worked as a double-edged sword, as neighbours had all too literally taken election campaigning into their own violent hands instead of engaging in peaceful democratic discussion.

On the whole, at the time of my fieldwork, counting and numbers seemed to play quite a big role in Renuga's life, registering as turbulence as in the case of the election time, or spurring social commentary as in the case of the ration shop. In fact, counting is also what provides part of Renuga's income. Her part-time job at a local school in Tharangambadi consists in overseeing the implementation of a government scheme for nutritious noon meals for all children in primary schools all over the state. Based on the carefully maintained records of the numbers of school days and of children attending, specific quantities of rice and dhal are allotted to the school, registered by Renuga and administered to the school's cook. Several times during my fieldworks, I have joined her at work on the two days a week when the children line up to be given a boiled egg at lunch time to raise the protein count in the diet.

Sometimes, however, people like Renuga are left to their own devices if they want to intervene against perceived unfair or unhealthy numbers and standards that collide with held values and with ideas about what can even be quantified. Lowering her voice slightly for the daughters not to hear us, Renuga tells me about yet another rise in the world market price of gold. We have often talked about gold during my fieldworks, and I know the metal weighs heavily on many people in Tharangambadi. The cost per gram of gold is announced daily on TV on the Tamil channels, and much to Renuga's worry the day had added to the price, amounting to a staggering 2,200 rupees for one gram. To her, gold is a present and pressing currency; the cost of it often seems a rock solid measure imposing on her world. For as long as I have known her, Renuga has put money aside to place in gold, and several times I have accompanied her to a trusted goldsmith in a nearby town where she keeps a kind of account measured in carats and grams. Her twin daughters were born in 1992 and a younger daughter was born in 2000, and within a foreseeable future she is likely to have to arrange for the marriages of the older girls to be settled. For the time being, the prospect of this looms, and none of the members of the family much like to talk about it.

On the day Renuga tells me about the alarming rise of the price of gold, the twins are in the room next to the hallway where we are, and I can hear the consistent murmur of their memorizing and discussing the homework for the next day's college class in the neighbouring village of Porayar. Disconcerted, Renuga tells me that in spite of widespread opposition to it, as well as of an official ban on the custom of dowry enacted by the Indian Federal Government in 1961, unsaid rules in the fishing villages now prescribe that the parents of the bride procure at least 200 grams of pure gold jewels as a kind of insurance, just as they are expected to provide the groom and his family with various other expensive goods, often a motorcycle and new furnishings for the home, before the marriage can be settled. Giving up on the maths of multiplying the price of gold with grams and number of daughters halfway, Renuga shakes her head and questions how on earth this has become the order of the day. She tells me about the sense that to her it is wildly unfair that such almost insurmountable financial burden should be put on parents of girls, and that the families of boys are free to make such a business out of their sons. What is worse, Renuga elaborates, is the implicit translation of human worth into economic value. As she tells me, the gold standard as an objective measurement of value ought not to apply to people.

Many of the boys' families, according to Renuga, share her opinion and agree that the custom is unjust and creates inequalities between families. This, too, is talk of the town. If this is so, I ask naïvely, would there be no chance of finding families who are willing to give up the claim of dowry and agree on marriage free of charge, as it were. "No chance, it's a prestige problem," Renuga says. Elaborating she goes on to tell me that before, when fishing families were poorer than they generally are today, dowry was not such a big issue, "but today with more money around, the families will demand and provide the dowry just because they can," Renuga says, again shaking her head at the apparent paradox. The boys' families, she explains, will simply be embarrassed if word gets out that they have relented on the claim for dowry; people will think that something is wrong with the groom. Often, people I talked to during fieldwork would express frustration with being locked into this pervasive order of specifying the value of people, while knowing very well and indeed agreeing that human worth cannot be captured in economic terms; to people like Renuga such gold standard appears as both absolute and oppressive and arbitrary and plainly wrong.

However, all hopes of circumventing the force of noble metal are not gone for Renuga and her daughters. On the day of discussing the most recent rise in the price of gold, the twins are in their final year of college, both completing a degree in mathematics. All three of them now place all possible effort into the course work, putting countless hours of work into their books, the girls getting up long before dawn to study, rehearse and repeat the calculations and results. So far the effort has been recognized, the twins ranking a shared first in their class in most of the tests. This, they hope and explicitly say, might pave their way to scholarships for further studies. Less explicitly, at least in the words of the girls, further studies and academic degrees just might postpone or somehow divert them from the concern with finding suitable spouses and sufficient funds. Faced with the overwhelming demand of resources to ensure the daughters' marital futures, Renuga and the girls work hard to generate an alternative world of numbers, entailing math degrees and top exam marks, as a possible way of outwitting the gold standard.

Analogue Analysis and Contingent Fields: A Revisit

In the two previous sections I have addressed how Sundt, the readers of "Friend of the People", amateur archaeologists, Renuga, Tamil shopkeepers and officials among others, attempt to portray, explore, analyse and indeed inhabit a liveable world, even though at face value things do not necessarily add up to a coherent or complete picture, at least not immediately. It may seem odd to combine the nineteenth century encouragement from Sundt to his fellow Norwegians to join in and supplement his analysis of houses and artisanal crafts across the country with, say, the twenty-first century discussions between Renuga and the ration shop manager about whether subsidized food meets its intended purpose in rural Tamil Nadu. There is a conflation of levels, it would seem, the example of Sundt addressing a tension between analysis as both complete and provisional; the Indian material being a discussion of how to balance contradicting features of village life. However, my point here is exactly to collapse what might appear as a theoretical or methodological problem in the first case and as a set of empirical findings in the other case – in order to qualify ethnography as inventive and as a creative juxtaposition of different features within one uninterrupted domain – and thus to perform analogue analysis. If, indeed, ethnography is a collaborative activity that brings non self-identical worlds to life through the analytical interrelating of different elements, it is perfectly possible to suggest that Sundt's ambivalence as to whether he can fully capture or even improve the well-being of the Norwegians by mapping housing customs is in an analogue relation to for instance Renuga's discussion about the widely acknowledged unfairness of the demand for gold as dowry. The continuous domain, if nothing else, that has these features working on one another, is my discussion of ethnography as relational and inventive analyses of unfolding life.

What is important here is that ethnography – the product of all who care to join the conversation about a particular concern – becomes both an empirical and a theoretical pursuit quite simply because of its inherent incompleteness and because it cannot map, count or classify the world from the outside and definitively. This of course has the effect that the distinction between theory and empirical material makes little sense – in any event ethnography comprises both a subject matter (housing, gold, hard-boiled eggs or whatever) and comments on what it means to do so by engaging contradictory scales at once. The reading of Sundt, the selection of the quantifying practices, and my recognition of Renuga's vital analytical contribution to my work in Tharangambadi are obviously conscious and partial choices on my part, not to argue that Eilert Sundt, Renuga and I are basically out to do the same or that we see the world similarly. Rather, by combining these bits and pieces I mean to perform the conflation of theory and empirical matter that I take ethnography to be about, when seen as someone's combination of different features working on one another in an inventive and indefinite conversation. By deliberately making what appears like a far-fetched connection between analytical work from different centuries, from far-apart places, and articulated in different genres, I am highlighting that all ethnography entails such combinatory efforts and ongoing processing, given less by empirical circumstances than by particular analytical perspectives. Fieldwork, accordingly, is just that – a *work* in which the fieldworker must argue for the connections she makes in a world that does not provide settled entities and obvious relations between them.

Consider, for instance, that the local quantifications played out in and around Tharangambadi are not just engaged with as given objective scales of numbers which are then applied to the world with greater or lesser accuracy. The externally given, and in Renuga's eyes colonizing, nature of the gold standard, is exactly the reason why it appears unacceptable as a definite working measure in social life and has to be challenged. Thus, rather than expressing imported and fixed scales coming from outside, the local quantifications create their own measurements provisionally and by way of encounters with other measurements in the very process of quantifying. This is also how I have attempted to read Sundt – not as measured against any established position as central (or peripheral, for that matter) in ethnology, but as someone who is also discussing what to make of interlocutors' analyses.

In light of this, one might understand the local quantifications that I met in Tharangambadi as practices of consciously shifting between different scales or perspectives to make their contingent nature apparent (cf. Strathern [1994]2004; Holbraad & Pedersen 2009). Let me for a minute look closer at this suggestion through Renuga's discussions of gold prices and marks in mathematics. If, in her world-making by numbers, Renuga can be said to grapple with her daughters' futures she does so through different coexisting scales, seeing her twins' future opportunities in more than one perspective at the same time. Putting her money in gold and encouraging her daughters to pursue further studies are at first glance contradictory strategies, based on two different ways of charting the twins' possibilities. What I want to suggest here is that Renuga's complex practice of scaling, with its inbuilt contradictory logic, is in itself an inventive ethnographic account of a feature of life in Tharangambadi, demonstrating that the here and now can take off in any which direction and does not comply with a settled measure. The numberings she articulates make a local social world appear, in which girls can be valued both as future wives in terms of gold and as potential scholars in terms of college marks, and because of the very coexistence of these two scales, quantification reveals itself as generative of a social world rather than evaluative or representative. The gold does not measure the girls' worth in any objective way, any more than their marks do, but both – and logically many other – scales play a part in Renuga's processing of how to envision a future and tell the visiting fieldworker about it. This is to say that her quantifications (and those of the other counting people I engage with here) articulate empirical description as well as analysis, imposing order and enabling protest, and as such the quantifications produce rather than reduce complexity. In that sense, Renuga's intervention by quantification does not just reside in the fact that she works to shift the balance from the alarming and uncontrollable price of gold to more controllable academic ambition, but equally in the fact that she generates a complex and indefinite local world on the basis of her analytical work. The (more or less achievable) shift from focusing on gold prices to focusing on marks in mathematics is thus not just a matter of finding a more suitable and more representative measure for her daughters' futures, it is equally a refusal to let any scale appear as absolute and as an abstract external yardstick.

As Holbraad and Pedersen have remarked, "for scales to be able to measure things they have to be more abstract than them" (2009: 378), and it is this kind of abstraction that Renuga circumvents by leaving no scale unchallenged exactly because it is, after all, just a scale that must incorporate the existence of other scales and things unaccounted for. What I argue here is that this is a prime instance of a refusal to live by digital standards, where discrete entities have a fixed value. Renuga knows only too well that the contingency and indeed emergencies of social life cannot be kept in check by such settlements.

Now, what does all this mean for the project of revisiting previously published ethnological work? My point here has been to explore the mileage offered by an approach to ethnography that takes seriously Sundt's encouraging others to join in the ongoing analytical work and that foregrounds the continuous nature of Renuga's analytical engagement with complex and even contradictory scales of living. I thus use the notion of ethnography as a product of analogue analysis to argue that, in principle, no one can possibly complete her own analysis. This, of course, has nothing to do with me assessing the analytical skills of Sundt, Renuga, myself or anyone else, but with a general claim about ethnographic knowledge as inevitably social and continuous. This point is vital for thinking about how a revisit to the work of Sundt and others can be paid and what it might yield. I have purposely not wanted to evaluate Sundt's findings on any subject matter against a present scholarly yardstick or to understand his work in its contemporary context, nor have I in any way attempted to portray Sundt's work as a coherent (or incoherent) oeuvre seen and read from a different domain. This would lead us straight back to the issue of representation and thus reinstall binaries, such as then/now, theory/empirical observation. What I wanted to do is to extend the notion of the field to also include, say, periodicals from nineteenth-century Norway – if, indeed, arguing for ethnography as a conversational inventive practice of addressing how to live and think with others is the main purpose. This implies that the field of any study is always carved out from a here and now and on the basis of a particular partial interest – in this case an inquiry into what ethnography might be. This is not, I would think, a controversial claim, but for thinking about revisits to former works of ethnology it is significant, because a focus on the partiality of fieldwork orchestrates revisits ethnographically, whereby revisits (like ethnography) cannot ever be complete. If inconsistency and unfixed scales feature in the field sites I explore, why would analyses – contemporary or historical – that explore these fields ever be seen as congealed into a uniform and settled fund? If revisits to founding figures in ethnology are productive, it is in my opinion not so much because we can classify earlier work under some heading or other, or read them as context or period pictures, with a view to either endorsing (…Sundt's admiration of Norwegian handicraft) or rejecting (…his evolutionist tendencies). Rather than such evaluation by hindsight or perhaps contextualization, a revisit is interesting because it adds new perspectives and questions to the here and now of any analytical undertaking – whether these emerge from talking with Renuga or from reading Sundt.

In consequence of these thoughts on the inventive nature of ethnography as explored through the analogue relation I have crafted between the very different work of Sundt and my discussions with Renuga, ethnographic work becomes what might be called a montage-like practice, adding to rather than depicting a world of complexity. On the notion and effect of montage-like ethnography, Suhr and Willerslev have stated:

> [S]trange things happen when two elements are brought together in montage. Never is the result simply the sum of the single components. Something extra, a surplus or an excess is always produced. This "extra" speaks back to the elements and produces a state of generative instability, where each part transforms and takes on new shapes within the wider constellation. (Suhr & Willerslev 2013: 1)

In the case at hand, I would like this surplus to be the idea that ethnography is ever about inventing liveable worlds by way of analogue conversation between different elements, voices and features. Although it may sound strange, I thus think that an interesting revisit is a matter of reading previous works as though they were different from themselves. Just as Renuga employs contradictory scales of measuring and charting her daughters' success, Sundt is here invoked in a conversation which transcends his time.

I like to think of ethnography as a motor for probing how things have come together in particular settings or fields of interest, and thereby as implicitly showing how things could have been and can be otherwise. Inventions rather than accumulation or meeting minutes, then, are what ethnography provides. Might this also be a way to read the classics? Do we miss out on important findings – such as the fact the researchers inclined to think in terms of cumulative natural scientific classification can still be humble and need assistance in their endeavours – if we relegate classical ethnological studies to a separate domain of, well, classics, each fitting into a school of thought? Would such a labelling not go against the very gist of ethnology, seen as an impulse to explore the contingent nature of social life?

Readers might object, saying, can anything be read as selectively? Does it really make sense to say that one conducts fieldwork in the texts of predecessor ethnologists? Or that Renuga is performing ethnographic work? And can any experiences and observations across times and places be combined, however disparate? Well, I for one would not want to police what can or cannot be brought into analogue interrelation. If, indeed, ethnology is a project about unsettled world-making processes that sees these as generated socially by people, ethnologists included, one basic ambition must be to keep curiosity alive, meaning that, yes, in principle I see no limit to what can be suggested, compared, juxtaposed, combined for the purposes of generating a field of a particular and occasional concern.

Ways of living with the knowledge that alternative ways are (logically, if not always actually) possible are what ethnography provides; theory, accordingly, must be equally accommodating of what is not already known and mapped, enabling analogue interrelation to do its thing. In fact, Sundt teaches us as much, and I end this article with his modest celebration of the curiosity that ethnographic scholarship might be all about:

> I have also come to think that it would amuse the inhabitants of the Norwegian wooden houses at some point to see how the art of building wood houses has developed in Sweden, Russia and Switzerland. (Sundt 1862: § 50)[6]

Notes

1 The original quotes in Norwegian/Danish are provided in the notes. All translations are by the author. "Skoleholder Holger Njelsen til Asminderup i Odsherred, havde til Biskop Mynter indsendt en smuk og med Zirater forsynet metalskive, som formodes at have været anbragt på et Skiold, der er fundet tillige med mange flere i en Mose ved Høiby. Skoleholderen takkes ved et Brev bedes at være opmærksom naar attes skjeres Tørv i denne Mose og efter Omstændighederne ville Commissionen tilstå Finderen en passende Douceur naar noget mærkværdigt fandtes" (Oldsagskommissionens Mødeprotokol 1807–1848: 268).

2 "At få fremstillet landets eller landsbygdernes bygnings-skik, det anser jeg for en sag af ikke så aldeles ringe national betydning, og mit arbejde var ingenlunde opgaven voxent; men jeg tænkte, at om jeg turde lade det trykke i Folkevennen, så kunde jeg få bistand

til med tiden at gjøre et nyt og bedre forsøg. Hver skrivkyndig mand kan yde mig bistand. En skolelærer eller bondemand f.ex. i Vegusdals sogn vil kunde sende mig oplysning om, hvorvidt jeg på hans kant har truffet det rette med hensyn til den mandalske stueforms udbredelse, om den nemlig er at se eller mindes at have været i brug i det nævnte sogn (…) Enhver sætersdøl, som måtte vide om et ildhus, der er beboet eller står igjen i uforandret stand fra den tid, det var beboet, vilde høilig glæde mig ved meddelelse derom (…) Folk, som kunde tegne, bygmestere og andre, vilde gjøre mig særdeles forbunden ved at sende mig rids og tegninger af huse, husgeråd osv" (Sundt 1862: § 50).

3 Man forstår altså, at mit arbeide er blevet til i modsætning til den trykkende mening og knugende påstand om almuernes ringe begreb og foretagsomhed. I Søndfjord kunde det fornøie mig, bare jeg så en flis udfor husvæggen, som mindede om det flittige arbeide med sildetønder der indenfor. Og om indberetningerne fra bygderne bleve aldrig så lange, så morede det mig dog linie for linie at se den mangeartede flid og opfindsomhed opregnet. Jo mere jeg speidede og stirrede, des mere så jeg af seirende flid og af udvortes hindringer og vanskeligheder, som man har havt at beseire, og som det endnu står tilbage at vinde bugt med" (Sundt 1867–1868: preface).

4 "Mange af disse ere medlemmer af Selskabet for Folkeoplysningens Fremme, så de altså både kunne se og rette manglerne I min fremstilling, og de skulle ikke tage det ilde op, at Folkevennen bestræber sig for at få opklaret ting, der stå i så nær sammenhæng med folkelivets historie og med folkets vel, som bygningsskikken i landet" (Sundt 1862: § 50).

5 "De, som have forsøgt sig i forfatterskab, kjende til, hvorledes det har sig: man kommer gjerne til at bruge så mange ord, når man ikke har rigtig herredømme over stoffet. Hefte for hefte kom jeg til at opfatte et og andet anderledes end fra først af (…) og idelig havde jeg med ting at gjøre, hvor jeg måtte ligesom famle mig frem med mine utilstrækkelige iagttagelser og erindringer" (Sundt 1862: § 50).

6 "Det har jeg også tænkt mig, at det skulde more de norske træhuses beboere ved leilighed at få se, hvorledes træbygnings-kunsten har udviklet sig i Sverige, Rusland og Sveits" (Sundt 1862: § 50).

References

Berggreen, Brit 1989: *Da kulturen kom til Norge*. Oslo: Aschehoug.
Brichet, Nathalia & Frida Hastrup in press: Sensationelle trivialiteter: Museer i vores eksotiske verden. In: T. Fibiger & U. Dahre (eds.), *Etnografiske museer i Norden: Visioner, holdninger, udfordringer*. Aarhus University Press.
Clifford, James & George E. Marcus (eds.) 1986: *Writing Culture: The Poetics and Politics of Ethnography*. Berkeley: University of California Press.
Hastrup, Frida 2011a: *Weathering the World: Recovery in the Wake of the Tsunami in a Tamil Fishing Village*. New York; Oxford: Berghahn Books.
Hastrup, Frida 2011b: Shady Plantations: Theorizing Coastal Shelter in Tamil Nadu. *Anthropological Theory* 11:4, 425–439.
Holbraad, Martin & Morten Axel Pedersen 2009: Planet M: The Intense Abstraction of Marilyn Strathern. *Anthropological Theory* 9:4, 371–394.
Jakobsen, Tove Benedikte & Christian Adamsen (eds.) 2007: Nationalmuseets oprindelse: Oldsagskommissionens mødeprotokol 1807–1848. *Acta Archaeologica* 78:1, 185–334.
Jensen, Jørgen 1992: *Thomsens museum: Historien om Nationalmuseet*. Copenhagen: Gyldendal.
Stoklund, Bjarne 2003: *Tingenes kulturhistorie*. Copenhagen: Museum Tusculanum Press.
Strathern, Marilyn 1999: *Property, Substance and Effect: Anthropological Essays on Persons and Things*. London: The Athlone Press.
Strathern, Marilyn [1994]2004: *Partial Connections*. Walnut Creek: Altamira Press.
Suhr, Christian & Rane Willerslev 2013: Introduction: Montage as an Amplifier of Invisibility. In: C. Suhr & R. Willerslev (eds.), *Transcultural Montage*. Oxford; New York: Berghahn Books, pp. 1–15.
Sundt, Eilert 1862: *Om Bygningsskikken på Landet i Norge*, Christiania: P.F. Mallings Bogtrykkeri.
Sundt, Eilert 1867–1868: *Om Husfliden i Norge: Til Arbeidets Ære og Arbeidsomhedens Pris*. Christiania: J. Chr. Abelsteds Bogtrykkeri.
Verran, Helen 2010: Number as Inventive Frontier in Knowing and Working Australia's Water Resources. *Anthropological Theory* 10:1–2, 171–178.
Verran, Helen 2012: Number. In: C. Lury & N. Wakeford (eds.), *Inventive Methods: The Happening of the Social*. London: Routledge, pp. 110–125.

Frida Hastrup is assistant professor at the Saxo Institute, Ethnology Section, at the University of Copenhagen. She has conducted fieldwork in coastal Tamil Nadu, south India, and her publications on this include a monograph entitled *Weathering the World: Recovery in the Wake of the Tsunami in a Tamil Fishing Village* (Berghahn 2011). Currently, she is leading a collaborative research project on natural resources (www.naturalgoods.saxo.ku.dk).
(hastrup@hum.ku.dk)

RETURNING TO THE ARCHIVE IN SEARCH OF EVERYDAY PRACTICES IN FIELDWORK

Karin Gustavsson

This article concerns itself with the early twentieth-century documentation of different phenomena in the Swedish countryside considered crucial to an understanding of rural lifestyle in the past. This research was motivated out of a concern for a vanishing peasant culture. Vast quantities of photographs, drawings and descriptions of houses and settlements were compiled into archives and later on, this material was used as the base for the Atlas of Swedish folk culture published in 1957. Inspired by Fleck's notion of "thought collective" and Latour's ideas of "craftsmanship", the article returns to the archives in order to examine the everyday practices of the fieldworkers and the different tools and techniques used to document the vanishing peasant material culture.

Keywords: fieldwork, history of discipline, technology, building documentation, archives

A young man is standing in front of a farmhouse, deeply concentrated, presumably making a drawing of it or taking notes. The suit and student's cap indicate that he is not part of the setting but is an outsider carefully observing the surroundings. The photograph with the young man working with a documentation of the farmhouse is dated 1921 and was taken at a small farmstead in the province of Scania (Skåne). In the archival text accompanying the picture, the farmhouse is described in terms of building techniques, materials and age.

What the Archives Contain

I have examined a large number of photographs of this kind as well as descriptions and drawings of old buildings and settlements, dating from about a hundred years ago, that are kept in Swedish archives.

This initial picture is one of many that caught my attention. It is pasted on a piece of cardboard. Topographical information can be found beneath the picture, together with the accompanying text about the building. The picture opens up a story on the practices of ethnographic documentation in the past and how documentary research was carried out.

The different buildings at the farmstead are described in words, accompanied by a plan of the setting that gives information about the size of the different buildings, their function and location. There are other things in this photograph, however, not described in the text. What was the name of the man at work? What kind of carriage is seen behind him? Is it an agricultural tool, or was it used for transportations? Who were the people living in the house, and how did they greet him when he arrived?

Ill. 1: A fieldworker at a small farmstead in the village Lya in Östra Karup parish in the province of Scania. (Photo: City museum of Helsingborg)

Or was the house abandoned – windows seem to be broken! And who was standing behind the camera, and how had this person composed this motif? No answers to these questions could be found in the file where this almost hundred-year-old photograph is kept. When this picture is viewed in the twenty-first century, it can be assumed that the viewer sees other things than the photographer in 1921 had in mind, and that quite different questions are considered. Questions like those listed here might of course have been asked by an early twentieth-century visitor to the setting, but the overriding set of questions at that time were related to the buildings as constructions, rather than what life was like at that place.

In the folklife archives in Sweden (as well as in many other countries in Europe) one can find a substantial number of files containing the results of documentation of what was looked upon as a vanishing peasant society. Such documentation was conducted during the first decades of the twentieth century. At that time, there was a strong belief that an old rural lifestyle was not only undergoing change but was doomed to vanish. Considerable efforts were therefore made to collect traditions and old customs, songs and dialects. Rural villages, buildings and settings were documented in descriptions, drawings and photographs. The underlying idea was that when the rural lifestyle eventually was abandoned, it would be possible to study it through this material. Time and changes in research ideals have, however, made this presupposition obsolete. When viewing the content of the records from the archives today it is easy to focus on what are now seen as deficiencies. We want to know other things than the explorers of 1921. This can direct our attention to the gaps rather than the content that nevertheless exist in the pictures. In spite of all these information gaps, these pictures are brimming with knowledge.

George W. Stocking, one of the pioneers in the writing of the history of anthropology, claims that anthropological fieldworks in the early years of the twentieth century were conducted with no questioning or analysis (1983: 8). The belief that neutral knowledge was gathered was strong. The same belief can be seen in the documentation conducted by the folklife archives in Scandinavia, where gathering was the primary task because of its perceived urgency. Evaluation and research were regarded as tasks that could be conducted later once the material was gathered in the archives. Thus, when the fieldworkers of the 1920s had completed their work, the archives were filled with material assembled with a set of empirical questions as a base. The aim at that time was to enable research of the presumed neutral material in the future. Research questions were based upon temporal and spatial connections between different types of buildings and settlements.

I have examined records from the archives in order to investigate if this voluminous material can be used in research today with other questions in mind. With texts from Ludwik Fleck and Bruno Latour underlying my reading I intended to subject the material to a reading of the importance of collective work in science. I also wanted to analyse the practical fieldwork of the early twentieth century in terms of materiality and technology. Both Fleck and Latour emphasise the importance of seeing research as a collective endeavour. From today's perspective, Sigurd Erixon (1888–1968), the ethnologist who initiated the documentation of vernacular architecture in Sweden, can appear as a solitary scholar, but he was surrounded by people like the fieldworker in illustration 1 (whose names are not always known to today's scholars) all working hard for the same aim.

Several scholars of European ethnology and other cultural sciences have returned to the history of their own disciplines over the last twenty or thirty years in order to understand their contemporary predicaments (Stocking 1983: 4). According to Regina Bendix it is possible to analyse how authoritative knowledge is produced by focusing on the inquiries within one's own discipline (Bendix 1997: 4). This is the main reason for my returning to these old investigations.

The archival material that constituted the results of the search for the "old peasant society", is the subject of this paper, which emphasises the documentation of vernacular architecture in particular. Erixon later became a main figure in Swedish ethnology and greatly influenced the development of European ethnology (see the introduction to this volume). Erixon was employed by *Nordiska museet* in Stockholm (Sweden's largest museum of cultural history), which was responsible for the fieldwork that was energetically carried out, especially during the 1920s. Public as well as private founders supported the efforts to "save" the lifestyle of the past by collecting and saving knowledge about it.

Erixon worked within a context where corresponding works were going on in several European countries. Magnificent books with many illustrations of old rural buildings, many in German, had been published since the late nineteenth century. The references in Erixon's works are not only to Scandinavian literature but also to contemporary European scholars, which shows that he was well-orientated internationally in this specific field of research. The documentation of vernacular architecture and rural lifestyle in Scandinavia carried out during the first half of the twentieth century was conducted with the same ideal as parallel work in the rest of Europe and within the anthropological discipline.

The documentation of buildings and sites yielded an immense volume of material as a consequence, easily accessible in different public archives and museums today.[1] The files with photographs, texts and drawings represent an impressive amount of empirical knowledge. They contain information about what kind of houses that were to be found in different regions, about different building techniques, as well as building materials, from full scale to small details; all the facts that the people responsible for the compilation of the material had in mind. In the archives a consistent order exists, based primarily upon topographical units. What was once considered as valuable knowledge about elderly buildings in the countryside can now be found compiled in files and cabinets, conveniently arranged and easily accessible.

Method

I have done a close reading of the material. This means that both texts and pictures (photographs and drawings) have been thoroughly examined for content. Information about what kinds of tools and equipment that were used by the fieldworkers is rare, but much can be detected from the pictures themselves. The size of the glass plates used is the most evident, but also other technical issues can be traced from the pictures. Some have dark shades in the upper corners, "corner shading" (e.g. illustration 4). It is a result of the use of an inferior quality lens, or a lens that did not match the camera very well. A lens of higher quality or better match would not leave these kinds of shades. Thus, this specific phenomenon in some pictures implies that the museum responsible for the fieldwork where these pictures were taken did not have photographic equipment that was optimal for the task.[2] One result of the close reading is that it is possible to learn from the photographs what kind of cameras that were used, and how skilled a specific fieldworker was in using it, a part of the knowledge about the interaction between man and technology. In this case, the close reading provides clues regarding the prerequisites for the knowledge production.

A close reading obviously focuses on the motifs of the pictures as well. Many traces of everyday life in the countryside in the early twentieth century can be seen in the pictures, features not described in words in any other sources. This is one of the reasons for returning to old material. The camera can only register what is contemporary, not the past, which was the original aim of the documentation. The photographer of 1921, who took the picture in illustration 1 at the little farmstead in Scania, was surrounded by features that were of less interest at that time, but which today can reveal a lot about everyday life in the countryside, about the conditions for farming, and livestock, etc. At the farmstead there was probably a diversity of sensory impressions – sounds, smells and sights – that were new and exotic for the man we see taking notes. But only the sights were possible to capture on paper (and in photographs). The other impressions that have not been depicted are not described in words. Behind the fieldworker some kind of carriage or farming tool on wheels can be seen. This is quite common in these pictures, but such features are never commented on in the descriptions of the different houses and settings. They represented, together with the sensory impressions, the contemporary everyday life, that was not in focus for these explorers of the peasant society.

I have examined both published and unpublished texts and manuscripts. In the archive of *Nordiska museet* there is a large number of small notebooks that originate from different fieldwork investigations. The notes were written while working in the field and contain immediate observations, not processed texts written at the office some weeks later or subjected to influence by later experiences. The material represents the work of many, not only those who later became scholars like Erixon. Many notes and manuscripts from fieldworking students that never made a career within folklife research or museum work have been neglected by succeeding ethnologists. For example, in 1920, there were 35 fieldworkers sent out by *Nordiska museet* (B. Nilsson 2000: 197). Some of them later became specialists, but it was not possible to know in advance who was to become a specialist, and who would give up the work and remain a non-professional in this kind of work. In addition to the printed texts, notebooks and archival manuscripts, my close reading also comprises studies of the relation between picture and text. All the photographs in the files are accompanied by an explanatory text. However, there is much more information in the pictures – facts that are not described in texts – which can be extracted and analysed.

Norms in Common, Working Together

The way the vanishing peasant culture was talked about was strongly established within society as a whole. In the Swedish parliament, the disappearance of folk culture was discussed in 1919 under the headline "Everything old is about to disappear". This discussion led the government to form the Official Committee of Folklife Research ("Folkminneskommittén") the following year, to work within the frame of the Swedish Government Official Reports with the aim of finding out how the work of documenting the vanishing remains of the peasant society should be organised (Gustavsson 2014: 53). While there was a widespread preconception that everything old was about to vanish, it coexisted with notions of what "old" represented in terms of value. What was old, was implicitly attributed a high value. It would be a great loss to society if the old disappeared. The importance of exploring and documenting what was considered as "old", and the efforts to collect folklore, can be traced to the nineteenth century (Bendix 1997). This assumption about the importance of "old" was strongly present during the following century, together with a prediction of the "vanishing primitive" (Stocking 1983: 4). The idea that different phenomena in rural lifestyle really were vanishing, not just undergoing change and development, was characteristic of folklife researchers as a group.

The fieldworkers who undertook the documentation of buildings and settings in the countryside within the commission from *Nordiska museet* were all young men who had studied folklife research, linguistics, art history or architecture, shared the same view of the past, and had the same sense of what was important to note and work with during the fieldwork. They shared the same norms, and were part of what can be defined as a "thought collective" as coined by Polish scientist Ludwik Fleck ([1935]1979). Sigurd Erixon gave both oral and written instructions to the fieldworkers. In the 1920s there were some books and leaflets that could serve as instructions, but they were quite schematic and did not give hands-on instructions for the daily work. This was instead achieved through letters over time as questions arose (Gustavsson 2014: 156). However, all the fieldworkers shared the same presumptions regarding the urgent need for a fast exploration of peasant culture. How were these presumptions formed and maintained?

Not only mutual norms within a group but also concrete "acting together" can create a sense of commonness (cf. F. Nilsson 2000). Travelling together, participating in the same meetings and so on creates a sense of togetherness among the different members of the group. Working together with various tools requires collaboration. Measuring, for example, could mean working in very incommodious positions that required both physical strength and ability to cooperate. When working together after bicycle rides that might have been spectacular, a specific fellowship based upon corporal activities, arose. This fellowship was of another degree than that between young men sitting at desks in the same office. Technical innovations affected the fieldwork, and the scientific process, when knowledge about the past was formed by the investigations of the vanishing peasant society.

The idea of the common way of thinking, "thought styles", and collective thinking in "thought collectives" as crucial in the forming of scientific facts, was presented by Ludwik Fleck in the mid-1930s (Fleck [1935]1979). The belonging to such a thought collective was formed not only by sharing ideological thoughts and norms, after reading the same books, for example, or undergoing the same theoretical education. A situation of fieldwork, when people really are doing things together, can also be crucial. French sociologist Bruno Latour has also emphasised the importance of the collective. According to him, the members of a group doing research together discipline each other (Latour 1999: 95). An even stronger sense of togetherness might appear when people not only participate together in the same events, but also really *do* things together, like handling tools for measuring buildings and cameras. Fieldwork entailed physical strains, with long bicycle rides with heavy equipment. The fieldwork situation also meant that the young participants lived together far away from home, mostly in a quite simple accommodation. After strenuous bicycle rides they were supposed to work with measuring and description-making. Although the measuring tools that were used were quite simple (yardstick, measuring tape), handling them was critical given the need for cooperation to produce reliable results. A camera consisted of several different parts (tripod, lenses, glass plates and cassettes containing the plates, tools for measuring light etc.). Cooperation between the fieldworkers was a prerequisite, given the weight of the equipment, and the number of complicated parts it sometimes consisted of, in addition to the tricky modes of operating it. Bruno Latour emphasises the importance of what he calls "craftsmanship" among

Ill. 2: Fieldworkers having dinner together when a period of work was about to end. Neither their names nor the place have been registered. (Photo: Sigurd Erixon collection at the Library of Linköping)

the employees at a laboratory where he conducted fieldwork with the aim of making a survey of a scientific process. Science derives not only from logical considerations but also from a set of devices that has to be skilfully handled (Latour 1990: 22).

In illustration 2 we see a group of fieldworkers having dinner together at a guesthouse, when their period at work was about to be finished. Only men conducted the fieldwork. No women participated, although there were many women working at *Nordiska museet* during its pioneer years (Klein 2013). One of the men in the illustration is wearing a wristwatch. Measuring time was important; the fieldworks were conducted with a sense of urgency. It was important to work fast, as there was a strong sense that the destruction of old buildings in the countryside was proceeding apace. As in the introductory illustration, their clothing can also be noted. It might look like they have dressed up for dinner, but they actually wore suits while working. The suits indicate the togetherness within the group, and signal that the young men belonged to another social class than the people they met in the countryside.

Technology, Research Questions and Gaze

At the beginning of the twentieth century, photographic technology had existed for several decades and portable cameras were now at hand. The photograph was an ideal medium that could mediate motifs to a beholder situated in a different place and different time. The technology was also compatible with the contemporary positivistic ideals in science (Petersen 2007: 24). In 1923, the fieldworker Mårten Sjöbeck wrote to the head of the Folklife archive in Lund, senior lecturer Carl Wilhelm von Sydow:

> Great demands ought to be placed on the quality of the photographic material, which in future

will be used to authenticate the validity of texts, drawings and plans. The photograph is the only impartial evidence that we have at hand.[3]

However, the photograph can hardly be "impartial evidence", as Sjöbeck claims. A photograph is the result of the photographer's active choosing – and thereby also ignorance – of what the motif should be (Garnert 1995: 169). The camera has a significant effect on the gaze (Urry & Larsen 2011: 155ff.). British sociologist John Urry points out photography to be "the most important technology for developing and extending the tourist gaze" (Urry & Larsen 2011: 155). He claims looking to be a learned ability. There is, according to Urry, no "pure and innocent eye" (Urry & Larsen 2011: 1). Looking is constructed upon already formed visual and linguistic experiences. The *gaze* is a way of looking at the surroundings that is based upon experience and knowledge. What is being *gazed* at and considered important to include in the documentation is the result of previously acquired experiences, norms and presuppositions. The fieldworkers' gaze at the time and the different modes in choosing objects for documentation were essential for what can be found in the archives today.

The content of the archives and the character of the photographs kept there are also dependent on different technical processes that had an impact on the final result. The focal length of the camera lenses influences the result; different filters could affect how colours and contrasts were converted in the black and white pictures, and dramatic skies could be emphasised and become even more dramatic. After taking pictures in the field, the plates would be developed in a laboratory and then copies made on paper – processes wherein the content in the picture could also be affected. To sum up, the camera technology was an innovation with vital effect on research questions.

There is little written evidence about how the photographing took place, or of the theoretical thinking influencing the selection of motives and the way that each photograph was composed. The common preconceptions of the fieldworkers resulted in a rather unreflected way of choosing motives. Consequently, as Swedish ethnologist Jan Garnert has pointed out, the photographs must be the basis for an analysis and evaluation of the work and the thinking in the past (Garnert 1995: 174). The pictures are, in a manner of speaking, sources to their own becoming.

For obvious reasons, the camera is seldom seen in photographs. In a drawing made by Gösta Selling in 1920 we see the fieldworker Harry Henschen handling the notebook and the camera, devices of different character but both crucial in the investigations of vernacular architecture. Selling mentions some materials that were essential: "Camera and notebook were the foremost devices during these research trips, that for the most part were made by bicycle" (Selling 1952: 58). Swedish-American professor in mass communication Karin Becker has called the camera "a companion in exploration and tourism" (Becker 1992: 4). This companionship is evident in a camera like this, mounted on a tripod that renders it as tall as a human.

Gösta Selling, a former head of the Swedish National Heritage Board, and himself a fieldworker in the 1920s, recounted some thirty years later that the "photograph was the primary medium in the documentation of vernacular architecture, with drawings and descriptions as important complements" (Selling 1952: 59), thus confirming the earlier claim by Mårten Sjöbeck. The camera appears as a crucial technique for the documentation of old buildings in the countryside. Without portable cameras, the documentation would hardly have reached the intensity and the focus that it did. The camera as a tool and the photographic technique made it possible to take photographs in the field. Hand in hand with the advances in camera technology, it is possible to observe an increasing need for taking photographs.

I shall return to the notebook later, but first I want to draw attention to another technology crucial during fieldwork, namely that of transport. The bicycle, that Selling mentions, was in combination with travel by train, essential in the investigations of the vanishing peasant society. The pioneers of folklife studies, working in the field in the nineteenth century, travelled in horse carriages or simply walked

Ill. 3: A fieldworker handling the camera and the notebook. (Drawing by Gösta Selling. Original in the Sigurd Erixon collection at the Library of Linköping)

while collecting artefacts and memories in the countryside. The bicycle, invented in the late nineteenth century, became an ideal vehicle for transportation in contexts that are central in this text, and made it possible to take the large cameras along, even though the weight of the equipment was considerable.

But however ideal, cars were soon in use. Selling describes how cars replaced the bicycles in the 1920s.

A revolution in fieldwork occurred in the mid-20s, when the bicycle was definitively replaced by the car as a means of transport. It was ironic that this should happen at the same time as cameras became smaller and the equipment lighter. This modern vehicle that seemed so convenient nevertheless had some disadvantages. Bad roads, and stiff springs sometimes made the glass plates come loose from their frames and fall forward inside the bellows when the magazine was opened: If the cassettes were loose in the case sometimes the glass plates would even crack. (…) The driver of the Ford was obliged to bed the camera down softly in the back seat. (Selling 1952: 64)

In this case, technology was both friend and enemy. It was easy to travel by car, and bad weather did not pose the same problems as when biking, and people who did not have the physical strength to ride a bike for days and weeks, could also participate. There were some unexpected disadvantages, however. Above, Selling describes one of many paradoxes that can be seen in the documentation; at the same time as lightweight cameras that would have facilitated the travels by bike were made available, the use of cars was introduced.

Selling also describes how the two technical systems, the car and the camera, do not match. Here, it was necessary for those who handled the different technologies to use their curiosity and ability to think creatively to find out how to solve this specific problem. In this case, bedding down the camera in the back seat of the car probably did not prove a major obstacle. There are other examples of different problems caused by technology, and how they required both skill and a great deal of creativity to make the tools work in a way that made the work efficient. The glass plates that were used were mounted in cassettes. After taking a photograph, the glass plate would be removed and replaced with an unexposed plate. This meticulous work had to be done inside a sack made of dark textile. Selling describes how he preferred to do this at night, in bed, with the cassettes and plates under the blankets to prevent light from reaching the glass plates (Selling 1952). This is not only an example of how technology has an impact on the people handling the device, but also an example of how man's ingenuity is capable of refining the technology with quite simple means.

As Gösta Selling points out, the notebook was one of two fundamental devices in the investigation of vernacular architecture. At the same time, he characterises the notebook as materiality, in addition to its knowledge content. The parallels to Bruno Latour's description of how the notebook was used by scientists in the forest of Boa Vista in Brazil in the late twentieth century are obvious. Latour conducted a study of natural science fieldworkers in the forest, with the aim of examining the relation between research results and technical devices. Here too, the notebook was of major importance for the fieldworkers. It created the sense of being in a laboratory, even though the research group was far out in a forest (Latour 1999: 58).

In Boa Vista Latour followed a fieldwork of natural science. The participants made conclusions of their observations by making a map where all the fluctuations in the qualities of the soil they had examined were highlighted with different signs. The result of several weeks of hard work of gathering soil was concentrated onto a large sheet of paper. They had created what Latour calls an inscription, that is, a materialisation of knowledge. It is possible for a beholder to point with the finger on the map – the inscription – and follow the inscription with a finger. The map contains concentrated knowledge, and is at the same time an artefact, a piece of materiality that shows the results of many years of fieldwork. When knowledge is transformed in this way into an object – here a map – it is possible to view the findings with a gaze (Latour 1999: 29).

The notes taken during fieldwork in the Scandinavian countryside were somewhat rough and ready material both for the files in the archives, and also for publishing. The notes were the first draft for manuscripts, that later became articles and books. In many of the notebooks there are traces of excerpts made later. Lines were drawn over the pages; small notes were made in the corners etc. As the notebooks contained knowledge from several weeks of fieldwork, they were very valuable and it was crucial that they should not be lost. In many of them, the name and address of the owner is written, sometimes including the information that a good finder's fee would be paid, in the event that the book was lost and found by someone else (Gustavsson 2014: 177).

The word photograph means "writing with light". A photograph can be seen as an inscription, though it is a picture and not a text. It is written not by words, but by light, and contains information that can be interpreted in a similar way to that of a text. At the moment of exposure, the photographer captures a glimpse of reality into a picture onto a highly light-sensitive material. The photograph becomes an inscription in the Latourian sense. It is both an artefact and a medium. Long after a fieldwork was finished, people other than those who were present at the moment of exposure, can put their fingers on the photograph, and in that way mark both the content of knowledge in the photograph, and its materiality.

Only stationary objects were the motives of the documentation, mainly houses, both from the exterior and the interior. There was little or no attention given to working processes, such as roofing with straw, for example, which was a recurrent work, and other building construction, or traditional farm work and so on. As the cameras were loaded with glass plates, the equipment was very heavy. The weight caused a limit for how many photographs that could be taken of each object, which meant that working processes consisting of many steps, that would require a lot of photographs if the process should be fully depicted, were neglected (Gustavsson 2014: 136). Illustration 4 is a photo of a straw-roofed house from the province of Halland in the south of Sweden, taken in 1921. The different shades of the roof make me curious – why does it look this way, how had that roof been made? Unfortunately, the pictures and the descriptions in the files made by the fieldworkers give no further clues. The description of the picture says that this is the farmstead viewed from the south side. A glimpse of the dwelling house is seen to the left, the building that dominates the picture is the stable. It is the stationary object that is pictured, and also described. Neither the daily work nor the processes when the house was being maintained and repaired are documented.

Some researchers in the late 1920s started to document on film the different working processes in the countryside. Danish museum inspector Kai Ulldal was a pioneer in making films with the purpose of mediating folklife. He began filming for the Danish National Museum in 1927 and was of the opinion that the films showed "living pictures of old manners and old times work". If there was a technology available, then there was also a need for using it (Gustavsson 2014: 195). In this specific case, it is possible to see that the interest among the fieldworkers to follow a working process arose when a suitable technology for documenting such processes became available.

The new technology of film made it possible to document processes such as timbering, and a need to make films was now expressed and justified with arguments that referred to the necessity of science. The costs for film-making were extremely high, which can be seen in the Swedish Government Official Report about the exploration of the peasant society presented in 1924, but that did not make it impossible to make films (Gustavsson 2014: 135). The high cost seemed to be just another obstacle to overcome.

There is an obvious paradox here – industrialisation was seen as the cause of the vanishing of the rural lifestyle, but it was the products of that industrialisation – railways, bicycles, cars, cameras etc. – that made it possible to document and in that way "save" peasant society for the future. The prerequisites for the investigation of rural lifestyle and vernacular architecture were the fruit of industrialisation, fruit of the same processes that caused the peasant society to vanish.

Mapping Folklife

The great national atlas projects that were going on in several European countries, and the striving to produce a European atlas of folk culture, are topics too extensive to be dealt with in this article (see Munk and Elgaard Jensen, and Sandberg in this volume).[4] There exist links, however, between the investigations of vernacular architecture conducted in the 1920s and the making of a Swedish Atlas of Folk Culture several decades later. It was Sigurd Erixon and Åke Campbell, taking part in the documentation in the beginning of their careers, who took ini-

Ill. 4: Farmstead in the village of Björkeröd, Hasslöv parish, in the province of Halland in southern Sweden. (Photo: City museum of Helsingborg)

tiatives to such an atlas in the early 1930s. The first part of the work was completed in 1957, the second was published in 1976 (Campbell 1957).

As mentioned above, a map is a picture that is a comprehension of reality. The results of the investigations of vernacular architecture could be concentrated in flat pictures, easy to overview. Erixon used maps in several of his articles from the 1910s and 1920s to show the distribution of different types of buildings, and in the 1930s he began the work with the earlier mentioned Atlas of Swedish folk culture, together with Åke Campbell, among others. He had presented the first ethnological doctoral thesis in Sweden in 1928. The thesis contains about 300 pages of text, but there are four maps in which he summarises the results of several years of work with the investigations of farmsteads and methods of fencing in the province of Scania (Campbell 1928). It is a parallel to what Latour describes in his studies of a laboratory – a long period of work that has engaged a whole group of people yields diagrams and plots on paper as a result (Latour & Woolgar 1986, 1990: 22). The use of maps to show results of the documentation of old rural buildings can be seen as a way of constructing a visual language for ethnology, an important factor in making it a powerful discipline (cf. Latour 1990: 36). Folklife research became a discipline where it was crucial to *show* things, not just to talk (and write) about them (cf. Latour 1990: 34). And the photographic and transportation technologies were essential in this.

Disagreements on the Task?

Thus far, this text has dealt with people working together and who shared the same norms and preconceptions. From the material examined I make the interpretation that the situation during fieldwork where young men from a similar background shared both hardship during work and commitment for the task formed a common thought style in the Fleckian sense. However, this interpretation also raises the question: did everyone really agree on the desirable outcomes and the methods at work? Were there not any individuals who participated in the fieldwork that had another way of working, with other technology and perhaps also other goals? In a study of the practices of archaeology, Swedish scholar Ola W. Jensen, who has studied the history of the archaeological discipline, claims, "new methods and new technology can be developed as a result of a conflict, to be used as an argument about the 'right practice'" (Jensen 2012: 26). According to Jensen, there is much to learn about scientific practice by studying the rejected practices. This can provide a perspective on the practices that became accepted and dominant in use (cf. Jensen 2012: 27). But are such conflicts and rejected practices also to be found in folklife research and in the documentation of peasant society? Perhaps there are – at a micro level – when it comes to how to measure a building, what kind of paper that was most convenient to use, or whether glass plates or film sheets would give the best results when taking photographs. But at another level, no. There was a consensus about the overall targets and about the methods – measuring, writing down the descriptions and taking the photographs that were to be compiled into records.

My interpretation, therefore, is that there may well have existed different opinions regarding camera techniques; for example, some preferred to work with the heavy cameras as in the sketch by Selling, while others found the lightweight cameras where film sheets were used more convenient and appropriate to the task. And the principals and the fieldworkers will no doubt have had different opinions concerning the appropriate amount of pictures of each object (Gustavsson 2014: 135). But the belief in technology, and the convictions about the importance of making the documentation were shared. The larger disagreements are to be found within the matters of organisation and how the responsibility was divided among the different actors, not in the fieldwork situation. Which organisation was best suited to take care of the important questions? Who should own the compiled archive files, who should have the rights of access to the contents of the files for further scientific processing? The Committee of Folklife Research mentioned earlier ("Folkminneskommittén") ended their work in 1924 in disagreement about matters of responsi-

Ill. 5: Picture found in a miscellaneous file. Having fun together and making light of the serious work is also a component in the "thought collectives". This fieldworker (name unknown) dared to indulge in pranks like this because of the existence of common norms and what Fleck calls a common "thought style". (Photo: Sigurd Erixon collection at the Library of Linköping)

bilities and organisation (Gustavsson 2014: 54). As said, there was a consensus, however, concerning the practical fieldwork. There was a shared conviction both among scholars and in Swedish society as a whole about the importance of documenting peasant society. The extent of the project and the great economic efforts that were made both from authorities and private founders are clear signs of consensus.

To claim that everyone agreed might be construed as making a heroic portrait of the group, instead of focusing on matters in which there were conflicts. On the other hand, this consensus in the group may have resulted in a situation in which new ideas had no impact. The stability of the group, formed both by a common education and during meticulous practices, had a preservative effect. "To convince someone, a scientist needs data (…) but also someone to convince!" (Latour 1999: 102). When everyone agrees, there is no one to convince, and therefore no sharp arguments are formulated. Scientific progress slows down and becomes less incisive in such a context, and a condition arises which Fleck identifies as a conservatism of thought (Fleck [1935]1979).

Let me return now to the thought style and how it can occur and be expressed in the material that I have investigated. In the files in the archives we find the "official" photographs – pictures of houses, villages and settlements. These were the tangible result of the documentation, and were the media that would redistribute knowledge about rural houses and settlements to scholars in other contexts – and in the future. It is possible to discern the "unofficial" side of the work, particularly in personal letters between fieldwork participants, in which the troubles of everyday life in the field are expressed, and also in the exchange of jokes about situations in the field, about flat tyres and lack of food and so on. There are unofficial pictures, too, sometimes found in "miscellaneous" files in which another side of the fieldwork can be seen – revealing a less respectful view of the serious mission, where fieldworkers go beyond the workplace boundaries of acceptable behaviour. These pictures show an obvious sense of fun (see illustration 5), which I want to suggest, in keeping with Fleck, was an important ingredient in the forming of a collective of knowledge. Both the "official" illustrations (such as illustration 4 above) and illustration 5 represent vital knowledge about how the investigations were conducted.

Conclusion

German cultural anthropologists Michaela Fenske and Antonia Davidovic-Walther use the expression "knowledge venue" to illustrate a discussion about ethnological knowledge practices (Fenske & Davidovic-Walther 2010: 1). The archive appears as such a knowledge venue in several respects as materials in archives can be used as sources for studies today with different aims.

One aim in returning to the archives is the possibility of exploring the content of photographs of the kind that has been used in this paper. There is a lot to see in them that is not explained in words in other sources. The empirical content can be used to tell stories about different phenomena from the past and be useful in a practical application, such as in studies of housing addressed to building history and building restoration. In a doctoral thesis in the discipline of heritage studies, Swedish Gunnar Almevik uses archival records like the ones described in this text in order to trace both the history and living conditions of an ancient farmstead in the province of Scania (Almevik 2012).

When examining the photo in illustration 1, we see many phenomena in the picture that are not mentioned in the accompanying text. The carriage and the curtains in the window that can be seen represented, together with the sensory impressions that surrounded the fieldworker in the picture, the contemporary everyday life, that was not in focus for the explorers of the peasant society. There is a constant lack of information about the everyday life in the countryside in the archive files. What is not written in words in the files can, however, be detected in the pictures. The way the roof of the building in illustration 4 looks is a result of continuous repair work – a small section of the roof was thatched every year. In other pictures, other traces of daily life in the countryside can be detected, that bequeath us valuable fragments of knowledge.

By detecting the preconceptions in texts and also in other sources like pictures, as well as studying the use of artefacts like cameras and bicycles, knowledge processes can be traced and new knowledge produced. When looking at the materials in the archives from different angles, different kinds of knowledge can be produced. Research processes in the past can be examined, as well as detailed empirical knowledge about building techniques, for example.

There are misconceptions among many ethnologists of today regarding these pictures. It has been claimed that the photographs taken during the investigations of the peasant society only show houses and settings, not people (Becker 1992; Garnert 1995). In my examination of a great many records in the archives, it is obvious that the presence of the inhabitants of the countryside in the pictures varies according to who was standing behind the camera. Different fieldworkers apparently had different ideals in this respect: some were eager to depict the buildings without disturbing features in front of the actual motif; for others this was not an obstacle (Gustavsson 2014: 117). The camera technique that was used cannot be overlooked when examining the pictures – sometimes the shutter speed was so long that it would have been impossible for a person to stand still.[5] The lack of people in the pictures is simply a result of the available technology.

The files that are filled with facts about buildings constitute sources of knowledge about the time and the context in which they were created, and the scientific processes in which they were produced. By studying the content of the files we can learn about the context and the contemporary research questions. Both the research questions and the practices of science are contextually specific as well as consequences of the surrounding society (Jensen 2012: 22). According to Regina Bendix, the archived collections of folklife and folklore have contributed to form the bulk of the discipline (Bendix 1997: 156).

The fieldworkers that collected the material that has been examined in this paper were working within an ideal that said that they were *finding* knowledge that already existed. By returning to this old documentary project it is possible to look upon contemporary projects with an awareness that reveals, in Bendix's words, that "knowledge is made, not found" (Bendix 1997: 220), and one can add that technology is one factor that contributes in the making of ethnographic knowledge, as well as in collective work.

Notes
1 In this case, material from the Folklife archive in Lund, *Nordiska museet* in Stockholm, and the City museum of Helsingborg has been used.
2 These corner shadows only appear in the pictures from the City museum of Helsingborg.
3 Mårten Sjöbeck in a letter to the Folklife archive in Lund, 1923 (Gustavsson 2014: 117).
4 The strive to make a European atlas has been described in *Ethnologia Europaea* 30:1.
5 In many photographs from the countryside, hens and cats are almost seen as ghosts – they were moving while the photograph was taken, and this blur reveals the slow shutter-speed.

References
Almevik, Gunnar 2012: *Byggnaden som kunskapskälla* (The Building as a Source of Knowledge, with an English summary). Dissertation. Gothenburg Studies in Conservation 27. Gothenburg: Gothenburg University, Institutionen för kulturvård.
Becker, Karin 1992: Picturing our Past: An Archive Constructs a National Culture. *Journal of American Folklore* 105, pp. 3–18.
Bendix, Regina 1997: *In Search of Authenticity: The Formation of Folklore Studies*. Madison: University of Wisconsin Press.
Campbell, Åke 1928: Skånska bygder under förra hälften av 1700-talet: Etnografisk studie över den skånska allmogens äldre odlingar, hägnader och byggnader (Rural Districts of Scania in the early 18th century). Dissertation. Uppsala: Uppsala University.
Campbell, Åke & Sigurd Erixon (ed.) 1957: *Atlas över svensk folkkultur* (Atlas of Swedish Folk Culture). Uppsala: Kungl. Gustav Adolfsakademien för Svensk Folkkultur.
Fenske, Michaela & Antonia Davidovic-Walther 2010: Exploring Ethnological Knowledges. *Journal of Folklore Research* 47:1–2, 1–5, January–August 2010.
Fleck, Ludwik (1935)1979: *Genesis and Development of a Scientific Fact*. Chicago: University of Chicago Press.
Garnert, Jan 1995: Rethinking Visual Representation: Notes on the Folklorist and Photographer Nils Keyland. *Nordisk museologi* 2, 165–190.
Gustavsson, Karin 2014: *Expeditioner i det förflutna: Etnologiska fältarbeten och försvinnande allmogekultur under 1900-talets början* (Expeditions into the Past: Ethnological Fieldwork and the Vanishing Peasant Culture at the start of the 20th century, with an English summary). Dissertation. Lund: Lund University.
Jensen, Ola W. 2012: A Thematic and Theoretical Introduction to Histories of Archaeological Practices. In: Ola W. Jensen (ed.), *Histories of Archaeological Practices: Reflections on Methods, Strategies and Social Organisation in Past Fieldwork*. Stockholm: National Historical Museum.
Klein, Barbro 2013: Women and the Formation of Swedish Folklife Research. *Journal of American Folklore* 127:500, 120–151.
Latour, Bruno 1990: Drawing Things Together. In: Mike Lynch & Steve Wolger (eds.), *Representations in Scientific Practice*. Cambridge, Mass.: MIT Press.

Latour, Bruno 1999: *Pandora's Hope: Essays on the Reality of Science Studies*. Cambridge, Mass.: Harvard University Press.

Latour, Bruno & Steve Woolgar 1986: *Laboratory Life: The Social Construction of Scientific Facts*. Beverly Hills: Sage.

Nilsson, Bo G. 2000: Folklivets upptäckare: Sigurd Erixons by- och bebyggelseundersökningar (The Detector of Folk Life: The Surveys of Villages and Buildings by Sigurd Erixon). In: Bengt Erik Eriksson & Roger Qvarsell (eds.), *Samhällets linneaner*. Stockholm: Carlsson.

Nilsson, Fredrik 2000: *I rörelse: Politisk handling under 1800-talets första hälft* (On the Move: Political Action During the first half of the 19th century, with an English summary). Dissertation. Lund: Lund University.

Petersen, Anja 2007: *På visit i verkligheten: Fotografi och kön i slutet av 1800-talet* (Visiting Reality: Photography and Gender at the End of the 19th century, with an English summary). Stockholm; Stehag: Brutus Östlings bokförlag.

Selling, Gösta 1952: Museifotografering (Museum Photography). *Fotografisk* årsbok 1952, 55–68.

Stocking, George W. (ed.) 1983: Observers Observed: Essays on Ethnographic Fieldwork. Madison, Wisconsin: University of Wisconsin Press.

Urry, John & Jonas Larsen 2011: *The Tourist Gaze 3.0*. Third ed. Los Angeles: Sage.

Karin Gustavsson, Ph.D., is a teacher and researcher in ethnology and museology at the Department of Arts and Cultural Sciences at Lund University, Sweden. She is also the Museum Inspector at the City museum of Helsingborg. Her research interests are heritage studies, the use of history and science and technology studies.
(karin.gustavsson@kultur.lu.se)

BORDER PRACTICES AND SPEED
Cultural Perspectives on Borders and Smuggling

Fredrik Nilsson

Understanding borders from different perspectives has been important to ethnological research since the beginning of the twentieth century. This article will revisit early discussions on borders as well as the more elaborated ethnological border studies of the end of the twentieth century. As some principal themes of these ethnological border studies are brought forward, the article demonstrates how a focus on speed informs contemporary border studies with insights regarding borders and border zones. The illegal liquor trade in the Baltic Sea during the 1920s will serve as the case being discussed, thus establishing analytical distance to contemporary European border processes.

Keywords: borders, practice, speed, inertia, smuggling

In 1921 several articles in the periodical *Lanternan* (The Lantern) – the Swedish Customs Federation's official organ – discussed an increase in the smuggling of alcohol into Sweden. The debate in *Lanternan* was concerned with the illegal border traffic, but also with speed and modernity. The smugglers used fast, modern motorboats and in comparison the coast guards' equipment was deemed dated: "Yes, it seems sad, not to say ridiculous, that the Swedish coast guard use unmodern yachts 'from old times'" (*Lanternan* no. 10, 1921). The polarisation between on the one hand fast smugglers and on the other hand slow coast guards carried an important message: Those who master new technology and speed are often afforded, or capture, the role of popular heroes, which allows them the opportunity to influence social and political change (cf. Marvin 1988; Tomlinson 2007). If the fast-moving smugglers were defined as heroes, even though they challenged the national border, then the representatives of the government risked losing their legitimacy. Thus, according to the debate in *Lanternan*, an effort to modernise and speed up the coast guard was of paramount importance. High velocity would stop the smugglers and turn the border zone into a controlled, inert landscape. The question of how speed destabilise (and stabilise) borders is at the centre of the discussion in this article: The aim is to investigate how the smugglers' use of fast, modern technologies challenged national borders thus forcing the authorities to establish new border practices. Through a discussion of the case, I will demonstrate how a focus on speed can provide ethnology and contemporary border studies further insights regarding the cultural dimensions of borders. The rereading of earlier ethnological border studies is important for the argument since it frames my understanding of borders and speed. I will, however, start with a discussion on contemporary ethnological border studies and will then introduce speed as an important aspect of this field of research.

Border Practices, Inert Border Zones and Speed

In *The Border Multiple* (2012) borders are conceptualised "as practices that are situated and constituted in the specificity of political negotiations as well as in the everyday life performance of them" (Andersen, Klatt & Sandberg 2012: 6). Accordingly, borders are the result of historical, political processes and agreements, but they are also a culturally complex matter. The position of territorial borders is quite often invisible (as for instance in cases where borderlines are drawn in water); therefore, borders need to be materialised in other locations where they must also be performed by different actors in order to manifest the inside–outside partition (cf. Donnan & Wilson 2001; Löfgren 2000; Nilsson 2007). For instance, tollbooths are rarely built on the location of a territorial border (cf. airports), and customs officials as well as coast guards are often working in vaguely defined border zones. This makes borders flexible and complex; they appear at different locations and in different (uni-)forms. Ethnologist Marie Sandberg argues, similarly, that border practices are performed by a variety of actors in an ongoing process of ordering. Such a perspective emphasise that borders are in a state of becoming, they are characterised by processes of stabilisation instead of stability, of ordering instead of order (cf. Sandberg 2012: 119–120). Understanding borders as practices, speed becomes an important element in de- or restabilisation of borders that should not be underestimated. For instance, it makes a difference if a person tries to run through the passport control at an airport or if this person slows down while approaching the counter, eventually stands still and presents the passport to the agent (who in this case of course is immobile inside her or his booth). Border controls are in fact quite often designed with slowness as a key feature (even though there might be a "fast lane" for some travellers); the narrow lanes in front of the passport control at airports; the speed bumps on the bridge between Denmark and Sweden; and the concrete blocks at "hot" borders forcing cars to slowly meander towards the border control. Thus, ideally borders and border zones are inert landscapes – even inside the Schengen area where borders are supposed to have disappeared (cf. Nilsson 1999, 2010). At borders, speed produces problems. Travellers who challenge inertia are defined as threats and accentuate the need for (new) border practices that encapsulate and slow them down.[1]

To analyse the relationship between speed-inertia and the re- or destabilisation of borders, I will employ the concept of "vector". According to Paul Virilio, a vector is a "transporter of speed" ([1984]1996: 54) that structures our understanding of distances, the way we interact with the world and transcend borders. Vectors such as cars, trains, aeroplanes and the Internet facilitate new border practices that allow more people to travel to, or communicate with, places that once were "far away" and "time consuming" to reach (and of course such distances in space and time are not absolutes, but relative). The function of vectors might be regarded as something positive: they produce speed as well as freedom to roam the city streets, the highways, and eventually the globe. From another perspective, of course, such acceleration potentially evokes feelings of dissolution, not only of time-space, but of identities, norms and moral. In this sense, the vector is a producer of anxiety, fear and uncertainty. In the preface to Virilio's *The Aesthetics of Disappearance*, Peter Handberg argues that vectors are "latent carriers of dissolution; they are the carriers of violence, shock and destruction" (1996: 10–11). From this understanding of vectors I will consider how different vectors, like boats, cars, and radio, destabilise (and sometimes stabilise) borders through speed. This argument is based on a research project on smuggling and speed I intend to publish in its entirety. In this forthcoming book a variety of sources are analysed, such as: police reports and interrogations; letters sent from local customs officials to the Swedish Customs Administration in Stockholm and other senior officials in major cities; articles published in newspapers and periodicals; and brochures and pamphlets addressing the problematic smuggling. Quotes below are all from this extensive material.

Even though border studies have developed as a highly dynamic field of research at the beginning of this new millennium, borders as well as speed have been an important theme in Swedish ethnology since the beginning of the twentieth century. As I will discuss in the following section, early Swedish ethnologists, such as Sigurd Erixon, were preoccupied with the inertia as well as the disappearance of borders; furthermore, this line of thought was still very much present and important towards the end of the century. Hence, I will begin by revisiting Sigurd Erixon's discussions on borders. As mentioned in other articles in this volume and elsewhere (cf. Arnstberg 1989, 2010), ethnology at its (Swedish) conception was practically defined by Erixon, making his publications (and conception of borders) an obvious point of departure. From this, I will move on to a discussion of how a renewed interest in borders emerged towards the end of the twentieth century. Although some lines of thought persisted from the earlier phase, this new wave also included some interesting elements. For practical purposes and in order to move this argumentation forward, I will mainly focus on Orvar Löfgren's contributions to the new wave. This enables me to distil an understanding of the foundations of contemporary border studies and leads directly to my conclusion, that speed is of crucial importance if we are to understand the cultural dimensions of borders. I will demonstrate this through my discussion of smuggling as a speedy border practice.

Border Studies in Swedish Ethnology

Sigurd Erixon published several studies in which discussions of borders are an integral part of the analysis: "Svenska gårdstyper" (1919), "Svensk byggnadskultur och dess geografi" (1922), and *Svenska kulturgränser och kulturprovinser* (1945). When the latter was published, Erixon had occupied himself with the project *Atlas of Swedish Folk Culture* since the 1930s. In *Svenskt folkliv* (1938) Sigurd Erixon even stated that the study of cultural borders was one of the most important tasks in ethnology (1938: 277). Through mapping Swedish folk culture and practices, ethnology as a discipline had to be interested in cultural borders – those between villages, vicarages, and provinces, but also those between cities and the countryside. The point here is that those early discussions established an ethnological understanding of borders (as well as of speed).

Using the Swedish province of Scania, once a part of the Danish kingdom, as an example, Erixon argued that cultural borders do not necessarily follow national borders. The so-called Danish-Scanian farm was, according to Erixon, a materialisation of a cultural border that separated different cultural areas in Sweden (1919: 28). However, Erixon did not elaborate on the border as such, or any sort of border practice that might have existed, as the primary focus of his analysis was the typology of culture(s). In *Svensk byggnadskultur och dess geografi* (1922) Erixon's arguments were almost identical, though slightly more elaborated. He argued that the southern parts of Sweden could be defined as a distinct cultural province, making the border between the provinces Halland and Scania in the south-west and the rest of Sweden "one of the most important and interesting borders in the country" (1922: 262). The diffusion of cultural elements, he argued, had been hindered by this border, hence making the folk culture north of this border more "authentic" Swedish (1922: 281–282). Some years later Åke Campbell, another leading ethnologist in Sweden at the time, refined Erixon's argument on the cultural borders and areas in southern Sweden. Campbell stated that the old Danish landscapes (Scania and Halland) were to be understood as a base, with cultural roots in continental Europe, from which cultural elements found their way to Sweden, but not without resistance: "The borderlines show where the foreign cultural streams had run into a dam caused by domestic nature and culture" (Campbell 1928: 2). Using the dam as a metaphor, borders and border landscapes were defined as inert matter, although not entirely impermeable. The idea of inertia was something to which Erixon would later return. He clearly understood the permeability of borders as anchored in historical circumstances and rationalities: "The population in one district was normally influenced by trends in other districts that for historical reasons were considered a role model" (1945: 14). Some borders were more stable than others and, thus, authentic folk culture was preserved in some archaic areas (Erixon 1945: 19). The lack of communication, due to vast distances or a difficult terrain, was defined as a factor that greatly decided the permeability of borders. The mind-set among the population – they could be "hostile" towards new trends, thus creating a "cultural barrier" – was another crucial element: "Even though the cultural diffusion is affected by geography, the defining power is to be found among the population, thus making cultural borders a compromise between nature and history" (Erixon 1945: 19).[2] However, as modernity, and acceleration, intensified, the cultural borders seemed to wither away. In *Atlas över svensk folkkultur* (Atlas of Swedish Folk Culture) (1957), Erixon stated that industrialisation and agricultural reforms caused cultural borders to disappear (1957: 9). This process was further intensified by new communications: "New impulses from big cities and abroad travelled faster and became more dominant than before" (1957: 10).

Thus, Erixon conceptualised borders as consequences of nature, history, political agreements and economy, but also considered them products of everyday life, habits and traditions. Borders were, furthermore, understood as regulators of flows making border zones inert landscapes.

This idea of inertia prevailed when at the end of the century political changes, in particular the dissolution of "Eastern Europe" and subsequently the collapse of the Soviet Union, triggered a new interest in borders and border practices among ethnologists. From the end of the 1980s, national identities or mentalities, thus, became a dynamic field for ethnological research. Borders and national identities became a hot topic as nations or regions tried to navigate in a transformed political landscape (cf. Nilsson, Sanders & Stubbergaard 2007). In a special issue of *Ethnologia Europaea: National Culture as Process*, Orvar Löfgren (1989) identified a need for research of the complexity of national culture. Compared to the early ethnologists, that is, Erixon and his contemporaries, during the following years, a different and more elaborate discussion of borders developed.

In a study of the nationalisation of Sweden Löfgren (1993) discuss how national borders are transformed into cultural borders. Borders are conceptualised as barriers, but also as a sort of actors: they direct the travellers' gaze towards differences and turn geographical landscapes into highly emotional national landscapes. Understood as actors, borders produce a desire for the strange and adventurous land on the other side as well as a longing for the home(-land) (Löfgren 1993: 86–87, 117). Convincingly, Löfgren argues that material culture is one important ingredient in the analysis of national borders and identities – but he claims this with a different twist from the early ethnologists. Whereas the early Swedish ethnologists wanted to map the distribution and diffusion of cultural artifacts to be able to identify cultural provinces, Löfgren focuses on how trivial things such as road signs and border crossings produce differences in an ongoing construction of culture.[3] Borders are still primarily seen as inert matter, as dams or barriers regulating flows, but new elements are added: borders are conceptualised as actors producing motion (migration and different sorts of transnational movements) as well as emotion.[4] In an analysis of the making of the Öresund Region, Löfgren (2000) addresses speed as an important *metaphor* in urban development and transnational region-building. Speed as a border practice, though, remains unexplored.[5] In the following sections, I will use a practice oriented border concept, but I will add a focus on speed as an important ingredient. Analysing the illegal liquor traffic during the 1920s, my aim is to demonstrate how speed, as an analytical concept, can provide contemporary border studies with further insights regarding border practices.

I will start with an overview of how this smuggling was organised; some structural foundations for its origins will also be brought forward as will a depiction of some actions taken to regulate smuggling. The smuggling and the state authorities' perceptions of these activities must first and foremost be related to Swedish alcohol policy and debate.

Smuggling – a Border Practice

After the First World War Sweden's borders had been tightened up and in conjunction with restrictive alcohol policy smuggling appeared as a lucrative branch (Lundin & Nilsson 2010). Denmark, Finland and Norway went through similar changes, and so did the USA. According to the historian Marc Mappen (2013), Prohibition, and thus smuggling, formed a new generation of criminals in the USA. They came from the margins of society but Prohibition gave them an opportunity to find a short cut to *The American Dream*: the possibility of social advancement, wealth, status and respect was alluring (Mappen 2013: 2–4).

In Sweden, anxiety for the negative influence of alcohol had grown strong at the beginning of the twentieth century. Misuse was extensive and the situation among the poor and vulnerable in society was especially bad (Larsson 1999: 53). Alcohol stood out as a grave problem and there were massive campaigns in action with the aim of forbidding, or alternately limiting, access to alcohol (Ambjörnsson 1988). To some degree, the keen supporters of sobriety were successful. In 1914 a ration book (the so-called *Motboken*) was introduced which limited access to alcohol, as the owner of the ration book was allowed only a certain amount of alcohol for a limited period of time. A specific application for a ration book had to be made and it was then decided by a special inquiry if the applicant was thought suitable to shoulder the responsibility (Johansson 2008). Some years later, in 1922, a referendum was carried out for a complete "Prohibition of intoxicating liquor" but the zealous supporters lost. The referendum as such, however, does illustrate the anxiety that alcohol caused.

The restrictive alcohol policy created the basis for comprehensive illegal alcohol dealing and an intensive alcohol smuggling. The deal between sellers and buyers was as a rule agreed beforehand. Informal contracts were established in special restaurants or hotels, for example the Hotel Savoy in Malmö, Hotel Kronprinz in Kiel, the restaurant Aalborgkælderen in Copenhagen, and Berns Salonger in Stockholm. The alcohol was transported by large vessels, depot ships, from Baltic and German ports to international waters. These depot ships usually anchored in shallow water, for example *Herthas Flak* in the Kattegat and *Plantagenet's ground* in the southern Baltic Sea. From theses marine nodes the alcohol was loaded onto smaller boats, which headed for the Swedish border. Just outside the border, the cargo was loaded into even smaller, but also much faster motorboats. In unguarded places, local recipients waited for the delivery and transported the alcohol by car or lorry to the buyers in towns. Of course, the Swedish State tried to stop the illegal border practice.

In order to counteract smuggling the legislation was changed. The most common punishment for smuggling was a fine, but in 1924 a law was brought into force that meant that smugglers of alcohol could be sentenced to harsh prison terms. During the 1930s, the legislation and sentences were once more toughened up (Larsson 1999: 59). Apart from these measures a police unit focusing on illegal dealing with alcohol (Spritpolisen), was organised and an international agreement on smuggling was eventually signed, the so-called Helsinki Convention. The states in the Baltic region agreed on sharpening the control of the export of alcohol and legalising inspection and seizing of vessels outside territorial waters. Initially only Sweden, Finland and Norway approved, but all the states round the Baltic Sea would later on affiliate themselves (Larsson 1992: 49–50). Even civil society was engaged in the war against smuggling. The Association against Smuggling (*Sammanslutningen för smugglingens bekämpande*), an association founded with the sole purpose of combatting smuggling, wanted to change people's attitudes towards smuggling. This would be achieved by "spreading fliers and brochures" but also "organising lectures in order to win support for their activities" (*Lanternan* no. 6, 1925). As we shall see, this help to protect the borders was needed.

Speedboats and "Liquor Racers"

At the end of 1923 a large smuggling "expedition" had been exposed in Scania, the most southern part of Sweden. A customs detective had had the opportunity to closely follow the planning of this expedition as well as the attempt to execute it.[6] According to plan the motor schooner Luna would approach the Swedish coast with 20,000 litres of alcohol on board. Naturally the authorities wanted to confiscate this substantial cargo of alcohol, but as Luna could make 12 knots there was a problem: "Swedish customs at the coasts of Scania did not have any vessel that could be used with any hope of success of commandeering the smuggler vessel Luna." After several failed attempts to borrow or hire fast boats, the customs detectives hired the steam-driven tugboat Hurtig (Jaunty or Spry).[7]

The tugboat had cautiously advanced to the area where the smuggling was expected to take place and after some hours Luna was discovered, even though the smugglers had tried to become invisible and soundless by putting out lanterns and only using sail. The smugglers' attempts to avoid detection were futile and Hurtig approached Luna. When only five metres separated them, the smugglers decided to head for international water using engine power and maximum speed. Hurtig was left far behind, and not even when "revolver shots were fired at the smugglers' vessel" did it stop. The customs detective concluded resignedly that Luna's high speed made it impossible to commandeer the vessel: "Had I had at my disposal a sufficiently fast vessel as well as the necessary weaponry, the smugglers' vessel would of course have been seized."[8] According to the customs detective, better technological equipment in order to prevent the dissolution of the nation's borders and thereby the morals was needed. The customs detective was not alone in calling attention to the authorities' sluggishness at sea and the smugglers' speediness. In another report for example, the speed of the smugglers' boats was in focus. It was concluded that transports from depot vessels "are made by motorboats which reach high speeds."[9] It was not unusual either for the smugglers' speed boats to be called "liquor racers". The denomination strengthens the impression of the authorities perceiving the smugglers as extraordinarily fast, making the question of speed interesting as an element in border practices.

Acceleration has, according to cultural sociologist John Tomlinson (2007) amongst others, been a characteristic of modernity. Even if modernity should not be perceived as synonymous with the

Ill. 1: The notorious smuggler Ernst Bremer managed to escape on several occasions and his speedy racers, such as Käthe above, gave him an iconic status during the 1920s and 1930s. (Photo: Tullmuseum, Stockholm)

nineteenth or twentieth century, yet the feeling of acceleration was intensified in the decades around 1900. A number of modern transportation and communication technologies such as railroad, telegraph, telephone, car and bicycle were developed around the turn of the century. Obviously trains and the telegraph had been in use for some time, but now these systems were extended simultaneously as new systems appeared and thus changed society. Faraway places suddenly were within reach (Kern [1983]2003: 111). This in turn made it possible for new groups of people to transgress borders in new ways. As a consequence, the historian Stephen Kern argues, a cult of speed grew among a generation that wanted to conquer time and space ([1983]2003: 111). As mentioned earlier, Paul Virilio uses the vector as a concept in order to understand this development. The vector is understood as a "transporter of speed" ([1989]1996: 54) which, to the extent that the speed increases, gives rise to new patterns of action and communities. The vector can take the form of cars and boats that continuously accelerate the transport of human beings, objects and information (Handberg 1996: 10). Vectors that favour higher speeds and new patterns of movement can represent an alluring future, but can also create anxiety. Since modernity and the cult of speed is linked to transformations, uncertainty is created; when "all that is solid melts into air," a need for security and safety arises (cf. Berman 1990). With a departure in this understanding of vectors a question has to be asked: Why did the customs detectives have to hire the steam-driven tugboat Hurtig in order to secure the border instead of using Swedish customs vessels? To answer this question, we need to return to the turn of the century.

"To Move Hastily" or Not – the Permeable Border

In 1902 a state inquiry was conducted which amongst other things assessed the Swedish customs' equipment and found that it was rather traditional: "For patrols at sea, in general larger or smaller customs yachts and other customs sailing vessels (...) even rowing boats are used" (1902: 163).[10] There were however exceptions, in Haparanda customs district in the most northern part of Sweden "patrolling is performed with steam vessels." This had started in the summer of 1900 in order to more effectively patrol the district's lengthy and sparsely populated coast (1902: 163). The inquiry also dealt with the question of whether rowing and sailing should be abandoned altogether in favour of the faster steam power.

The Swedish Customs Administration argued that steam vessels were a superior technology as they, regardless of the weather, quite easily would "be able to move hastily." But, certain stretches of coast were shallow and therefore the deep-going steam vessels rapidly lost their advantages. The Swedish Customs Administration was therefore hesitant towards an increased usage of steam-powered vessels (1902: 164).[11] As smuggling seemed to be on the increase in Stockholm's archipelago, steam vessels could be tried out in this area but with caution: "For this reason the committee has found the question deserves closer investigation, however, the change must have the character of an experiment" (1902: 166). It is not unusual that uncertainty arises when a new technological system is introduced (cf. Marvin 1998) and the authorities' hesitant stance would characterise the discussions on this technological equipment in the following decades.

In 1914 a commission was set up with the purpose of investigating the customs' and the coast guards' organisation. At that time the coastal areas were patrolled by boats that achieved higher speeds than had been the case at the turn of the century, but they were still regarded as slow since it had become common with motorboats in coastal traffic. The commission therefore suggested that fast, so-called customs yachts should be used (1917: 13, 24).[12] The customs yachts would, in order to reconnect with Virilio ([1989]1996: 54), become a vector that compressed time and space and created preconditions for the surveillance of the national territory and borders. Still, the Swedish Customs Administration hesitated. According to them only five customs yachts should be purchased and these would first be tried out in two districts (1920: 127).[13] Once again, a

Ill. 2: In the beginning of the twentieth century, the Swedish Coast Guard primarily used "slow" technologies such as small sailboats. Although the situation changed gradually during the 1920s, they still had to chase the smugglers with rather slow, unmodern technologies. (Photo: 1907, Tullmuseum, Stockholm)

cautious experimental activity can be discerned in the authorities' attitude to modern technologies and higher speeds.

The discussions on higher speeds continued for some years and were also concerned with psychological warfare. In a debate in the parliament the Director of the Finance Department, F.V. Thorsson, claimed that high speeds were more important than ever since the smugglers had "moved on to using vessels that reached much higher speeds than 14 knots" (quoted in *Lanternan* no. 16, 1922). For that reason Thorsson pleaded that faster moving customs cutters must be ordered. It was thought that the bare knowledge that the coast guards used new, fast vessels would make the smugglers more hesitant. The same train of thought was taken up by yet another speaker during the debate: "It is obvious that the knowledge that the state has possession of fast moving vessels in order to keep pursuing the smugglers must be, in itself, a deterrent" (quoted in *Lanternan* no. 16, 1922). The speakers touched upon a basic foundation in warfare. The arms' race after the Second World War can serve as an example. A prominent element in warfare is the opportunity to influence the feelings of the enemy, which was evident in nuclear weapons policies. The plain knowledge that an attack with nuclear weapons would lead to massive retribution should have a deterring effect (Virilio [1984]1996: 6–7). After yet another period of debates, parliament agreed to order six customs cutters, but there was a delay until the 1930s before the boat materials had been modernised and speed at sea had increased. Thus, the borders of the 1920s were indeed permeable even though the authorities tried to stabilise them.

The Car – Speedy Transports and Status

The smugglers did not only move speedily at sea but also on the Swedish main roads. In police interrogations, investigations and written communication, a pattern emerges: The car created preconditions for effective, speedy transport of alcohol from major towns in the south of Sweden, such as Malmö and Helsingborg, to smaller communities in the vicinity, but also to more distant cities such as Gothenburg and Stockholm. In 1934, the alcohol police unit in Malmö conducted an investigation regarding this illegal traffic, "as to whether Danish citizen Gaarden Jensen at some time in the past was a passenger in a hearse travelling through the police district of Finja parish." According to witnesses the "hearse had been black in colour and equipped with corner pillars but otherwise open." Inside there had been a "yellow coffin on which a wreath had been placed." The same car had been observed on the streets of Hässleholm and it had been "driven exceedingly fast and to a great extent recklessly."[14] In reports like this the smugglers appear as speed merchants, or to quote Virilio, *dromomaniacs*, who have been blinded by the opportunity to drive speedily. The term was used by Virilio in a discussion of the Nazis' taking over public space in Germany in the 1930s. The opportunity to drive around in fast cars made the Nazis into "agents of terror" ([1977]2006: 45). Of course the smugglers, as far as is known, had no such political motive but the term can be said to ring in the Swedish authorities' view of their rampaging border practices. The car acted as a projectile, which penetrated national borders and moral boundaries. But the car was also an important symbol.

The car was one important technology among others in a wave of modernism that swept over the Western world at the beginning of the twentieth century. After the First World War, the import of cars to Sweden increased and it was above all American cars that were attractive. The American car was, according to Tom O'Dell, closely connected to dreams of freedom, escape and social as well as geographical mobility (1997: 114–122, 138). Even if the car became more common during the first decades of the twentieth century, it was a technology that was coupled with the upper class (Ingmarsson 2004: 25–27). The car's coupling to modernity and freedom, but also the upper class and luxury, was doubtless of importance to the smugglers. In 1923 customs detective Asp sent word that two smugglers had been arrested in Malmö and that a "7-seat automobile of the make Hupmobile" had been confiscated. The car's value was considerable, 4,400 Swedish crowns,[15] and the import of the Hupmobile did not occur until some years later (Ingmarsson 2004: 80). In other words, the smugglers had bought a car that was expensive and unusual. It appears as paradoxical that they chose to drive a car which probably attracted attention, but as mentioned, the car was an important symbol and it is likely that the smugglers had been influenced by the dreams that surrounded this specific make of car: "A Hupmobile becomes a little more than just a car (…) He'll act! Give you fact after fact, not in words but in deeds, in bullet speeds and 'Big Bertha' power!" The quote is from a flier for a somewhat later model but it is obvious that the car should represent powerfulness, strength and high speeds, which was repeated in adverts for other models: "But even more striking is this car's ability to flash ahead of traffic with lightning speed." A similar message is found in the adverts for the American cars that were used by some of the central figures in smuggling, Edvin Jönsson and the above-mentioned Niels Carl Gaarden Jensen.

Jönsson and Gaarden Jensen regularly exchanged cars, sometimes with very short time intervals. In the beginning of 1929, they bought an "automobile of the make Anderson."[16] Anderson was a popular make at this time. In the adverts for the different models of this make of car its "power and speed" are emphasised but it was also a car that signaled status: "It is a car you will be proud to park at the golf links or club." Apart from this feature, the car's dependability was highlighted as an important characteristic: "Yet it is a car for business too, and in dense traffic, or when there is an appointment to be kept, it will serve you faithfully and dependably." If one wanted to be certain of arriving at a destination and with a businessman's punctuality then this was the car one should choose. Two days later Jönsson and Jensen replaced this car with a Chandler. In November a second hand Ford was purchased and the next month a "transport automobile of the make Chevrolet." In the same month, yet another car was bought, this time a Chrysler: "Jönsson had herewith paid 300 [Swedish] crowns in cash and as part exchange handed in a second-hand automobile of the make Willys Knight."[17] Similar to many other makes of cars, Chrysler wanted to represent speed. In one advert speed was emphasised in the following way: "It flashes in and out of traffic, nimbly outdistancing the fastest and the finest." Thus, the symbolic value of the car should not be underestimated, nor should the symbolic value of speed.

The cultural sociologist John Tomlinson claims that high speed, from a historical perspective, is associated with positive values such as success, wealth, vitality, energy, intelligence and being dynamic (Tomlinson 2007: 3–4). Therefore, in the time of Prohibition in the USA it was not unusual that the gangsters – not least those who came from environments characterised by poverty and social misery – regarded expensive, fast cars as kinds of trophies (Gorn [2009]2011: 171). The historian David E. Ruth argues in a similar vein in an analysis of how the gangster became "a paragon of technological modernity" as he used fast cars (and modern machine guns) (Ruth 1996: 53). It can thus be reasonable to

Ill. 3: Feverish car chases were not unusual. Sometimes they ended in horrible, fatal accidents due to high speeds and poor roads. (Photo: 1925, Tullmuseum, Stockholm)

presume that cars not only offered smugglers a means to transport alcohol over larger geographical areas in a short space of time, but also status. Driving American cars is in itself to be regarded as a border practice stating: I am different, modern and cosmopolitan. It was however not only the smugglers who seemed to be in the grip of a need for speed at this time.

Confiscation and Spike Strips – Stabilising the Border

In order to prevent the illegal border practice the police regularly confiscated the smugglers' vessels and vehicles. In a written communication to the Swedish Customs Administration from the police officer John Nilsson the following information was given.

> Herewith through confiscation and the informant's claims an automobile of the make Dodge with the registration mark M12797 is handed in with approximately 50 litres of alcohol illegally brought into the country contained in three 10 litre tin cans, as well as three suitcases, in which the cans have been placed.[18]

The confiscated cars (yet also boats and goods) were a self-evident part of a compensation system, which was to be found within both the customs and the police force. Police officers who seized goods had the right to one third of the worth that the items were valued at. Within the alcohol police unit, individual officers could thus make a substantial profit as the right to one third of both alcohol and cars as well as one third of fines was theirs (Andersson 2001: 316, 320). But the confiscation system also created competition between the customs and the police, which made collaboration more difficult. They did not freely share information and sometimes anonymous informants directed both of them to the same border area which left other sections of the border unguarded (Blomberg 1968: 136).

The seizures meant the disarming of the smugglers in both a symbolic and a factual meaning. They were deprived of access to fast technologies and symbols of success, modernity and perhaps freedom. The confiscations were, expressed in a different way, important elements in stabilising the borders. A precondition for the seizures was that it was possible to stop the speedboats, and, as we have seen, this was not an easy task. The same goes for the cars.

In October 1921, the coast guard in a smallish coastal town had confiscated a car that transported 200 litres of alcohol. A day or so before the seizure some "suspicious persons" had been observed and for this reason, the surveillance of the main road had been tightened up. After a while, a car with no lights had been spotted and the customs officers had to intervene. In order to stop the car, the local coast guard's supervisor called out to the driver but to no effect: "The speed rather increased than decreased" (*Lanternan* no. 10, 1921). The increase in speed meant that the car went through a metamorphism – from simple transport technology to the projectile that regularly and repeatedly was described in the advert material for the cars of the 1920s. Vectors with higher speed is, as a rule, more efficient and terrifying (Virilio [1989]1996), and the supervisor decided to use his revolver.

> A blank warning shot was fired but was not able to hinder the car. When a sharp shot was fired, that caused a hole in the car's body and roof, (…) the chauffeur hit the brakes and gave up the game. (*Lanternan* no. 10, 1921)

Shots fired at sea were not unusual in connection with hunts for alcohol smugglers, but occurred in connection with car chases too. The shots were fired with the purpose of paralysing the driver and thereby stopping the car. As has been mentioned previously, warfare is characterised by a will to paralyse the enemy by terrifying them and this was a war against smuggling.

Firing shots could, however, result in increased speeds rather than lower ones. This was something that amongst others a customs detective in southern Sweden had noted. In a letter to the Coast Guard Director in Malmö, the detective told of vessels and vehicles that refused to obey the "stop signals". In order to deal with the threat other strategies were suggested and used.

The National Committee against Illegal Alcohol Trade (Rikskommittén mot den olagliga smugglingen) presented a proposal of using spike strips. Such beds of nails would, the committee argued, effectively stop the speeding smugglers in their modern cars.[19] The customs detective was doubtful about this suggestion: "That the use of spike strips would lead to catastrophes and outrageous mistakes is obvious." A risk existed that the use of spike strips could put innocent road-users in danger.

The spike strip demonstrates a paradox in what Virilio calls the dromocratic development. The infrastructural planning has aimed at evening out irregularities in the terrain; tunnels have been dug through mountains and under waterways; bridges have been built over valleys; and crooked roads have been straightened out with the aim of transporting people and goods more quickly (1997: 79–81, 84). Similar tendencies can be seen in Sweden during the 1920s. Concurrently with the car becoming more common there were demands for straighter, more even and more hardwearing roads that would make higher speeds possible. But, Virilio points out, at the same time as state authorities around the world have acted for quicker, friction-free traffic flows, new obstacles have been "invented": "Thus, everywhere, the mobile mass's vehicular power is repressed and reduced, from limits on speed or fuel to the pure and simple suppression of the personal auto" (Virilio [1977]2006: 141). There is, on the one hand, a will to homogenise the road surface and on the other hand a need to keep irregularities in order to create friction and the preconditions for lower speeds. I have discussed similar processes in the border zone where cars cross the border between Denmark and Sweden (cf. Nilsson 2010): Speed bumps simulate natural irregularities in the road at the same time as they perform or materialise the border. In a similar manner the spike strip of the 1920s simulated both natural irregularities in the road and on the border. When cars were used as a kind of barricade, they can be regarded as a simulation of dams in waterways. In April 1926, Gaarden Jensen had attempted to smuggle alcohol into Scania.

As he was on his way to receive the alcohol, he was stopped on the road by a couple of customs officers, who had placed a couple of cars directly across the road to stop his car from continuing. Gaarden Jensen however had jumped out of the car and by running off had got away.[20]

The authorities did not only try to stop the smugglers' cars; it happened that they themselves used cars. But, as in the case of faster vessels, it was not self-evident if, or how, this modern technology should be utilised in order to stabilise the border.

The Car – "a Trial Appliance"

In several written communications to the Swedish Customs Administration a chief of one of southern Sweden's coast guard districts described the problematic situation. The chief concluded that the war against smuggling had moved from sea to land. The smugglers' ability to bring alcohol ashore made it impossible to hinder them at sea, so therefore the battle took place on Swedish soil. The border was to be protected or stabilised on *terra firma*. As was apparent above, the smugglers had more or less adopted the car in their activities as it offered fast transport over relatively large areas, but the district chief took a watchful stand when faced with this new technology. In 1927, he considered the possibility of "patrolling the roads along the coast with one automobile". But purchasing a car was not of immediate interest; instead the local supervisor in a coastal area should be persuaded to use his own car when on duty. If the smuggling traffic were to change he could consider "taking this question under perusal once again."[21] He was not convinced that the car could be of real use, but this watchful attitude would change.

In a report written later the same year, the chief reiterates about the local supervisors' car and in a balanced enthusiastic manner concludes that: "On a couple of occasions the automobile in question has been utilised during awaited attempts at smuggling."[22] Starting out from experiences, he pleaded for a continued use, against reimbursement, of this private vehicle. The next year, 1928, the situation changed even more. The number of cars employed on customs' duties in the district had been doubled and the chief applied for funds for this seemingly revolutionary move: "This measure is to be regarded as a kind of trial device and has only come into use on occasions when first-hand information has been involved in smuggling attempts."[23] Yet again, a cautious attitude comes to light; using modern technology in order to stabilise the border was difficult to relate to. In the inquiries that were conducted at this time, the car is in no way self-evident. This hesitation must be related to the discussion regarding the authorities' equipment and the discussion on savings that were ongoing at this time.

"Automobiles should not, in any Scenario, be allowed to be Used"

According to the 1914 Customs Commission (1914 års tullkommission), cars had become more common in society and this made the investigators reflect upon their use within the customs: "Automobiles should not, in any scenario, be allowed to be used for coast guard duties. They are too expensive to purchase and to maintain and can tempt to misuse" (1917: 26). The commission was tainted by its assignment, as the assignment was to suggest a reorganisation, which would entail lower costs. But their perception of the car was also influenced by the stiff opposition towards the car that was present in society. The car and motorism were considered as dangerous and a threat; others meant that the car mainly was a toy for the upper class. There were yet others who pointed out that the car made too much noise and that it was a pleasure machine "meant for sport and competitions" (Ingmarsson 2004: 12). If the coast guard was equipped with cars there was, according to the Commission, a risk that they would use the cars in an irresponsible way (1917: 26). Naturally, the Swedish Customs Administration brought up the question of the car's place in the organisation and they took an equally hesitant stance towards the use of cars (1920: 112).

With hindsight, one could banter about the insecurity that the car gave rise to, but the past did not have the answers at hand. In this light, it is therefore not particularly strange that the Swedish Customs Administration hesitated. Besides, there was a similar insecurity within other organisations at this time. For example, it was not until 1915 that the Swedish military realised that the car had a strategic value and it took yet another couple of years before the car was a self-evident part of the army (Nerén 1937: 430–434). It was not only in Sweden that the authorities hesitated. In the USA, the police's technical equipment – particularly outside the big cities – was not as modern as that of the criminals (Gorn [2009]2011: 33).

The cautious attitude that the Swedish Customs Administration advocated successively gave rise to yet more stiff criticism from the customs and coast guards, but during the 1920s, the car remained a rare technology in the stabilisation of borders and the war against alcohol smuggling. The smugglers in comparison seemed exceedingly modern, or even hypermodern, as they almost invisibly transcended borders.

Ill. 4: The bicycle was a rather quiet, fast and, compared to cars, cheap technology. Here, the local coast guard in the small village of Domsten in the 1930s. (Photo: Tullmuseum, Stockholm)

"Hypermodern Tools"

In connection with an attempted smuggling on the southern coast of Scania in 1929, it was shown that the alcohol smugglers could communicate rapidly over great distances with the help of another modern technology. One of Sweden's major newspapers reported : "The whole day the racer had been hindered by the customs' vessels from getting close to the mother ship [Herkules] which had a radio on board and was hidden somewhere far out in the Baltic Sea."[24] It was no coincidence that the radio was mentioned in the article.

One decade earlier radio communication had become an important part of shipping, but far from all vessels had this equipment on board. When the technology was developed, the interests of the navy were in the foreground, and these were further strengthened during the First World War when wireless telegraphy was an important means of communication. Now it was possible to correct the movements of the vessel even if there were great distances between units, but this development was infested with problems. Communications were performed with Morse code which required trained and competent personnel (Keegan [1998]2006: 278). As special equipment and special competences were demanded, the Swedish merchant navy awaited further developments for a long period of time. Only 47 Swedish vessels had a radio on board in 1913 and of these 31 belonged to the navy. Radio communication would remain a relatively undeveloped area during the 1920s (Heimbürger 1974: 340–343, 593–597) making the radio on board Herkules important to mention. It was even more remarkable that a radio was to be found on board the Herkules since it was a technology closely connected with the navy.[25] The smugglers' radio communication was perceived as something exceptional and dangerous.

At some time during the year 1935, a hand-written letter was sent to Police Superintendent Ernst Wessman. The letter writer was Johanna Nilsson, a teacher in the small coastal town of Kivik.

Since I suspect that my abode, the preschool teacher's abode in Kivik, was used as a signal station for a gang of smugglers I wish to hereby advise you of this. I comprehend neither radio nor radio equipment, yet I believe that some sort of such equipment is to be found. In one place there has been some damage where I think fingerprints could be found. If my suspicions are correct then this gang must surely belong to a widespread organisation that works with the most hypermodern tools. If therefore an investigation is undertaken, it should take place without too much delay.[26]

It is not apparent if Nilsson had found a radio hidden in the house or not, but obviously she was afraid of this "hypermodern" technology used by the smugglers to transcend borders. Their use of modern technologies contributed to the fascination mingled with terror that surrounded them, but their border practices rested on other foundations as well.

Well Organised and Well Informed

The large amount of alcohol that has been smuggled in and confiscated during the past months bears witness to unusual audacity. The names of the persons involved and their social status underlines the perception of organised smuggling, which even for a longer period of time has been flourishing without protests. (*Lanternan* no. 18, 1920)

Lanternan published articles that dealt with different aspects of the illegal alcohol trade. They focused, as shown earlier, on speed and technology, but also on organisation as such: The smugglers were portrayed as dangerously well organised. Similar opinions were expressed by the previously mentioned Association against Smuggling (Sammanslutningen för smugglingens bekämpande). A report published by them informed the reader of what had happened as a large car had been stopped in the town of Malmö. Guards had been placed so that the police could not surprise them and then "boxes of alcohol were taken from the car and bottles and cans were noted down on a list kept by a man in a raincoat" (Bergvall 1927: 49). The man in the raincoat checked the goods almost with the zeal of a bookkeeper or store foreman.

The impression of smuggling being a well-organised enterprise was also connected to the smugglers access to important information.

A letter to the chief of the nineteenth coast guard district informed him that the motor vessel Nena had arrived in Klagshamn. On board was amongst others J.P. Jensen who was employed by a ships' chandler in Copenhagen and therefore very familiar with the work of the customs: "[Jensen] is very familiar with the Danish customs officers and their work (…) as well as having good knowledge of the Danish customs vessels' movements, the times they were in dock for repairs etcetera, as well as being acquainted with Jörgen Hansen on the 'Lübeck'."[27] It is not apparent how Jensen had acquired knowledge of the activities of the customs, but it is plausible that he through his work in the ships' chandlers had a network that provided him with information. Jörgen Hansen is not unimportant either in this context. Hansen's network and capacity for collecting information had almost mythical features and could even surprise customs officers who had infiltrated his activities.

> Jörgen Hansen's principal strength however lies in his having at his disposal a widespread reporting system both in Germany and Sweden. Thus, for example, Hansen could tell me the positions of the different posts with an accuracy that surpassed my own knowledge in that way.[28]

Resigned and at the same time impressed the customs detective pointed out that "nothing concerning our coast guards was unknown to Hansen."[29] It seems as if the border practices of the smugglers were impossible to stop, the border remained porous and there was a lack of inertia.

Concluding Remarks on Borders, Speed and Inertia

As modern technologies were introduced at the turn of the twentieth century, a cult of speed, as well as new border practices, emerged. Places that had previously been far away, suddenly felt reachable, and some borders transformed from barriers to mere thresholds. The alcohol smugglers of the 1920s were affected by these transformations, and so were the early ethnologists.

Cultural borders were understood as consequences of nature, history, political agreements and economy, but also as products of everyday life, habits and traditions. Besides, borders were perceived as regulators of flows, making border landscapes inert, although not impermeable. Modernity and speed, though, challenged inertia and the idea of stable borders. According to early ethnologists such as Sigurd Erixon, the cultural borders of traditional society withered away as modern, fast communications were established. Similar processes of destabilisation triggered a new interest in borders among ethnologists in the late twentieth century. Borders were still understood as complex consequences of economy, political agreements and social interaction. The idea of inertia also prevailed, but new elements were added. Borders were conceptualised as non-human actors, turning geography into emotionally laden national landscapes. Eventually this border concept moved one step further as speed was introduced as an important metaphor in transnational region-building. Speed as a distinct feature of border practices, however, remained unexplored. Therefore, my aim was to demonstrate how speed, as an analytical concept, can provide contemporary border studies with further insights regarding border practices and the inertia of border zones. For that reason, I applied a practice and speed-oriented border concept in an analysis of the illegal liquor traffic during the 1920s.

Using speedy motor racers, fast cars and radio, smugglers transcended national borders with ease. They traversed borders in a time when Swedish society began to recognise the consequences of what modernity could offer, and this is probably why they were perceived as hypermodern. As the national borders were de-stabilised by such illegal border practices, representatives of the state tried to re-construct inertia and hence stabilise the border. Confiscating the smugglers' racers and fast cars was one strategy used, but they also tried to stop them with the aid of spike strips and weapons. Hesitantly they even adopted high-speed technologies of modernity in order to create inertia. Thus, high velocity de-stabilise borders, but there is a parallel process of re-stabilisation and strive for inertia.

There is a need for further investigations of how speed affects processes of de- and re-bordering in contemporary Europe as well as in other parts of the world. Borders and border zones are, ideally, inert landscapes – even if some nations and transnational regions make bold rhetorical claims on fast and friction-free flows of goods, information, money and people. Travellers who challenge inertia are, nevertheless, often defined as threats, leading to border practices that encapsulate and domesticate them. Thus, we need to deepen our understanding of speed as a border practice imbued with culture, and power. Speed is intimately connected with modernity and freedom, but the distribution of speed is unevenly distributed in society. Applying historical perspectives on speed as a distinct feature of border practices can provide us with more knowledge concerning such asymmetries.

Notes

1 Not all fast-moving travellers are defined as problems though; when the president of the USA visit different countries, speed is "required" in order to keep him safe. He moves fast on and off Air Force 1, and just as quickly to and from foreign airports.
2 Early ethnologists' seemingly naïve perspective on diffusion was heavily criticised in the 1960s and 1970s as the so-called new ethnology emerged. The older generation, it was said, did not pay any attention to the social context (Bringéus [1976]1990: 44, 93). But perhaps Erixon, and his colleagues, were dismissed a bit too easily.
3 Similar ideas inspired Anders Linde-Laursen in his doctoral thesis (1995). Linde-Laursen studied how the political border between Denmark and Sweden, agreed upon in the seventeenth century, gradually turned into a cultural border. He was intrigued by a border that appeared in different social contexts or situations, such as kitchen habits and the everyday practice of doing the dishes.
4 This border perspective would eventually become more prominent and a quick glance into the rather important text book *Kulturanalys* (Ehn & Löfgren 1982) can serve as an example of this change. In *Kulturanalys*, borders are briefly touched upon and mainly treated as mental maps. In the sequel, *Kulturanalyser* (Ehn & Löfgren 2001), the border concept was elaborated defining borders as "cultural signal systems" that acted upon people as they reminded them of differences, endings and starting points (2001: 56). Cultural analysis should therefore focus on borders that "are visible and become dominant in different contexts" (2001: 55).
5 Speed as a metaphor was of paramount importance in the invocation of the Öresund Region (Nilsson 1999).
6 Report, December 24, 1923: Rickard Bengtssons tullhistoriska samling, vol. 40, Malmö stadsarkiv.
7 Report, December 24, 1923: Rickard Bengtssons tullhistoriska samling, vol. 40, Malmö stadsarkiv.
8 Report, December 24, 1923: Rickard Bengtssons tullhistoriska samling, vol. 40, Malmö stadsarkiv.
9 Spritpolisens anteckningar m.m. år 1935. Landsarkivet Lund.
10 Underdånigt betänkande afgifvet den 29 oktober 1902 af komitén för granskning af Tullverkets stater. 1. Betänkande och förslag. Stockholm: K.L. Bergmans boktryckeri.
11 Underdånigt betänkande afgifvet den 29 oktober 1902 af komitén för granskning af Tullverkets stater. 1. Betänkande och förslag. Stockholm: K.L. Bergmans boktryckeri.
12 1914 års tullkommissions betänkanden 1917: I. *Förslag till omorganisation av tullverkets kust- och gränsbevakning*. Stockholm: K.L. Beckmans Boktryckeri.
13 Generaltullstyrelsens underdåniga utlåtanden över 1914 års tullkommissions betänkanden. 1 (A) 1920: Utlåtande över förslaget till omorganisation av Tullverkets kustbevakning. Stockholm: Isaac Marcus Boktryckeri Aktiebolag.
14 June 5, 1934: Spritpolisen i Malmö. Inkomna skrivelser. 1934, A: 1.
15 Report, October 24, 1924: Rickard Bengtssons tullhistoriska samling, vol. 40, Malmö stadsarkiv.
16 Report, January 22, 1930: Kungliga generaltullstyrelsen II, Kanslibyrån, E3:13.
17 January 22, 1930: Kungliga generaltullstyrelsen II, Kanslibyrån, E3:13.
18 October 27, 1930: Kungliga generaltullstyrelsen II, Kanslibyrån, E3:13.
19 Kerwing's letters to the head of the Coast Guard in Malmö, November 8, 1932. Rickard Bengtssons tullhistoriska samling, vol. 40, Malmö stadsarkiv.
20 The story was printed in one of the major newspapers in Sweden (*Sydsvenska Dagbladet*, SDS, February 2, 1930).
21 Borgs skrivelser till Kungliga Generaltullstyrelsen i Stockholm. Landsarkivet, Lund.
22 Borgs skrivelser till Kungliga Generaltullstyrelsen i Stockholm. Landsarkivet, Lund.
23 Borgs skrivelser till Kungliga Generaltullstyrelsen i Stockholm. Landsarkivet, Lund.
24 The story was published in *Sydsvenska Dagbladet*, SDS, May 16, 1929.

25 New technology is often used for reasons the inventors or the state authorities had not foreseen nor desired (Andersson-Skog 1998: 277).
26 Spritpolisens anteckningar m.m. år 1935. Landsarkivet Lund.
27 Tullkammarens i Helsingborg arkiv –1981. Ämnesordnade handlingar, huvudserie, 1920–1930, F1:4. Landsarkivet Lund. Tullförvaltare B. Borgs hemliga handlingar rörande spritsmugglingsärenden omkr. 1920–1930. Rapporter, förhörsprotokoll m.m. Smuggelfartyg Saml. 1.
28 Rickard Bengtssons tullhistoriska samling, vol. 42, Malmö stadsarkiv.
29 Rickard Bengtssons tullhistoriska samling, vol. 42, Malmö stadsarkiv.

References

Ambjörnsson, Ronny 1988: *Den skötsamme arbetaren: Idéer och ideal i ett norrländskt sågverkssamhälle 1880–1930*. Stockholm: Carlssons.

Andersen Jagetic, Dorte, Martin Klatt & Marie Sandberg 2012: *The Border Multiple: The Practising of Borders between Public Policy and Everyday Life in a Re-scaling Europe*. Farnham: Ashgate.

Andersson, Hans 2001: Spritsmuggling i mellankrigstidens Stockholm: Illegala entreprenörer i ett komparativt perspektiv. In: Leif Appelgren & Hans Sjögren (eds.), *Ekonomisk brottslighet och nationalstatens kontrollmakt*. Stockholm: Gidlunds.

Andersson-Skog, Lena 1998: De osynliga användarna: Telefonen och vardagslivet 1880–1995. In: Pär Blomkvist & Arne Kaijser (eds.), *Den konstruerade världen: Tekniska system i historiskt perspektiv*. Stockholm; Stehag: Brutus Östlings Bokförlag Symposion.

Arnstberg, Karl-Olov 1989: *Utforskaren: Studier i Sigurd Erixons etnologi*. Stockholm: Carlssons.

Arnstberg, Karl-Olov 2010: Sigurd Erixon. In: Mats Hellspong & Fredrik Skott (eds.), *Svenska etnologer och folklorister*. Uppsala: Kungliga Gustavs Adolfs Akademien för svensk folkkultur.

Bergvall, John 1927: *Den olaga rusdryckshanteringen och samhället*. Utgiven av sammanslutningen för smugglingens bekämpande. Stockholm: Bokförlags A.B. Tidens tryckeri.

Berman, Marshall 1990: *Allt som är fast förflyktigas: Modernitet och modernism*. Lund: Arkiv förlag.

Blomberg, Gustaf Adolf 1968: *Bakom polisens kulisser*. Stockholm: Nordiska museet.

Bringéus, Nils-Arvid [1976]1990: *Människan som kulturvarelse: En introduktion till etnologin*. Stockholm: Carlssons.

Campbell, Åke 1928: *Skånska bygder under förra hälften av 1700-talet: Etnografisk studie över den skånska allmogens äldre odlingar, hägnader och byggnader*. Uppsala: A.-B. Lundequistska Bokhandeln.

Donnan, Hastings & Thomas M. Wilson 2001: *Borders: Frontiers of Identity, Nation and State*. Oxford: Berg.

Ehn, Billy & Orvar Löfgren 1982: *Kulturanalys*. Malmö: Liber.

Ehn, Billy & Orvar Löfgren 2001: *Kulturanalyser*. Malmö: Gleerups.

Erixon, Sigurd 1919: Svenska gårdstyper. *Rig: Tidskrift för Föreningen för svensk kulturhistoria* 1. Stockholm.

Erixon, Sigurd 1922: Svensk byggnadskultur och dess geografi. *Ymer: Tidskrift utgiven av Sällskapet för antropologi och geografi* 3–4. Stockholm.

Erixon, Sigurd 1938: *Svenskt folkliv: Några kapitel svensk folklivsforskning med belysning av dess arbetsuppgifter och metoder*. Uppsala: J.A. Lindblads förlag.

Erixon, Sigurd 1945: *Svenska kulturgränser och kulturprovinser*. Kungliga Gustav Adolfs Akademiens småskrifter 1. Stockholm: Lantbruksförbundets Tidskrifts AB.

Erixon, Sigurd 1957: Materiell och social kultur. In: Åke Campbell, Sigurd Erixon, N. Lindqvist & Jöran Sahlgren (eds.), *Atlas över svensk folkkultur*. Part 1. Uddevalla: Bokförlaget Niloé.

Gorn, Elliot J. (2009)2011: *Dillinger's Wild Ride: The Year that made America's Public Enemy Number One*. Oxford: Oxford University Press.

Handberg, Peter 1996: Förord. In: P. Virilio: *Försvinnandets estetik*. Gothenburg: Korpen.

Heimbürger, Hans 1974: *Svenska telegrafverket: Historisk framställning*. Part 5. Telefon, telegraf och radio 1921–1945.

Ingmarsson, Niklas 2004: *Bilkultur i Malmö: Hur en bilstad blir till*. Hedemora: Gidlunds Förlag.

Johansson, Lennart 2008: *Staten, supen och systemet: Svensk alkoholpolitik och alkoholkultur 1855–2005*. Stockholm: Brutus Östlings bokförlag Symposion.

Keegan, John (1998)2006: *Det första världskriget*. Stockholm: Natur & Kultur.

Kern, Stephen (1983)2003: *The Culture of Time and Space 1880–1918*. With a new preface. Cambridge, Massachusetts: Harvard University Press.

Lanternan: no. 18 1920, no. 10 1921, no. 16 1922, no. 6 1925.

Larsson, Ulf 1992: Mellankrigstidens anti-smugglingspolitik. *Argus: Årsbok för tullmuseum och Tullhistoriska föreningen*.

Larsson, Ulf 1999: Smuggling of Liquor in the Baltic Sea Area during the Interwar Period. *Argus: Årsbok för tullmuseum och Tullhistoriska föreningen*.

Linde-Laursen, Anders 1995: *Det nationales natur: Studier i dansk–svenske relationer*. Copenhagen: The Nordic Council of Ministers.

Löfgren, Orvar 1989: The Nationalization of Culture. *Ethnologia Europaea: Journal of European Ethnology* XIX, 1989.

Löfgren, Orvar 1993: Nationella arenor. In: Billy Ehn, Jonas Frykman & Orvar Löfgren (eds.), *Försvenskningen av Sverige: Det nationellas förvandlingar*. Stockholm: Natur och Kultur.

Löfgren, Orvar 2000: Moving Metaphors. In: Per-Olof Berg, Anders Linde-Laursen & Orvar Löfgren (eds.), *Invoking a Transnational Metropolis*. Lund: Studentlitteratur.

Lundin, Johan A. & Fredrik Nilsson 2010: Smugglarnas och statsmaktens nätverk – Gränslandets kulturella dynamik. In: Anders Palm & Hanne Sanders (eds.), *Flytande gränser: Dansk-svenska förbindelser efter 1658*. Gothenburg: Makadam Förlag.

Mappen, Marc 2013: *Prohibition Gangsters: The Rise and Fall of a Bad Generation*. New Brunswick: Rutgers University Press.

Marvin, Carolyn 1988: *When Old Technologies Were New: Thinking about Electric Communication in the Late Nineteenth Century*. Oxford: Oxford University Press.

Nerén, John 1937: *Automobilens historia*. Stockholm: Motor-Byråns Förlag.

Nilsson, Fredrik 1999: *När en timme blir tio minuter: En studie av förväntan inför Öresundsbron*. Lund: Historiska Media.

Nilsson, Fredrik 2007: "Nationalitet og landegrænser er os ligegyldige": En studie av ungsocialister och gränsöverskridande vid tiden kring 1900. In: Fredrik Nilsson, Hanne Sanders & Ylva Stubbergaard (eds.), *Öresundsgränser: Rörelser, möten och visioner i tid och rum*. Gothenburg: Makadam Förlag.

Nilsson, Fredrik 2010: Öresund Plaza: Om konsten att passera. In: Orvar Löfgren & Fredrik Nilsson (eds.), *Regionauterna – Öresundsbron från vision till vardag*. Gothenburg: Makadam Förlag.

Nilsson, Fredrik, Hanne Sanders & Ylva Stubbergaard 2007 (eds.): *Öresundsgränser: Rörelser, möten och visioner i tid och rum*. Gothenburg: Makadam Förlag.

O'Dell, Tom 1997: *Culture Unbound: Americanization and Everyday Life in Sweden*. Lund: Nordic Academic Press.

Ruth, David E. 1996: *Inventing the Public Enemy: The Gangster in American Culture, 1918–1934*. Chicago: The University of Chicago Press.

Sandberg, Marie 2012: Border Orderings: The Co-existence of Border Focusing and Letting Border Issues Take the Back Seat at the German-Polish Border. In: Dorte Andersen Jagetic, Martin Klatt & Marie Sandberg (eds.), *The Border Multiple: The Practising of Borders between Public Policy and Everyday Life in a Re-scaling Europe*. Farnham: Ashgate.

Sydsvenska Dagbladet, SDS: May 16 1929, February 2 1930.

Tomlinson, John 2007: *The Culture of Speed: The Coming of Immediacy*. London: Sage.

Underdånigt betänkande afgifvet den 29 oktober 1902 af komitén för granskning af Tullverkets stater. 1. Betänkande och förslag. Stockholm: K.L. Bergmans boktryckeri.

Virilio, Paul (1977)2006: *Speed and Politics: An Essay on Dromology*. New York: Semiotext(e).

Virilio, Paul (1984)1996: *War and Cinema: The Logistics of Perception*. London: Verso.

Virilio, Paul (1989)1996: *Försvinnandets estetik*. Gothenburg: Korpen.

Virilio, Paul 1997: *Open Sky*. London: Verso.

1914 års tullkommissions betänkanden 1917: I. *Förslag till omorganisation av tullverkets kust- och gränsbevakning*. Stockholm: K.L. Beckmans Boktryckeri.

Fredrik Nilsson, professor and Head of the Centre for Oresund Region Studies (CORS), Lund University, has written extensively on the Öresund region and the cultural dynamics of national borders.
(fredrik.nilsson@ism.lu.se)

RUPTURE AND CONTINUITY
Reflections on the Relationship between Synchrony and Diachrony in Ethnology, in Memoriam Bjarne Stoklund

Signe Mellemgaard

In this article, Professor Emeritus Bjarne Stoklund's research spanning more than sixty years is revisited. Trained in the historical-geographical method, Stoklund saw it as his task to mediate between this approach and new trends after 1971. The article pursues three lines: 1) the change of focus from relatively isolated cultural traits to a broader cultural history, 2) the introduction of an ecological perspective focused on functioning totalities, and 3) the transformation of "relic areas" to areas seen within a world system. The revisit to Bjarne Stoklund's publications also addresses his revisit and revitalisation of his own earlier research. His efforts to address the question of continuity and transformation have made lasting impressions in Danish ethnology in terms of an interest in cultural history and long term processes.

Keywords: Bjarne Stoklund, ethnology, historical-geographical method, paradigm shift, cultural history

European Ethnology Revisited

In May 2013, Professor Emeritus Bjarne Stoklund, the long-standing editor of *Ethnologia Europaea*, passed away, bringing a long life in and with ethnology to a close. This in itself is reason enough to revisit his publications, which span a period of over 60 years, from 1952 to the present day. However, this return to Bjarne Stoklund's work is also a return in a different sense. Indeed, as a museum curator and later as a professor and a productive professor emeritus, Bjarne Stoklund was characterised by his willingness to take new directions while still retaining the positive aspects of earlier research and knowledge, which makes revisiting his work pertinent to an assessment of the present and future of ethnology. As a former student and later colleague of Stoklund I have witnessed how he was continuously engaged in refining his research: its subject matter, approaches, preconceptions and methods. Rather than simply abandoning his earlier studies – thematically and theoretically speaking – in order to plunge into new topics or methods, he constantly honed his topics and methods, departed from them and supplemented them. In his career as a professor, Stoklund had to navigate through dramatic shifts and transformations. In this process, Stoklund also revisited and further developed an earlier tradition within cultural history.

In this article, I examine how, by adopting new perspectives and by refining his point of departure, Bjarne Stoklund retained a firm grasp on the productive aspects of earlier insights. Doing so, he brought them into a new "paradigm", at a time when others were simply breaking away from traditional folklife research completely.[1]

Danish ethnology profited from Stoklund's endeavours to build a bridge between the diffusionist ethnology that characterised large portions of ethnology in Europe from the 1920s onward, manifested in the extensive atlas projects, and the ethnology oriented towards the present, inspired by social anthropology, which gained ground in ethnology in Europe at varying speeds. Bjarne Stoklund was Denmark's only professor in the subject and his continued interest in the diachronic and cultural historical perspectives had a substantial impact upon research and teaching in Danish ethnology, where a focus on cultural history and a long-term perspective remained central. This was in contrast to, for example, the neighbouring country of Sweden, where the departure from traditional ways of working at the time meant a clearer focus on contemporary ethnology (Ehn & Löfgren 1996; Daun 2003).

How continuity and rupture interact in historical processes remains a problem in ethnology, as well as the problem how we should deal with material and knowledge generated in an earlier "paradigm". I should therefore like to discuss the relationship between synchrony and diachrony in Stoklund's work, putting special emphasis on his role as mediator between the diffusionist paradigm and social anthropology inspired studies of the present. However, first a brief note on Stoklunds biography.

A Short Academic Life History

Originally trained as a historian with a special interest in medieval history, in 1949 Stoklund got "one of the most sought-after student jobs at the National Museum" (Stoklund 2003b), where he worked with the National Museum's Ethnological Investigations (NEU, Nationalmuseets Etnologiske Undersøgelser), which had been established in 1939. This was an outright apprenticeship in ethnology, which was not yet a subject at the university in Copenhagen, where ethnological methods and subject areas were frowned upon by the history faculty, as Bjarne Stoklund humorously recollected on several occasions (2003b, 2010; Henningsen 2002). Ethnology had its base at the National Museum and, for Stoklund, working here was a training in ethnological methods, but also meant the accumulation of a comprehensive expertise. Based on a model from Sweden, which had equivalents in many other places in Europe, the work involved gathering material using lists of questions sent out to informants throughout the country.

After only a few months at NEU, Bjarne Stoklund became involved in the National Museum's Farm Building Survey, which was initiated in 1944 as a systematic registration of Danish smallholdings and houses from before 1850. The survey was carried out via inspections – each year in a specific region – and Bjarne Stoklund spent the subsequent summers with other staff members, cycling around to different parts of the country, describing farms and houses. He also spoke to the locals on the farms – old people in particular – about the farms' history and use. In 1949, the inspections were in Læsø, where the seaweed roofs were under threat of being turned into mattress fillings during the years of material scarcity following the war (Henningsen 2002).

The head of NEU, Svend Jespersen, who knew of Bjarne Stoklund's family affiliation with the island of Læsø (his grandfather was from there originally), gave him the task of commencing a so-called "point survey" on the island in conjunction with the Farm Building Survey on the island. The idea was that the broad ethnological studies that gathered material from the whole country – and which could provide a general overview of the dispersal of cultural elements – should be combined with close-up studies in selected areas, which could provide the contextual background for the former. Bjarne Stoklund continued to work on this locality throughout the 1950s and 1960s, whenever the opportunity arose. In later decades, he also worked to summarise these extensive studies in between his other projects.

After completing his studies a few years before, in

1958 Bjarne Stoklund was employed by the Open Air Museum under the National Museum. Even during his time as a student assistant, Bjarne Stoklund had published short articles based on the National Museum's ethnological research, the Farm Building Survey, and his own work. As a museum curator, Bjarne Stoklund continued to write, publishing guides to a number of other houses and farms at the museum (1959, 1961, 1969a). In particular, the museum's smallholding from the southern Zealand village of Kalvehave and a house from the Faroe Islands became the subject of publications which were based on the individual houses but which opened up to broader cultural historical perspectives. Generally speaking, Bjarne Stoklund's interest in the houses and farms at the museum was never limited to building customs; they were always considered in their cultural-historical context.

Bjarne Stoklund was curator at the Open Air Museum from 1958 to 1971, and it was by no means self-evident for him or for others that he should take on the professorship after Axel Steensberg, the professor at the time. He had not had much to do with the institute, as he considered Steensberg's "Material Folk Culture" to be somewhat rigid and very narrow in scope (Henningsen 2002).

When he was inaugurated as a professor in 1971 following Steensberg's sudden resignation due to a local student protest, it was important for Bjarne Stoklund to turn the discipline into something other than a museum discipline and to depart from the narrow focus on material culture (Stoklund 1971a; Henningsen 2002). Thus, he ensured that the subject was given its current name of "European ethnology" and, not least of all, drew inspiration from Swedish ethnology, which became a model for the reorganisation. He brought Swedish lecturers to Copenhagen: Orvar Löfgren, Jonas Frykman and Gunnar Alsmark. The result was a lasting impression on Danish ethnology, both with regards to new inspiration and to the preservation of a historical perspective. There was now space to explore new forms of ethnology as well as to revisit the history of the discipline, for example, the earlier cultural-historical tradition, which provided the inspiration for a different type of cultural-historical study than those that were carried out by NEU and the Farm Building Survey.

As a professor, Stoklund influenced not only Danish ethnology and several generations of students, including my own, which profited from his inspiring and erudite teaching and insight; his influence also spread to other disciplines and abroad. In his teaching, he always linked his comprehensive and often detailed knowledge of a variety of subjects with broader structures and transformations. As an author he is known and admired for his eloquent and unpretentious style, making his works worth reading to a broader public.

During the twenty years between 1984 and 2003, Bjarne Stoklund was the editor-in-chief for *Ethnologia Europaea*. The previous editor, German Professor of ethnology Günter Wiegelmann, was forced to leave the position due to ill health, and the Swedish ethnologist Nils-Arvid Bringéus, among others, suggested that Bjarne Stoklund – not least due to him being the head of Danish ethnology and having a broad network in Europe – should take over the position. At that time, the journal was 15 years old, and following the change of editor, it was renewed with a new editorial line and layout (Stoklund 2010; Sandberg 2012). For Bjarne Stoklund, this provided an opportunity to strengthen the European network and facilitate the exchange of knowledge and discussions across linguistic and national boundaries.

In 1996, Bjarne Stoklund retired after 25 years as a professor, during which he had received numerous national and international accolades. During his 17 incredibly active years as emeritus, he worked on and published a number of his life's works, starting with a book on Faroese houses (1996a) and including several studies on the history of the discipline and museum history, building customs, and world exhibitions. In 2000, the material from his dissertation was published in an expanded and revised form, and in 2015 there are plans to publish Bjarne Stoklund's last (and in some respects, his first) large study, the synthesis of 64 years' intermittent work on the cultural history of the island of Læsø (Stoklund, forthcoming).

European Ethnology between Monsters and Maelstroms

Two aspects of Bjarne Stoklund's academic work stand out. The first is his ongoing efforts to unite a long-term diachronic perspective with the explanatory potential of a synchronic context. His point of departure is that the synchronic and the diachronic, or functional and historical explanations cannot be used in isolation. Indeed, at a time when ethnology was becoming increasingly characterised by contemporary issues in line with a shift that was also taking place in other ethnological institutions throughout Europe (Wiegelmann, Zender & Heilfurth 1977; Löfgren 1996; Kaschuba 1999; Daun 2003), Stoklund maintained an approach that was tuned in to changes over long periods of time. For Stoklund, who had studied the Middle Ages and Renaissance as a student, long periods of time could easily mean five, six, or seven centuries.

Due to the conflicts about the aim of ethnology around 1970, Stoklund had to navigate in troubled water. Students pushed for ethnology to engage in studies of contemporary cultural phenomena and to play an active role in society. This meant an increased focus on community studies, working-class culture and urban locations. New inspiration mainly came from anthropology and community studies, mostly via Swedish ethnology. This was similar to changes in ethnology in other European countries. In Denmark, as in many other places[2], it was connected with the student protests after 1968, which pushed for more student influence regarding the content and form of teaching. In Copenhagen, students wanted to reform what they saw as an outdated training for the museums of cultural history, and the result was two contending parties that found it difficult to get on.

In his inaugural lecture in 1971, Bjarne Stoklund depicted this balancing act between the synchronic and the diachronic as a voyage between on one side Scylla, a monster with multiple heads which threatened to devour Odysseus and his men, and on the other side Charybdis, whose maelstrom sucks in and crushes everything in its vicinity. In this case, Scylla is the earlier ethnology with its focus on the elements of material culture and its pronounced specialisation in these matters, whereas Charybdis symbolises inspiration from anthropology and sociology, which, in Stoklund's view, represented a threat in the years around the student protest and the collapse of the old ethnology. Ethnology was in danger of losing its uniqueness and being blended beyond recognition into an indistinguishable mass of undifferentiated social sciences (Stoklund 1971a). Ethnology in the German-speaking countries and in Sweden; the two places from which Ethnology in Copenhagen was mainly influenced, also took up a position between a traditional focus on artefacts and a social science, as portrayed by for example W. Kaschuba (1999).

For Bjarne Stoklund, the argument was that the historical perspective was central to explanations of cultural forms and processes, because those are established in one period and can be maintained in later periods. Thus, these cultural products or cultural elements – objects or habits, for example – are often "inherited from earlier generations and therefore emerged under different economic and social circumstances than those that are now predominant" (1971a: 669[3]). In other words, history matters. Further, Stoklund points to the fact that materiality provides this continuity. We take on material forms that were formed in other time periods than our own, but which – also quite literally – force us to handle them in particular ways.

However, just as the synchronic perspective cannot do without the diachronic, Stoklund argued, the historical perspective must also be qualified by an analysis that includes the synchronic context. Thus, cultural element studies are not complete without a study of the totalities of which these elements are a part. In the light of the one-sided focus on cultural element studies in the years leading up to his inauguration, Stoklund considered it to be "good and right that total studies are prioritised today" (1971a: 667). Indeed, the point is that both aspects are necessary. For him, the relationship between synchrony and diachrony appeared to be a relationship between cultural elements and studies of functioning totalities.

The second characteristic trait in Stoklund's writings is his continuous refinement of his own point of departure. Raised with the historical-geographical method's understanding that explanations are to be found in the historical perspective – manifested in the attempts to trace the histories of individual cultural elements and map their routes of dispersal – Stoklund continually attempted to unite this perspective with synchronic explanations, which took the form of various departures from this diffusionism. These departures included the criticism of the element-based way of thinking – the idea that the point of entry to studying culture was via individual elements, whose dispersal and distribution could be analysed – and of the idea of relic areas, as well as a problematisation of the mechanisms that underlie this dispersal, which remained untheorised in diffusionism.

Inspired by the work of Thomas Kuhn, Bjarne Stoklund on several occasions described the history of the discipline as being characterised by paradigms and ruptures, whereas diffusionism represented "the closest this discipline has ever come to what Thomas Kuhn called a 'normal science'" (e.g. Stoklund 2006: 28) for a long period of time, from the 1920s to the 1960s. Indeed, during this period there was a great degree of consensus with regards to ends and means, rationality and relevance, and individual researchers saw their research as the building blocks of a greater shared project, such as the great atlases of folk culture in Scandinavia, Finland, Germany and a number of Eastern and Central European countries. In Denmark, the change or "scientific revolution" occurred in the form of persistent criticisms of the existing ethnology by students and young scholars who joined with students in other Nordic countries, centred on the journal *Nord-Nytt*, to promote a new ethnology. The borrowing of social anthropological approaches was "a large paradigm shift" (Stoklund 2003a: 87) and of radical importance for what could be studied and how, as the object of study now became cultural totalities in synchronic contexts – often in the form of contemporary studies – and this meant that many of the traditional themes had a tendency to disappear.

Indeed, it makes sense to follow Stoklund and describe diffusionism as a normal scientific paradigm. For Kuhn a paradigm is defined by certain rules and standards for a science, and by research that is focused on particular problems. A consensus prevails regarding the relevance of the research, and most of the concepts in use are well-known, their meaning is largely undisputed. All of these points apply to diffusionism. According to Kuhn, propagation of the paradigm often takes the form of tacit knowledge, and this corresponds to, for example, Bjarne Stoklund's own description of his initiation into the historical-geographical method (Stoklund 2003b, 2010; cf. Ehn & Löfgren 1996: 37).[4] Kuhn's description of normal science as a puzzle almost seems to have been written with diffusionism in mind: it is a matter of filling in gaps, finding the missing pieces and finding ways to fit them in to the general picture. In the case of diffusionism, this general picture includes cultural boundaries and routes of dispersal. Normal science does not seek out the unpredictable, but rather that which can be assimilated. However, there is just one of Kuhn's points that does not correspond with folklife research in the period between the 1920s and the 1960s: according to Kuhn, in periods when normal science predominates, science is largely unconcerned with the general public and research is almost exclusively addressed to academics from within the same field. However, folklife research has always held the public's interest and has been dependent on this in a variety of ways.[5]

But does Kuhn's description also encapsulate the situation following the student protest in Danish ethnology? In one way it does not, since there was no consensus regarding the means and ends of the discipline. Rather, there was what could be called a pre-paradigmatic situation with competing schools that criticised each other's objectives and standards. In one sense, however, there was a consensus when it came to viewing the objects of the old ethnology as problematic, and a different set of problems was now at the centre of the analyses. Despite the disagreements, this provided a common foundation.

For Kuhn, the transition between two paradigms takes the form of a revolution; it is irreversible but takes place gradually and can only ever be partial, since some of the language and instruments used will remain the same. The revolution occurs when members of the scientific community gradually convert to the new paradigm. A few may hold on to the old, but if they do, they will eventually be pushed out of the profession and ignored. This was certainly not the case for Bjarne Stoklund. On the contrary, as a professor he spearheaded new initiatives and movements while also making a connection to the previous paradigm.

If Kuhn is to be believed, then paradigms are incommensurable. This means that an earlier paradigm is partially incomprehensible to its successor because they disagree when it comes to the nature of problems as well as the standards and relevance of scientific work. However, as revolutions are never complete, this incommensurability does not render conversation between the paradigms impossible, although misunderstandings are likely since the content and meanings of concepts change to some extent. In these paradigm shifts, some members of the scientific community may become translators between the two paradigms if they are able to familiarise themselves with which concepts cause tensions and translate between the two (Kuhn 1996: 202).[6] Bjarne Stoklund was able to incorporate new perspectives and generate new insights within the themes of earlier research in ways that lay beyond the reach of the previous paradigm. In the following I will discuss how Bjarne Stoklund's efforts to test the potential of new perspectives while at the same time maintaining a firm grasp on the insights and themes of earlier research might be interpreted as the role of translator between paradigms.

A Translator between Paradigms?

A number of different subject areas have been at the centre of Bjarne Stoklund's works. Examples of these are his interest in the history of ethnology, exhibitions and museums and how these have played a part in nationalisation and national struggles, rural building customs within a long historical perspective, medieval fishery, peasant diaries, cultural landscapes and peasant ecotypes.

In the following, I focus on three areas in which the relationship between synchrony and diachrony is central, and which thematise the difficult navigation between what Stoklund portrayed as Scylla and Charybdis. Stoklund revisited these three areas, taking up a critical stance in relation to the previous paradigm, which is even more precarious here because, to a great extent, it represents the context for the collection of material which was gathered within the very same framework of understanding that the analysis attempts to overturn. Thus, the material I use is taken from a selection of Bjarne Stoklund's publications from over sixty years' work. Therefore this paper is both idiosyncratic and entirely incomplete, and the discussion is exclusively about Stoklund as a writer, rather than a professor for a discipline, a teacher or an editor. All of these aspects are, however, worthy of attention in a different forum. The discussion that follows is structured along three lines.

1) The conflict between cultural element studies and general cultural studies viewed within the framework of the relationship between the micro and macro levels. Here, the point of departure is building customs, with particular focus on the works about the Open Air Museum's house from the southern Zealand village Kalvehave. Even if Bjarne Stoklund, via his approach to building customs, may not entirely have turned the study of cultural elements into a historical study of totalities, he nonetheless managed to deal with the relationship between the micro and macro levels by convincingly placing houses and building customs into a larger cultural-historical perspective.

2) The ecological perspective as a qualification of diffusionism. For Bjarne Stoklund, the ecological perspective became, from the early 1970s onwards, an approach which could solve some of ethnology's problems with the historical-geographical method and its strong focus on diachrony and cultural elements. Ecotypes became a new – or rather a revitalised – and promising approach to peasant economy and everyday life.

3) Finally, world system theory also represents an alternative to the idea of "relic areas". Drawing inspi-

ration from Fernand Braudel and Immanuel Wallerstein, among others, Bjarne Stoklund shed new light on the cultural history of the North Atlantic region, in particular the Faroe Islands. In contrast to earlier ethnological research which had seen the region as a prime example of a relic area, is was seen as an area that had changed position from centre to periphery in a global economic system.

Cultural Elements or Cultural Totalities: "Dead and Dissected Houses" or "Living Human Dwellings"

In the historical-geographical method, the idea of continuity usually took the form of, and was maintained by, a focus on cultural elements. In order to analyse the distribution of cultural forms, they had to be divided into elements, such as particular forms of joints in timber houses, specific thatching methods or types of traditions related to harvesting, which could be traced back in time and distributed in space. A fundamental principle in diffusionism was also that small, unheeded characteristics were particularly suited as point of entry into a study. Indeed, it was in these selected form-related aspects, preferably of a type for which no functional explanation could be found, that relations between cultural areas could be identified; for example, via the small, unnoticed solutions used in the construction of tools, which could function as "clues" in an analysis of the history and geography of a cultural product. Therefore, cultural elements were prioritised over totalities (even though these were expected to emerge in the synthesis of the atlas works), just as continuity was prioritised over rupture. In the historical-geographical method, the perspective was both geographically and historically broad, but this long historical perspective presupposed that culture should be viewed via its elements. In this respect, a discussion of how the parts relate to the whole is also linked to a discussion of how synchrony relates to diachrony.

Bjarne Stoklund was a firm critic of both his predecessors' and his contemporaries' one-sided focus on cultural elements (e.g. in Stoklund 1987, 1988a, 2003a). In his inaugural lecture, the point was that one does not have to choose between traditional cultural element studies or social sciences-inspired total studies, and nor should one select elements from each of them. Rather, one should strive to do both (Stoklund 1971a). As a student, he was rooted in a paradigm which prioritised knowledge about elements. In one of his fist publications, a very brief, popular and humorous introduction to the Farm Building Survey, he discusses the working practices of the folklife researcher. Here he expresses a desire to understand traditional cultural as a totality: as a "whole, in which every cultural element, new and old, has its own specific role" (Stoklund 1957). The Farm Building Survey was never published as intended. Svend Jespersen, who headed the survey from 1944, died in 1958 and it was at risk of ebbing to a close (Stoklund 2010). It was Stoklund who, with his *Bondegård og byggeskik* (Farm Building Customs, 1969b) attempted to summarise the results. The book is true to its historical-geographical genesis and in its conclusion, and Stoklund points out that the study of farm buildings not only has intrinsic value, but is also a means to a deeper understanding of "the nature of culture and its pathways". Farm buildings in their local variations cannot be studied in isolation; they must be compared to those in other localities. Thus, the houses must be detached from their respective environments and their components must be analysed. This is the method used in the book and, as a result, the houses appear to be more "dead and dissected houses than living human dwellings" (1969b: 78). Bjarne Stoklund notes that the overall cultural pattern is best understood via a study which takes a holistic approach to the chosen locality; that is, it should seek to understand the interplay between the individual components, living patterns and societal structure (1969b: 77–78).

One can gain a sense of what this might mean by comparing Bjarne Stoklund's two books about the Open Air Museum's house from Kalvehave. The first, published in 1960, was occasioned by the moving of the house to the museum. The second, published twenty years later, is a significantly revised version of it, supplemented with extensive archive work (1980a). The publication from 1960 deals with the reconstructed environments in the house's two dwellings as they appear at the Open Air Museum, with a focus on the building customs. In the publication from 1980, the building customs are consistently placed within the context of the larger society. In this way, the diminutive smallholding from southern Zealand becomes a prism for a broader understanding of economic, ecological and social conditions. In particular, the focus here is on peasant economy and particularly the use of the forest, to which the title also refers.[7] However, neither the house nor the forest can be understood in isolation from a wider Danish and North European context: economic, political, ecological, and demographic factors as the medieval herring fishery (resulting in a boom in the demand for barrows and hoops from hazel wood), the increased power of the nobility (resulting in changes in the distribution of rights to the forest), the agricultural reforms and the emergence of new landowners and new smallholding craftsmen, and the cultivation of a new cultural landscape and the impact of industrialisation on rural craftsmanship.

Thus, the house is a comprehensive piece of cultural and social history, representing continuity, because of the existence of a complex smallholder economy throughout the entire period, and rupture as the house must be understood in constantly new contexts throughout the almost 400-year-period covered by the book. This anticipates more recent attempts to integrate the micro and macro perspectives in cultural history, and in line with microhistorical proponents one might say that it is not a matter of seeing things small, but to see through small things. It is however not a modern microhistory peeping through the text, but more likely efforts to integrate a macro perspective, informed by an earlier tradition of cultural history. As I mentioned earlier, the historical-geographical method was by no means narrow in its outlook; the perspectives used were both spatially and temporally expansive. However, in *Huset og skoven*, the outlook is one of an entirely different character: Changes in a long historical perspective are narrated through the changing conditions on a smaller level, creating a well-told piece of cultural history.

Ill. 1: The folklife researcher at work. An old farmer gives information on the history and use of the farm to the recording, almost autobiographically depicted, researcher in his leather shoes, plus fours, and beret. (Drawing: Bjarne Stoklund [Stoklund 1957])

Temporally, the latter publication coincided with two other efforts by Stoklund. On the one hand, the return to the rich traditions of earlier, primarily Nordic cultural historians (e.g. T.F. Troels-Lund, V. Grønbech and E. Sundt [Stoklund 1979a, 1979b, 1981a, 1987]) and, on the other hand, attempts to introduce new cultural history approaches. For Bjarne Stoklund, these two things were closely connected. In 1980, he arranged an interdisciplinary Nordic seminar in collaboration with two other Danish ethnologist-folklorists. The aim of the seminar was to introduce historical anthropology into the Nordic context. The participants were researchers in a range of disciplines from the five Nordic countries, and the speakers included leading international researchers from the burgeoning discipline of historical anthropology: Peter Burke, Alan Macfarlane, David Sabean, E. le Roy Ladurie and Bjarne Stoklund himself, who gave two lectures – one on early exponents of cultural history in Denmark and one on peasant diaries (1981b). Like other sorts of "ego-documents", these received increased scholarly attention internationally with Stoklund as a leading proponent. Taking wider international tendencies as a point of departure, the old cultural historical tradition could now be revisited and given new significance as an inspiration to understanding culture and cultural change.

Arguably, the interest in historical anthropology along with the return to the cultural historical tradition contributed to the creation of a particular profile for ethnology in Copenhagen, which retained the diachronic perspective in both teaching and research. This was also particularly significant to Stoklund's own studies which drew inspiration from both new and old cultural history approaches in the studies of long-term changes in local communities (in Læsø, in particular) and his studies in museology and the history of the discipline. In the rapprochement between history and anthropology, he saw a revival and a reinforcement of ethnology's efforts to reconstruct historical communities and the living conditions, ways of life, and world views of the past. The conjunction of anthropological and historical methods could provide a sort of "quasi fieldwork" ("fingeret feltarbejde", Stoklund 1981b), which would revitalise the study of communities in transformation.

From Studies of Distributions to Studies of Ecological Systems

In his inaugural lecture, Bjarne Stoklund had suggested the ecological perspective as a possible solution to the dilemma of how to combine a diachronic perspective with a synchronic perspective. "In local studies, especially those conducted from an ecological perspective, European ethnology's tendency to work with a historical approach is successfully combined with the social anthropological method," he claimed (Stoklund 1971a). In the 1970s, the ecological perspective represented for Stoklund an opportunity to bring cultural element studies together into an environment study which could explain how cultural phenomena worked together synchronically: it could help to explain how the relationship between part and whole could be seen in a perspective of change, supporting the efforts to view the small society within the large one.

In the same year as the inaugural lecture, an edition of the Nordic ethnology and folklore journal *Nord-Nytt* was published with the theme of *Ecology and Culture*. This served to introduce cultural ecology to Nordic ethnology and included an article by Stoklund on ecological adaptation in a Danish island community (1971b, cf. 1968). It contains the first outline of a synthesis of many years of Læsø studies. In the article, these studies are placed into the framework of an ecological perspective, which understands developments in Læsø as the result of an ecological process of adaptation. However, Stoklund also notes that such "a synchronic analysis will quickly prove to be inadequate. An ecological system will always be the result of a process of adaptation, and this can only be studied diachronically" (Stoklund 1971b: 174). Although the inspiration from cultural ecology is not particularly explicit, the argument is nonetheless clear in that in local studies the ecological perspective has the potential to bring the historical perspective together in synchronic cross-sections, illuminating functional relationships between the following aspects: work, economy and gender roles. In each of these temporal cross-sections, things are synchronically linked. They also explain the continuity of cultural forms; that is, the relative immutability in agricultural technology and gendered division of labour, the continuity of which can both be explained by durable structures and the new functions they acquire in relation to first trade at sea with small vessels and, later on, via international shipping.

In 1975, this perspective was taken up once again in conjunction with the Nordic ethnology and Folklore Congress, and was published in the form an article: "Ecological Succession" (1976). Here, Stoklund, informed by previous depictions of peasant economies and by Julian Steward's cultural ecology, identifies a number of "ecotypes" pertaining to Danish peasant economies in the early modern era. He stresses that ecotypes are not only based on variations in soil and climate, but also on macro (economic) conditions, especially the trade opportunities available to farmers in a given region. Furthermore, he emphasises how important non-agrarian subsistence has been in different ecological, economic, and social contexts.

In the article, another analogy from biology is employed with the aim of integrating the temporal dimension; namely, the concept of "ecological succession", which, in biology, denotes the process by which plant and animal societies within an ecotype develop in a particular direction due to changes in the ecological conditions. In the article, the succession is a sequence of specific forms of interaction between people and the environment in a given geographical area; that is, a transition from one ecotype to another. Particular attention is paid to the woodland peasants of southern Zealand, who used to exploit the forest for grazing, pig breading, wheel making, the production of hazel hoops and apples – which were sold in Copenhagen along with pork and butter. Thus, they lived on a varied livestock production and resources from the forest, and this had its basis in not only the ecological conditions but also in the distribution of rights and in the conditions of the market economy. This changed after the agricultural reforms by which the peasants were transformed to arable farmers, but they still grew fruit in their gardens and, to some extent, continued to make trade journeys to the capital with pork and fruit.

In a much later article (1998), Stoklund takes stock of the use of the term "ecotype", although the focus is now partially shifted to "non-agrarian subsistence". Overall, the point here is that a peasant should not be viewed as someone who has farming as his primary source of income, but rather as someone who, thanks to his farm or house, has access to a range of resources that can be exploited: the fertile land, the sea, heathland and forests. This perspective enables us to avoid an evolutionist interpretation of rural economies as stages in a several-hundred-year-long development process culminating in a typical farmer, as well as an equally evolutionist interpretation of a "natural" movement in the direction of (proto-)industrialisation. The ecotypes and non-agrarian subsistence should be understood as co-existent adaptations to specific natural geographical, economic and social conditions, with no innate destination – neither pure arable farming nor industrialisation (cf. Stoklund 2003b, 2000).

Firstly, in Bjarne Stoklund's use of the ecological perspective, it is characteristic that earlier cultural element studies are linked to the broader and complex historical, geographical, ecological and economic conditions. This does not mean that knowledge established within the historical-geographical paradigm is invalid; rather, the perspective provides it with new explanations. Seeing the object of study as co-existent adaptations is rather different to seeing it as element studies with a focus on variations of form as part of a relative chronology of innovation and relics. Secondly, this is not a matter of ecological determinism. Rather, cultural, economic and social conditions on both the macro and micro level are involved. The lifestyles of farmers not only reflect the landscape, they also form this landscape to a great extent. Indeed, it is the heath peasants' use of the heath that maintains it as it is, just as the open woodlands of the era prior to the agricultural reform are a result of the woodland peasants' use of them. Thirdly, the studies demonstrate that the ecological perspective facilitates both a synchronic and a diachronic way of observing – but, as is typically the case, the diachronic view is made up of a range of synchronic cross-sections, which can each be analysed as functioning wholes. The transformation process in itself is more difficult to pinpoint. The ecological perspective's ability to explain differences, however, is also linked with an awareness of (global) economic conditions and thereby also true history; that is, that things can change and that they do so in unpredictable ways.

Relic or Peripheral Area? The Faroese House from Centre to Periphery

The transport of a house from Múli to the Open Air Museum in 1959 and 1961 had prompted Stoklund's research interest in Faroese and North Atlantic building customs in general. In a contribution to the discussion about "Western Nordic building customs" (1980b, 1981c), Bjarne Stoklund made it clear that there was a need for an alternative to the two existing dominant models of explanation regarding cultural development in the North Atlantic and, in particular, building customs in the Faroe Islands. Until then, research into North Atlantic building customs had, on the one hand, been considered from an evolutionist perspective – as a unified process from primitive forms of housing (such as houses built entirely of stone and turf with just one room) to more complex types of house (such as houses clad with wooden panelling and windows). It was thought that because of its remote location, the area would provide good opportunities to find relics from previous stages in this development. On the other hand, research into houses had been approached in a diffusionist manner, where elements were studied and analysed separately, and their age and origins were determined. From this perspective, the North Atlantic was interesting because it was thought to be the meeting place for cultural elements originating in different areas. In this perspective, the resemblance of the house forms are analysed as originating from either the Nordic or the Celtic World (as in Stoklund 1963). The functionalist local studies that had replaced evolutionism and diffusionism completely ignored building customs, and there was now a need for a, "for want of a better term," sociocultural interpretation, which could rediscover them, "but not continue with its evolutionary/diffusionist innocence intact, as though nothing had happened." Such an approach would have to include ecological and economic changes and should also see building customs in their context of social structures and the symbolic functions of the house.

The article "Das färöische Haus" (1974) introduces such an interpretation. Faroese building customs are related to other western Nordic stave constructions and also have parallels with similar timber-frame houses in the North Sea coastal areas. This reflects a time when the North Sea brought regions together. Later, the North Sea area became more fragmented and North Atlantic building customs developed in several separate directions. This was also due to ecological changes: the settlements in Greenland were abandoned due to climatic changes, and timber and fuel shortages in Iceland presented the population with new challenges. In the Faroe Islands, this resulted in buildings being adapted to the local conditions; that is, the specific trade conditions and the supply of building materials. This means that what could be observed on the islands were not old forms, but specific adaptations to ecological, economic, and social conditions.

From the 1970s on, Immanuel Wallerstein's world system theory, which viewed local characteristic features as connected to global systems, was employed by anthropologists and ethnologists in studies that also found their way to for example *Ethnologia Europaea* (Cole 1985; Hofer 1987). In 1981, Stoklund (1981c) drew attention to the fact that shifts in the economic centres in Europe in a long temporal perspective were important when it comes to explaining cultural process in the North Atlantic, and this idea was later expanded (1991, 1992, 1996a), influenced by the works of Braudel, Wallerstein and Wolf. The idea was that in Viking times, the area was characterised by Western Nordic culture, introduced by an extremely mobile elite of peasant-trader-seamen. Even though the Norse area was rather atypical in terms of its centre formation as it did not have dense settlements, it had pronounced trade activity and was effectively held together by superior transportation technology and a written language, which allowed for communication over long distances. As a centre, the area was typical in that it was the basis for an expansion in the form of the Viking era's colonialisation of England etc. and the related collection of taxes.

Even in the High Middle Ages, the area around the North Sea represented a culturally cohesive region, but when the global economic centre of gravity shifted to the Hanseatic cities and the Netherlands in the period prior to 1600, the North Atlantic gained the status of periphery as a supplier of cheap mass products and raw materials in the form of dried fish and later knitted woollens. However, a subsistence economy continued with livestock, fishery, and wild birds, but the market economy also left its mark on this, and the area was gradually brought into the capitalist market economy via a process which turned the area into a peripheral region, and caused it to splinter into smaller areas with their own individual cultural processes of transformation. This also applies to house building and is manifested in the specific building types that had previously been explained from an evolutionist or a diffusionist perspective as relics or primitive characteristics. These were ascribed the function of representing earlier developmental stages which were preserved due to one-sided and late outside influences. In this alternative, ecological-economic interpretation from a global system perspective, it is not a question of isolated cultural elements but, on the contrary, related processes, which are the effects of a structure of exploitation. What previously appeared to be non-simultaneous – that is remains and relics – now became simultaneous effects of a co-existing system, in a perspective that allows things to be synchronically linked, but which also explains the continuity of cultural forms. Stoklund's efforts represent an interpretation which both utilises the insights from an earlier paradigm and transforms them so that they can be relevant within a new paradigm.

Læsø's Culture and Ecology – Synchronic and Diachronic Analyses

2015 sees the scheduled publication of an extensive, comprehensive publication of the studies of the Danish island of Læsø in a long historical perspective.[8] The situation in which the rich material for this publication was collected – especially the records from around 1950 – was marked by the historic-geographical method with its painstaking descriptions of work and life, tailored around traditional themes. Efforts to transgress the boundaries of the investigation, so to speak, and establish an alternative framework of interpretation, permeate the entire volume.

The Læsø studies started in 1949 with the so-called "point survey" under the auspices of the National Museum's Ethnological Survey, for which Læsø was considered particularly useful as old cultural forms appeared to have been able to survive there for a long time. In the point surveys, the data collected through lists of questions to a selection of people were to be combined with photographs, measurements and archival studies (Højrup 1962), but these surveys were carried out on the basis of the same guidelines, goals and aspects as other work done by the NEU, and were therefore far from being "total studies" of functioning wholes.

As the island of Læsø represented a "relic area", the systematic investigation of the unique culture was thought to preserve the material of value for folklife studies at large, and attention was drawn to the old-fashioned farming traditions on the island, which were thought to provide more general insights into times past. In this respect, the island's culture appeared not only to be disconnected from the world at large – this isolation being the very justification for the study – but also from the social, economic and ecological contexts. In the early stages of the investigation, Stoklund (1971b) realised that geographical isolation did not account for the preservation of earlier forms, which were instead due to a specific gendered labour division in which women were responsible for farming, resulting in the conservation of elements. A "paradigmatic rupture" in the understanding of the island, however, came with the application of an ecological perspective which led to Læsø's cultural form being understood as adaptations to specific ecological conditions, combined with a view to external economic and political conditions (1985, 1988b, forthcoming).

The ecological perspective supported the division into a series of synchronic cross-sections, each of which is characterised by different ways of exploiting both the macro-economic conditions and the natural resources of the island. From the Middle Ages to the 1500s, salt production on the island had a great economic value, but also required large amounts of fuel, and this led to a shortage of fuel, deforestation and peat-digging, and later resulted in sand drifts and the destruction of the ecological stability of the island. Both (external) economic and (internal) ecological conditions put an end to salt production, which was replaced from the end of the 1500s to around 1700 by boat trade in Norway, whereby farming products were exchanged for timber from trade ports in the Oslo fjord and the Bohuslän coast (now Swedish west coast), which was traded all over Denmark. Following an economic, ecological and demographic crisis, there was a period from the second half of the 1700s when the male part of the population was mainly hired in a growing international trade fleet, and the ecological system found a balance via heath farming. Back on the island, the increased international trade and shipping also meant increased opportunities to earn money from strandings.

In the whole era from the Middle Ages onwards, these sources of income were supplemented with subsistence economy on the island. The farms were the legal basis for the exploitation of the island's other resources – salt production, salvaging and so on – but even early on, in the timber period and perhaps also during the salt production era, farming was carried out by the female population, resulting in a gendered division of labour, which became only more pronounced during the shipping period. This was an effect of both internal ecological adaptations and external economic and political conditions (the requirement that fees be paid in salt in the Middle Ages, the demand for Norwegian timber as well as the trade regulation of agricultural products in 1500–1700, and the inclusion in the international division of labour and its requirement for qualified mariners from the 1700s onwards).

Stoklund chose to see what was earlier perceived as old traditions and retardation due to isolation (that is, as a matter of non-simultaneous relics) as simultaneous adaptations to radical changes over the past 400–500 years in the geographical environment and the external conditions for trade and industry. Thus, "old fashioned" farming on the island is not only an effect of ancient traditions and durable cultural norms for the gendered division of labour. Rather, it is an adaptation to specific local ecological and macro-historic conditions. Old cultural forms, the remains of which were documented in around 1950, can only be understood within a long historical perspective as processes in which some aspects change (adaptation to different economic conditions and changing ecological condition), whereas other aspects are more stable (the subsistence economy and the gendered division of labour).

Because *Læsø Land* is conceptualised and based in the specific context of the historical-geographical method, it very clearly carries this legacy forwards, even though, as argued here, it is further developed and thereby positions Læsø within the wider world and considers the island's position within the global economy, and takes an ecological approach to the island's history. This bears witness to Bjarne

Ill. 2: A Læsø woman in her typical clothes in front of one of the farms with its heavy seaweed roof. She is carrying the equally typical spade, used for the extensive turf cutting for fuel and manure as well as for tilling the land. The dung that one of the cows is about to drop, in one period of the history of the island represented an important form of fuel for the islanders. (Drawing: Bjarne Stoklund [Stoklund 1965])

Stoklund's translation work between two paradigms, but also points to the differences and the incommensurability between the two.

In Conclusion

This article takes the form of a return visit to some parts of Bjarne Stoklund's extensive research. It traces three different paths, which all can be said to thematise his efforts to bring relevance to insights that were gained via what can be called an earlier paradigm. The three pathways address the following questions: How can studies of cultural elements be made into studies of cultural wholes, with studies of building customs as a point of departure? How can the ecological perspective be used to prioritise the study of synchronic systems in a diachronic process? And finally, how can relic areas be transformed via a global system perspective from non-simultaneous remains to simultaneous relations? Finally, the question of how these pathways can also be used to characterise the work on Læsø's ecology and culture in a long historical perspective is dealt with.

As always, this return visit to the history of the discipline is structured on the basis of a contemporary question. And the question raised is relevant today: How do we understand the relationship between rupture and continuity, synchrony and diachrony? This is addressed on two levels: Firstly, the problem of how to understand cultural phenomena both synchronically and diachronically – as structure and transformation – and secondly, the question of how scientific insights can be made relevant across "paradigmatic ruptures". Thus, this paper revisits the problem of continuity and change on both the empirical and theoretical levels.

However, this return visit also leaves us with questions regarding the concept of culture. For Bjarne Stoklund, the concept of culture denotes a process (more than a structure) in which people continually attempt to bring order and meaning into the world (e.g. in Stoklund 1996b). In analyses of objects, this translates to an insistence upon taking the symbolic content and cultural classifications of artefacts into consideration (Stoklund 1990, 1996a).

Nonetheless, material culture is not included in this explicit concept of culture, but becomes a form of cultural expression. However, in the concrete analytical practice, there is another concept of culture in play. Bjarne Stoklund stressed many times that materiality is significant because it actually has a practical influence on people's lives. Furthermore, to a certain degree, materiality creates continuity over time because people inherit material forms that were created in different social and cultural contexts, and must interact with them. This point has been made a number of times, but as yet remains to be developed in analyses and thematisations. Thus, it is appropriate to end this return visit with the question of the relationship between materiality and continuity – and also to base our work going forwards on this question.

This return visit has illuminated the problems of translating between "paradigms". When cultural processes are viewed as totalities in transformation, diachrony tends to become sequences of synchronic cross-sections; in the cases discussed, successive ecological adaptations or successive ecotypes. This discussion of Bjarne Stoklund's published work has shown that the translation between paradigmatic assumptions is relevant, but also troublesome and always only partial.

Notes

1 I want to thank not only the reviewers and editors of *Ethnologia Europaea*, but also Annette Vasström and Orvar Löfgren as well as other contributors to this volume for their helpful and generous comments on earlier versions of this article. I would also like to thank Luci Wolfdale for her help with the translation.
2 But unlike in Sweden (Ehn & Löfgren 1996).
3 Also printed in a German version with the title "Europäische Ethnologie zwischen Skylla und Charybdis" (1972).
4 See also Karin Gustavsson's contribution to this volume, which is concerned with the question of how working with tools that require collaboration is a way of founding shared norms and knowledge.
5 See also Frida Hastrup's article in this volume.
6 Thomas Kuhn presents these considerations in his 1969 postscript to the book *The Structure of Scientific Revolutions*, which was first published in 1962.
7 *Huset og skoven* translates to The House and the Forest (Stoklund 1980a).

8 The manuscript, entitled *Læsø Land*, was left almost completed by Stoklund, and will be published by Museum Tusculanum, Copenhagen, with Marie Stoklund, Anders Møller and myself as editors.

References

Cole, John W. 1985: Culture and Economy in Peripheral Europe. *Ethnologia Europaea* XV, 3–26.

Daun, Åke 2003: *Med rörligt sökarljus: Den nya etnologins framväxt under 1960- och 1970-talen*. Stockholm: Symposion.

Ehn, Billy & Orvar Löfgren 1996: *Vardagslivets etnologi: Reflektioner kring en kulturvetenskap*. Stockholm: Natur och Kultur.

Henningsen, Peter 2002: Vejen til Thrinakria: Samtale med Bjarne Stoklund om europæisk etnologi i fortid og nutid. *Fortid og nutid* 4, 306–321.

Hofer, Tamás 1987: Agro-towns in Peripheral Europe: The Case of the Great Hungarian Plain. *Ethnologia Europaea* XVII, 69–95.

Højrup, Ole 1962: Etnologiske undersøgelser. *Budstikken. Årbog for Dansk Folkemuseum og Frilandsmuseet*. Copenhagen.

Kaschuba, Wolfgang 1999: *Einführung in die Europäische Ethnologie*. München: Verlag C.H. Beck.

Kuhn, Thomas S. (1962)1996: *The Structure of Scientific Revolutions*. Third Edition. Chicago: University of Chicago Press.

Löfgren, Orvar 1996: Linking the Local, the National and the Global: Past and Present Trends in European Ethnology. *Ethnologia Europaea* 26, 157–168.

Sandberg, Marie 2012: Unpublished Interview with Bjarne Stoklund. University of Copenhagen, December 12.

Stoklund, Bjarne 1957: Suler og stolper. *Skalk* 4, 18–27.

Stoklund, Bjarne 1959: *Truegården*. Copenhagen: Gyldendal.

Stoklund, Bjarne 1960: Kalvehavehuset: Et sydsjællandsk landhåndværkerhus på Frilandsmuseet. *Budstikken. Årbog for Dansk Folkemuseum og Frilandsmuseet*, pp. 67–90.

Stoklund, Bjarne 1961: Loftsboden fra Småland. *Budstikken. Årbog for Dansk Folkemuseum og Frilandsmuseet*, pp. 7–30.

Stoklund, Bjarne 1963: Den færøske Hjallur. *Budstikken. Årbog for Dansk Folkemuseum og Frilandsmuseet*, pp. 32–62.

Stoklund, Bjarne 1965: Deres bedste brænde. *Skalk* 6, 8–11.

Stoklund, Bjarne 1968: Mehrberuflichkeit und Gesellschaftstruktur auf einer dänischen Insel. In: Reinhard Peesch & Wolfgang Rudolph (eds.), *Kolloqvium Balticum Ethnographicum 1966*. Veröffentlichungen des Instituts für Deutsche Volkskunde. Bd. 46, pp. 131–136.

Stoklund, Bjarne 1969a: *Gården fra Lønnestak*. Copenhagen: Nationalmuseet.

Stoklund, Bjarne 1969b: *Bondegård og byggeskik*. Dansk historisk Fællesforenings Håndbøger. Copenhagen: D.H.F.

Stoklund, Bjarne 1971a: Europæisk etnologi mellem Skylla og Charybdis. *Fortid og Nutid* XXIV, 633–676.

Stoklund, Bjarne 1971b: Økologisk tilpasning til et dansk øsamfund. *Nord-Nytt* 3, 35–42.

Stoklund, Bjarne 1974: Das färöische Haus und die Wohnkultur Nordwesteuropas. *Ethnologia Europaea* VII, 193–222.

Stoklund, Bjarne 1976: Ecological Succession: Reflections on the Relations between Man and Environment in Pre-Industrial Denmark. *Ethnologia Scandinavica* 7, 84–99.

Stoklund, Bjarne 1979a: Etnologiske lokalstudier. *Fortid og Nutid* XXVIII, 26–34.

Stoklund, Bjarne 1979b: Europæisk etnologi. *Københavns Universitet 1479–1979* XI, 87–120.

Stoklund, Bjarne 1980a: *Huset og skoven: Et sjællandsk husmandshus og dets beboere gennem 300 år*. Højbjerg: Wormianum.

Stoklund, Bjarne 1980b: Houses and Cultures in the North Atlantic Isles: Three Models of Interpretation. *Ethnologia Scandinavica* 11, 113–132.

Stoklund, Bjarne 1981a: To danske kulturhistorikere i grænselandet mellem historie og antropologi. *Folk og Kultur. Årbog for dansk etnologi og folkloristik*, pp. 55–72.

Stoklund, Bjarne 1981b: Historisk Antropologi på Schæffergården. *IEF Information*. Institut for europæisk folkelivsforskning, no. 18.

Stoklund, Bjarne 1981c: Tre modeler for studiet af vestnordisk byggeskik. In: Bjørn Myhre et al. (eds.), *Vestnordisk byggeskikk gjennom to tusen år*. Stavanger: Arkeologisk Museum, pp. 15–30.

Stoklund, Bjarne 1985: Economy, Work, and Social Roles: Continuity and Change in the Danish Island Community of Læsø ca. 1200–1900. *Ethnologia Europaea* XV, 129–163.

Stoklund, Bjarne 1987: *Hvad er kulturhistorie? Troels-Lund og den kulturhistoriske strid i Tyskland i 1880'erne*. IEF Arbejdspapir 2. Institut for Europæisk Folkelivsforskning, Lyngby.

Stoklund, Bjarne 1988a: Was ist Kulturgeschichte? Troels-Lund und die kulturgeschichtliche Meinungsstreit in Deutschland in den 1880er Jahren. In: Nils-Arvid Bringéus, Uwe Meiners & Ruth-E. Mohrmann (eds.), *Wandel der Volkskultur in Europa: Festschrift für Günter Wiegelmann zum 60. Geburtstag*. Münster: Coppenrath, pp. 3–16.

Stoklund, Bjarne 1988b: *Arbejde og kønsroller på Læsø o. 1200–1900*. Læsø: Læsø Museum.

Stoklund, Bjarne 1990: Ethnological Interpretation of Implements: The Hayrake as an Example. *Ethnologia Europaea* XX, 5–14.

Stoklund, Bjarne 1991: Fra center til periferi: Hovedlinjer i den nordatlantiske kulturudvikling fra middelalder til nyere tid. In: Jóan Pauli Joensen et al. (ed), *Nordatlantiske foredrag*. Tórshavn: Annales Societatis Scientiarum Færoensis. Supplementum 15, pp. 54–62.

Stoklund, Bjarne 1992: From Centre to Periphery: Main Lines of North Atlantic Cultural Development from Medieval to Modern Times. *Ethnologia Europaea* 22:1, 51–65.

Stoklund, Bjarne 1996a: *Det færøske hus i kulturhistorisk belysning: Selskabet til udgivelse af færøske kildeskrifter og studier*. Færoensia 14. Copenhagen: C.A. Reitzel.

Stoklund, Bjarne 1996b: Etnologi. In: *Den store Danske Encyclopædi: Danmarks Nationalleksikon*. Vol. 6, pp. 56–57.

Stoklund, Bjarne 1998: Bønder og binæringer: Bondens mange næringer. Bol og By. *Landbohistorisk tidsskrift* 2, 8–47.

Stoklund, Bjarne 2000: *Bondefiskere og strandsiddere: Studier over de store sæsonfiskerier 1350–1600*. Copenhagen: Landbohistorisk Selskab.

Stoklund, Bjarne 2003a: *Tingenes kulturhistorie: Etnologiske studier i den materielle kultur*. Etnologiske studier. Copenhagen: Museum Tusculanum Press.

Stoklund, Bjarne 2003b: Kulturgrænser og økotyper. In: Inge Adriansen & P.O. Christiansen (ed.), *Forskellige mennesker? Dansk Folkemindesamling og Forlaget Skippershoved*. Ebeltoft, pp. 15–37.

Stoklund, Bjarne 2006: Bygder, aktivitetsfelter og økotyper: Etnologien og de regionale variationer. In: P. Grau Møller & Mette Svart Kristiansen (eds), *Bygder: Regionale variationer i det danske landbrug fra jernalder til 2000*. Auning: Landbohistorisk Selskab, pp. 25–39.

Stoklund, Bjarne 2010: Private noter og bemærkninger: Svend Jespersen og den etnologiske faghistorie. Unpublished manuscript.

Stoklund, Bjarne (forthcoming): *Læsø Land: Økologi og kultur i et øsamfund 1550–1900*. Copenhagen: Museum Tusculanum Press.

Wiegelmann, Günther, Mathias Zender & Gerhard Heilfurth 1977: *Volkskunde: Eine Einführung*. Berlin: E. Schmidt Verlag.

Signe Mellemgaard, Ph.D., is associate professor in the Department of Ethnology, The Saxo-Institute, University of Copenhagen. Among other things, she publishes research on the history and methodology of ethnology.
(signem@hum.ku.dk)

COMMENTS

HAUNTED PLACES

Valdimar Tr. Hafstein

"On n'habite que des lieus hantés," Michel de Certeau (1980: 196) noted in a work I often find reasons to revisit. It is one of the more inspiring attempts from the last quarter of the twentieth century to reinvent ethnology and the study of everyday life: "Haunted places are the only ones people can live in" (1984: 108). Michel de Certeau's oft-quoted dictum came to mind more than once as I read the articles in this special issue on *Revisiting Ethnologia Europaea*. As Marie Sandberg explains in her introduction, revisiting may mean "to visit again, return, reexamine, revise, recycle, or even retire." In the context of the present issue, however, the use of the term refers primarily to considering something again from a perspective altered by the passage of time. But revisiting also refers to coming back. And sure enough, the revenant comes back to visit the living. If nothing else, his visit makes them consider things again from a different perspective. Reading the contributions to this special issue, both senses of the verb ring true.

The guiding concept of revisiting is thus a rich one and the authors put it to many interesting uses: from bringing long dead Norwegians into contemporary conversations on fieldwork, collaborative research, and dialogic knowledge production (Hastrup) to waking up the ghost of the once mighty ethnocartography to contend with the highly current practice of controversy mapping from science and technology studies (STS) (Munk & Elgaard Jensen). These revisits presuppose in every case, however, that there is a relevant past to revisit and a disciplinary context in which such time travel makes sense, with the journal as its vehicle. In turn, revisits such as these, in their recurrence, perform the discipline: they give it (an air of) substance and continuity; they trace its boundaries and reaffirm its difference, even if the terms in which they do so change slightly (or tremendously) over time. They are among our more interesting border practices (to borrow a term from Fredrik Nilsson's article in this issue). They instantiate our spectral imaginations.

Revisiting follows an earlier departure. In European ethnology, the revisit is the counterpart to the farewell: the "Abschied vom Volksleben" of the 1960s and 70s. That this is the case is very much in evidence in the authors' contributions to this issue: contemporary ethnology can here be seen reaching back across the "new ethnology" of the last forty years to the "old ethnology" of the early and mid-twentieth century, sometimes directly, as in Karin Gustavsson's "Returning to the Archive", and in other cases by way of mediators, as in Signe Mellemgaard's article on Bjarne Stoklund's "translation work between two incommensurable paradigms" (Mellemgaard, this issue). Bringing old debates and arguments back into the present to confront current challenges begs the question of who is visiting whom: are we visiting our disciplinary ancestors or are they visiting us?

"Such visits can take many shapes and forms," the editor states matter-of-factly, as if introducing a collection of ghost stories. And in one sense, that is exactly what she is doing. This issue reveals European ethnology as a haunted ground, its ghosts lurking in the library, in the dusty pages of old journals and in books that the authors read in their student days, but also hiding in the nooks and crannies of concepts, ways of doing, and in deep-seated attitudes and assumptions, as the authors reveal in their respective contributions. Reading the special issue from front cover to back cover, one is struck by the time depth of ethnological practice and perspectives; the field is, to quote Michel de Certeau once more, "haunted by many different sprites hidden there in silence, spirits one can 'invoke' or not" (1984: 108; "hanté par des esprits multiples, tapis là en silence et qu'on peut 'évoquer' ou non," 1980: 196). This issue invokes them.

In addition to departments, societies, congresses, and journals, one of the hallmarks of a scholarly discipline is surely a temporality in argumentation; a mode of writing, analyzing, and arguing that revisits and brings into the present previous writings, analyses, and arguments. Through the very act of revisiting, they are brought into the same conversation-writ-large and the contours of that conversation are thus defined.

Another way to put this is to say that a discipline is a haunted place; the revenants help form the discipline, or better yet, turning from the noun to the verb, the dead discipline the writings of the living, who summon them precisely for that task. Their invocation adds a dimension to topical questions, namely depth of the temporal kind. It corrupts current theories with history; it disrupts new orthodoxies by stirring up old heterodoxies.

There is a notable difference, however, between the ghosts who discipline the ethnologist and those who discipline, for example, her neighbor from sociology. The haunting that makes sociology inhabitable comes in the guise of familiar names and faces: the specters of Marx and Durkheim and Weber, to name some of the more famous revenants. Rereading them and writing yet another exegesis of their work seems as common and ordinary in sociology as one imagines that going to a séance must have been in Victorian London. Ethnologists seem less often to be visited by individual, named ghosts; the rather exceptional nature of the present issue of *Ethnologia Europaea* is a testament to this. After all, how often do we actually revisit the writings even of someone like Sigurd Erixon, the major player in mid-twentieth century European ethnology?

To be sure, as Tine Damsholt and Astrid Pernille Jespersen make evident in their article on "Innovation, Resistance or Tinkering", ethnology is a haunted ground. Its haunting, however, is less individualized, more anonymous. It takes the form of disciplinary tradition, apparent in a special kind of sensibility, a way of doing, and in more or less implicit assumptions, perpetuated in part through conceptual kits (regardless even of changing terminologies). Another way to put it is that ethnology's ghosts are less likely to be invoked through the author function than those of some neighboring disciplines; one might say that the subject of ethnology resembles in this regard its objects of study. The time-depth and longue durée of ethnological practices and perspectives reflect to some extent "the inertness and resistance of everyday life" (Damsholt & Jespersen, this issue) that the ethnological toolkit helps to pry apart and hold up for inspection.

But to be honest, the anonymity of ethnology's ghosts may be indicative of something else as well: that compared to some of its neighbors in the humanities and social sciences, ethnology is fairly undisciplined. Its disciplinary unity is not as coherent and confident as that of its more securely institutionalized neighbors. I suggested above that a certain temporality in argumentation is characteristic of a unified discipline. Taking a note from Heidegger, one might take that argument a step further and maintain that the unity of a discipline, its existence and identity, is grounded in temporality. The past (or, in Heidegger's terms, *Gewesenheit*, having-been-ness) is projected out of a future toward which our actions in the present aspire and with reference to which they matter and make sense ([1953]1996: 299–304; [1975]1988: 265). For the sake of argument, let us read Heidegger's "Being" in the sense of being a discipline (I will be the first to admit that this is an unorthodox reading, but for present purposes I find it an interesting one). We might then say, following Heidegger, that being a discipline involves making analyses and arguments in the present that aspire to a future in which we better understand the discipline's objects, and that out of that future we project a disciplinary past, on which we rely or from which we take distance, while always recognizing it as our own. Seen through this lens, our ethnological having-been-ness, our disciplinary past, is less palpable and not as well defined as that of some neighboring disciplines. That is not for a lack of it; there is more than enough to go around. Rather, if the past is projected out of a future to which our present actions aspire, I would suggest that perhaps this future is not as well conceived of as it might be. To some extent, this may be explained by the partial and differential institutionalization of the field, with its many names and identities. But part of the reason surely lies with us, its practitioners.

The depth of the discipline's temporality is of course relative, depending to what we compare it. I have drawn a comparison to sociology, but a very different picture emerges if one compares ethnology instead to recent formations like cultural studies or STS. While these are sometimes content to present themselves as interdisciplinary, its practitioners also grapple with projecting a disciplinary past out of a future to which they aspire. To that end, they summon ghosts whose historical relation to the disciplines they are awakened to uphold is tenuous at best. In this issue, Anders Kristian Munk and Torben Elgaard Jensen note that STS/actor-network theory (ANT) in the past couple of decades has been building a "gallery of forefathers" that includes William James, John Dewey, and Gabriel Tarde. Taken together, these "possible inspirations and forerunners (...) might define ANT as part of a specific tradition in the humanities and social sciences" (Munk & Jensen, this issue). The example makes clear that as far as scholarly disciplines are concerned, Heidegger's analysis of temporality is spot on: the future comes first, and the past projects from it. What STS may have been is a function of what it might become. Such temporalization is at the heart of the disciplinarization of knowledge, or the formation and reformation of scholarly disciplines.

Speaking for myself, I find it interesting to belong to a discipline with an overabundance of ghosts, a discipline haunted by a rich and varied and not always exemplary past, one characterized by "an uncanniness of the already there", to borrow another phrase from Michel de Certeau (de Certeau, Giard & Mayol [1994]1998: 133); one that need not hunt for all of its ghosts in other fields. I hasten to add that I say this not out of purism or prudishness, both of which I think would be misplaced; ethnology's intellectual promiscuity is one of its great virtues. There is nothing wrong with summoning ghosts from other times and places, but to my mind it is most interesting to summon them into a house that is already haunted – our house. To end where we began, "haunted places are the only ones people can live in."

References
de Certeau, Michel 1980: *Arts de faire: L'invention du quotidien 1*. Paris: Union générale d'éditions.
de Certeau, Michel 1984: *The Practice of Everyday Life*. Translated by Steven Rendall. Berkeley: University of California Press.
de Certeau, Michel, Luce Giard & Pierre Mayol 1994: *Habiter, cuisiner: L'invention du quotidien 2*. 2nd ed. Paris: Gallimard.
de Certeau, Michel, Luce Giard & Pierre Mayol 1998: *The Practice of Everyday Life. Vol II: Living and Cooking*. Translated by Timothy J. Tomasik. Berkeley: University of California Press.
Heidegger, Martin (1975)1988: *The Basic Problems of Phenomenology*. Translated by Albert Hofstadter. Bloomington: Indiana University Press.
Heidegger, Martin (1953)1996: *Being and Time: A Translation of Sein und Zeit*. Translated by Joan Stambaugh. Albany: State University of New York Press.

Valdimar Tr. Hafstein is an associate professor in the Department of Folkloristics/Ethnology at the University of Iceland. His research interests range from cultural heritage to copyright and from the body to surveillance, as well as the histories of knowledge in ethnology and folklore studies. Since 2013, he serves as the president of SIEF, the International Society for Ethnology and Folklore. He is currently a visiting researcher in the Department of Conservation at the University of Gothenburg and a KNAW visiting professor at the Meertens Institute in Amsterdam.
(vth@hi.is)

AT THE ETHNOLOGISTS' BALL
Changing an Academic Habitus

Orvar Löfgren

Revisiting – what does that mean? What are we able to recognise when we travel back to earlier periods. What seems familiar, alien or exotic? And why should we bother to revisit?

Some disciplines have developed a firm tradition of revisiting – like sociology, where a canon of classics exists, and founding fathers such as Durkheim, Simmel or Weber are constantly being rediscovered. This is hardly the case in European ethnology; there is no canon of "must read" classics. The idea of rupture, of irreversible breaks with the past, seems more common here. Still, I like the idea of revisiting as opposed to writing yet another disciplinary history. Revisiting, to me, brings forward the idea of a dialogue with the past.

Reading these articles, I am struck by the fact that they deal with an often understudied aspect of academic life. Discussions of the history of research often tend to focus on paradigm shifts in theories and methods, the making and unmaking of new "turns" in research, and less on the everyday habitus of actually doing research and being an academic. In a Bourdieuan sense, these papers present us with insights into such everyday workings, the frequently silent knowledge surrounding "the way we do research here." It is a kind of disciplinary habitus, a mundane undercurrent of well-established routines that have to do with how to structure a paper, how to search for materials and create one's own mini-archive in the office, but also with learning to ignore and overlook.

The articles tell us how different generations of ethnologists have acquired research skills. These ethnologists have learned to navigate in the field, in archives and later on the Internet; they can judge a book by holding it in their hands, or quickly grasp "the gist of the matter" in a given situation. They have learned what is interesting or uninteresting, important or not. Such mundane but crucial competences are rarely explored in studies of academic life. Most studies of tacit knowledge and non-verbal academic learning have focused on the laboratory experiences of the natural sciences. How do you acquire what is sometimes called "lab fingers": learning to work quickly and efficiently but also innovatively in a given laboratory setting (Löfgren 2014)?

On the surface, the academic everyday of an ethnologist may seem less material, but as is shown here this is hardly the case. Rolls of maps, boxes of excerpts, filing cabinets, photos and styles of doing fieldwork do something to lofty theories. In their collection, *Inventive Methods*, Celia Lury and Nina Wakeford emphasise the often overlooked dimensions of "the materiality and tingishness" of methods. By using the concept of "devices" – from lists and screens to photo-images and tape recorders – they explore the surprising ways in which methods and objects are related and constitute each other (Lury & Wakeford 2012). The authors here force us to reflect on how we can become aware of such relations and mundane practices, which often rest more in the body than the conscious mind. Many of these practices have slowly become invisible over time, and are no longer seen as parts of the theoretical and methodological baggage scholars carry with them. It is an acquired knowledge, working as reflexes rather than conscious actions. The fact that they are often seen as personal habits, or are just taken for granted and not problematised, also means that they may carry hidden charges of power and authority.

The examples in this issue are mainly from Scandinavia and although there has sometimes been talk of a Scandinavian style of doing ethnology, there are also striking and interesting local differences between national settings as well as between different universities. If we look at Europe, we can find similar differences. The phenomenologist Sarah Ahmed (2006) once asked, how does the world look from the philosopher's desk? What's on the research horizon, what seems close and noticeable, distant or alien, important or unimportant? Reading these authors, I become more interested in knowing what the world looks like from the desk of an ethnologist in Berlin, Amsterdam, Budapest, Tartu or Zagreb – whether it is today or fifty years ago.

Who Controls the Dance Floor?
In his discussions, Bourdieu tends to focus more on the stubborn reproduction of the acquired habitus of primary socialisation, rather than changes later in life. In one of his early and now classic studies, *The Bachelors' Ball* (2007), he returns to his old home village and vividly captures a scene in which an old habitus is hopelessly contrasted with a new one. He depicts a village ball in the 1960s; the bachelors have walked from their outlying farms in order to take part, but they end up lining the wall, hopelessly out of place. Not only can they not dance, but their clothes, their clumsy body language and their ways of talking set them apart from the younger ones who take to the dance floor already self-assured in mastering the habitus of the modern world and its popular culture.

Bourdieu's text comes to mind here. I remember an ethnologists' ball in the 1960s, a Christmas party at the *Nordiska museet* (the Nordic Museum) in Stockholm, where older and younger ethnologists were gathered. The young generation took control of the dance floor, they were ready to show off their new talents – they represented the new and modern in the discipline, while the old school lined the walls, talking with colleagues. A young woman, slightly drunk, walks up to the doyen of Swedish ethnology, Sigurd Erixon, long retired but still in a sense the old king and the Founding Father. She is in a provocative mood and asks him: "So what are you doing that is of interest to ethnologists today?" Erixon seems at a loss and begins to talk, slightly defensively, about his still ongoing atlas projects, but she cuts him short: "That's old stuff."

In the Sweden of the 1960s, there was a sharp rupture between the old and the new ethnology. I was a young student then, eavesdropping, a little embarrassed, on the exchange between Erixon and the student. At my Institute of Folklife Studies – soon to be renamed the Department of European Ethnology – the ruins of Erixon's many projects were still visible. His atlas project seemed to us students like an old ocean liner, which kept moving forward even when the engines were burned out. On the abandoned desks we found boxes of excerpts, half-finished maps and long protocols of evidence collecting dust. We never had a chance to experience the enthusiasm and the exhilarating feeling that went with the idea of a common project uniting the discipline. For us, much of the earlier knowledge was dead. We wanted to develop a new utopian project.

Many of the papers here discuss this turning point in Scandinavian ethnology, but this was not just a local thing. All over Europe the discipline was reorganised, albeit with different timetables, aims and directions. We could begin by comparing how ethnologists' balls were reorganised in different settings. What kinds of new choreographies emerged? What happened when different dance styles were confronted, and who started to line the walls and leave the dance floor to others? Some of the new styles may have been short-lived fads, or their stylish performance could hide the fact that it was the same old movements just dressed up a bit.

Reading about paradigm shifts from different corners of Europe, it is this that strikes me. Let me just give a few examples. In a volume on "Umbruchszeiten", a number of the authors discuss ethnological paradigm shifts and upheavals. Martin Scharfe (2012) scrutinises the metaphorics of "Umbruch", and different takes on ruptures, revolutions, discontinuities and turns. When and how is a shift visible and for whom? Some ruptures are only noticed first in retrospect.

The volume also makes me think of the strong national framing of paradigm shifts; there is no smooth process of globalisation here. Take Germany and Sweden, for example. The *Abschied von Volksleben* and the farewell to folklife studies occurred quite simultaneously, but with little contact. In Sweden, the influence of British and Norwegian social anthropology meant that material culture, as well as the study of "cultural elements", was out. In German *Volkskunde*, the shift had a stronger political dimension, in which the Nazi past was confronted. New theoretical ideas came much more from critical theory than from Anglo-Saxon anthropology, meaning, among other things, that a traditional cultural history approach survived better, and closer ties were maintained with the world of the museums.

The importance of the national becomes even more striking when one looks at the other German-speaking countries, where the dramatic years in the German Volkskunde of the late 1960s and early 1970s had a very slow and gradual impact (see Bendix 2012). "The quiet and late (r)evolution" is the title of Johann Verhovsek's discussion of Austrian Volkskunde. As a student in the 1980s, he read about the radical transformations and conflicts in Germany and kept asking himself: "Why don't we have a revolution, instead of only this slow and very gradual change of research" (Verhovsek 2012: 80). A similar non-dramatic and slow process of change is depicted from Switzerland (Hugger 1994).

France is a different story again (see Bromberger & Segalen 1996). Martine Segalen's study of the birth and death of a national folk museum, the Musée des Arts et Traditions Populaires in Paris, illustrates the French context and the problems that traditional folklife and folklore studies had in re-inventing themselves in a situation where new generations of ethnologists increasingly turned to the contemporary world and new theoretical approaches (Segalen 2005). The topics proper to an ethnology of France merge today with the general topics of anthropology. There was never a strong disciplinary division of labour in France between ethnologists working abroad or at home, as there was in the Scandinavian countries and Germany. It must be added that in France there is no dedicated chair for European ethnology, even though some researchers are dubbed "européanists".[1]

In Eastern Europe the big upheaval came with the crumbling of the Soviet empire. Here, there was often an invasion of mainly British and American anthropologists doing fieldwork, who sweepingly and rather patronisingly defined the local ethnologists as backward or contaminated by the politics of the past (Buchowski & Domininguez 2012; Köstlin & Niedermüller 2002).

My point is that the local dance floor – the ways in which ethnology is done – depends on an entanglement of different factors, both local and global. For an outside visitor to German Volkskunde departments in the 1980s and 1990s, this was very striking. To me it sometimes felt like a journey through Germany before unification. Many departments attended to their local profile, often in fierce dissociation from others. There was a Tübingen, a Berlin, a Münster or a Frankfurt style of dancing. (Small and proud nation-states, sometimes ruled by very strong professorial personalities.) These differences seem to have become much less marked in later years.

All over Europe, the style of doing ethnology has also been determined by the local academic division of labour. (Who, at a given time and place, is defined as a close and interesting neighbouring science, or as a dangerous competitor? What kind of job market is there for students?) The recent *Companion to the Anthropology of Europe* (Kockel, Nic Craith & Frykman 2012) shows how the contemporary European research landscape has changed, in the blurring of old disciplinary boundaries, for example, between European ethnology, folklore, social anthropology and cultural studies.

Reading the contributions to this issue and looking at earlier paradigm shifts, I am, however, also reminded that the tabula rasa of the 1960s and 1970s (or 1989) maybe was not so total as it was experienced at the time. What parts of the ethnological habitus were carried on between generations?

Fieldwork as Habitus

All over Europe there are silent rooms in folklife archives with neat rows of boxes of ethnographic documentations. They are biding their time, waiting for someone to enter and start leafing through the materials, which often have not been used in decades. As Karin Gustavsson points out, they represent decades of countryside fieldwork, in attempts to salvage what was seen as a dying peasant culture. Much of this material is the result of enthusiastic fieldwork expeditions, followed by time-consuming reports. Opening these binders one might be struck by the order and aesthetics of the documentation, with its painstaking details, drawings and photos.

For younger generations of ethnologists, these materials seemed dead and those great efforts wasted. What was the use of all this? But, as several of the authors here show, this era has left important imprints on contemporary ethnology. Parts of our modern habitus were forged during these intensive fieldwork decades, from the 1920s and up to the 1960s. What does that legacy consist of?

Karin Gustavsson focuses on the craftsmanship that the pioneer decades of intensive fieldwork created. These were the years when ethnology became a discipline heavily defined by doing fieldwork, with skills that were rarely taught formally but were learned in the field. A new habitus emerged, based on exploration, improvisation and curiosity – what might be waiting around the next corner: a unique farm construction, a barn with old tools, a folk singer? Fieldwork created a brotherhood of researchers. This was a male activity, a bit of a military campaign in which one had to rough it out in ways that tended to exclude women. Women were delegated to the less heroic and visible tasks of organising the materials back home in the museums and the folklife archives. At a later stage, they became part of the fieldwork campaigns. I also think Gustavsson's focus on the role of technology is important here. What impact did the bike, the camera, the measuring tape and the sketching set have on ethnological practice?

The crisis came in the 1950s when the traditional rural culture was seen as gone, with nothing left to document or save. This was a crucial situation for ethnology. Like other fields in the humanities that had a fieldwork tradition, such as art history and cultural history, the discipline could have chosen to withdraw from the field, to become an archival science, no longer exploring a contemporary world. But by then, the fieldwork habitus seems to have been so strongly established that European ethnology was not transformed into just another historical discipline, but maintained its important asset of combining contemporary and historical studies. In a similar manner, the fieldwork habitus, with its special mindset and analytical gaze, was also used in archival study – fieldwork in the archives, as Rebecca Lennartsdotter (2011), among others, has discussed.

The meticulously gathered materials on farm buildings may appear as a dead legacy from the past (although one never knows when that will change), but the fieldwork habitus, the way of doing ethnology, is a strong legacy from the 1920s and 1930s.

These transformations of old and new paradigms are also discussed in Signe Mellemgaard's "Rupture and Continuity". Her discussion of the work of Bjarne Stoklund reminds us of the importance of bridge builders in a discipline. In retrospect, it is possible to see how important his efforts were in keeping up a dialogue between research generations – often a thankless task. We could probably identify similar brokers in other ethnological settings in Europe.

What's the Use of Maps?

In "Revisiting the Histories of Mapping", Anders Kristian Munk and Torben Elgaard Jensen in a sense take over where Gustavsson stops in their discussions of the grand comparative atlas projects that developed out of the documentations of peasant cultures – the historical-geographical paradigm from the 1930s and into the 1960s. It is both surprising and refreshing to see them discuss what was lost in the cultural revolution of the 1960s and 1970s, when new social and cultural theory vigorously attacked the old paradigm. Is there anything that can be learned from these atlas projects?

Munk and Elgaard Jensen, as well as Mellemgaard, discuss what was lost when the idea of cultural elements was abandoned for a view of culture as a system and a pattern in the 1970s, under the heavy influence of British anthropology. In those days, one had to choose – in the tough battle between two paradigms. Today we might be more open to alternating between different definitions of culture and see them as supplementary analytical tools rather than theoretical credos. In a similar manner, we might see more of a combination of qualitative and quantitative data in the future. For students of everyday life, the enormous output of Big Data provides a challenge and a possibility (see, for example, the discussion in Pantzar & Shove 2010; and Mayer-Schönberger & Cukier 2013). There are staggering amounts of knowledge on rhythms, routines and decision-making in the everyday (sometimes jealously guarded by large corporations). When do people call home on the cell phone, swipe their credit cards, or log in to the Netbank or Netflix? Facebook contains unparalleled amounts of material on everyday life (Rudder 2014). Here is a chance for ethnologists to strike up new analytic partnerships, but also to take a critical look at how Big Data is used by those who control the material.

The Magic of the Everyday

The magic of the everyday is still with us, as Damsholt and Jespersen discuss. In interdisciplinary collaborations, and in situations where ethnologists are brought in as consultants, they are expected to unravel the secrets of everyday life and make the mundane exotic and surprising. In the fast growing world of applied ethnology, it is for this skill of doing ethnographies of the everyday that ethnologists are most often hired by corporations and government agencies.

As Damsholt and Jespersen point out, "the everyday" often stands for inertia, boring routines and status quo. This becomes very striking in discussions of technological change, in which the everyday is often relegated to the role of a passive backdrop, a scene-setter, but not an active actor. There is a constant talk of how innovations, from digital media to nano-technology, will revolutionise everyday life. As ethnologists, we should turn the question around for a change. How does the everyday revolutionise new technologies? Everyday life can be seen as a machinery that drastically changes the forms, functions and futures of new media, for example. It chews and devours new technologies, some of which are spat out rapidly because they cannot be integrated into quotidian practices and needs. Others are digested, tested, adapted and changed. There is a lot of tinkering going on here, as Damsholt and Jespersen show.

We still know surprisingly little about how this machinery works. One could argue that everyday life is still the black box of ethnology. We like to market ourselves as the masters of its study, but our understanding is still piecemeal and fragmented, a thought I find comforting. There is still much to be discovered (to stay with our favourite metaphor). We live in an academic world of theoretical "turns", the material, the spatial, the affective, the practice, the sensory, the ontological... Without getting trapped in turn hunting, this search for overlooked dimensions in the study of everyday life could help us to focus more not only on "new dimensions" but on what Doreen Massey (2005) has called the throwntogetherness, and what Tim Ingold (2011) calls the entanglements, of everyday life. How do objects, people, emotions, sensibilities or activities come to co-exist?

The Mysteries of Fieldwork

Another theme of Damsholt and Jespersen's concerns researchers' relations to "the folk", that is the informants, the locals, the collaborators. They point to the two traditions, to the enlightenment of the eighteenth century, seeing the need to study the people in order to be able to understand and change their peculiar customs and stubborn traditions, to the romantic discovery of "the folk" in the early nineteenth century as the true basis for a national culture. Both these traditions came to shape ethnological praxis into the twentieth century. A strong dialogue between laymen and academic scholars had been established, networks of informants created through the folklife archives, etc. This tradition of collaborating and co-authoring was sometimes seen as a problem; a real science needs to distance itself from amateurs, but as Frida Hastrup says in her discussion of ethnography as an intensive conversation, there is also a strength in this tradition. She talks about ethnography as a conversational product, an inventive and collaborative sociality.

Both anthropologists and ethnologists have been accused of mystifying the methods of ethnography. A professor in organisational studies once remarked that the quickest way to identify an ethnological dissertation is through the fact that it usually lacks a chapter on method. Ethnography is described as a mystic skill that ethnologists acquire together with their magic "ethnological gaze", through which they discover new worlds in the everyday.

I like Hastrup's discussion of the ethnographic process as open-ended, inventive and messy, and the ways in which she revisits the fieldwork of Eilert Sundt, a nineteenth-century scholar who has many parallels in Europe. What we see here is another analytical asset, using history and earlier studies as partners in dialogue.

Finally, there is a balancing act here in any discussion about practising ethnography. There is always a risk of fetishising fieldwork as a trade secret, which cannot be turned into textbook instructions, and then, on the other side, trying to discipline it into a set of methodological procedures.

Borders

Borders are another analytical category central to much ethnological research, both past and present. As Fredrik Nilsson shows, it is a concept that has changed form and function in ethnological research. What kinds of work do borders carry out in different ethnological eras and fields? Reading Nilsson, I am struck by how culturally productive borders and boundaries are as concepts (these twin terms open up for a more flexible perspective than the single Scandinavian *gräns/grense* or German *Grenze*). Boundaries are often soft, fuzzy and porous, while borders can be sharp, based on the modern magic of the thin line.

Nilsson's empirical example of smugglers and smuggling is a good way of approaching questions of national borders. There is still much energy to be drawn from comparative historical studies here. What or who must the nation be protected from, in a given situation and at a given time in history: contraband, luxury goods, political pamphlets, illegal immigrants, drugs, or terrorist threats?

Like Karin Gustavsson, Fredrik Nilsson shows the potentials of the return of the material in ethnological research. His focus on smuggler's speedboats, fancy cars and new radio transmitters as not only icons of modernity but as ways of reorganising cross-border activities is rewarding. Moving into contemporary times, we can see the intense material investments in border surveillance and border passages, gigantic sorting out machines for goods, ideas and people. Ivaylo Ditchev, writing about travelling in the Balkans, points to how closely forms of mobility interact with social hierarchy. The Mercedes with grey-toned windows is waved across quickly by the border guards, while the battered van next in line is taken apart. Lorry drivers wait in long queues and the suitcase traders travelling by bus have to get out and line up for border inspection. At the bottom of the transport hierarchy are the illegal immigrants avoiding the checkpoint and crossing over the mountains, led by local and expensive guides (quoted in Morley 2011: 753).

Back to the Dance Floor

Ethnology and folklore are, like anthropology, very habitus-oriented disciplines, containing many, often silent agreements on "how to be a scholar" and a wide range of embodied skills. This collection has focused much on the Scandinavian experience, and especially Denmark and Sweden, but it provides a platform for further discussions. By focusing on the mundane ways of doing ethnology in different generations there are a number of dialogues with the past established in these papers. There are also constant navigation problems – the dangers of Scylla and Charybdis constantly change and it is not always the best strategy to keep to the middle road.

Reading these papers, I was struck by the importance of two choices that the discipline has encountered. In the 1950s, ethnology in Scandinavia could have turned into an archival and purely historical discipline, as the fieldwork salvage operations seemed to be finished. Ethnology might have become purely cultural history. In the 1970s, the risk was the opposite. The interest in ethnographies of the contemporary world carried the risk of ethnology abandoning its old historical interests and competences. Back then, the discipline could have turned into a study of the present, a kind of cultural sociology or anthropology. Looking back, I find it lucky that the discipline kept this twofold interest in studying the present and the past. It has created analytical strategies of using the past to problematise the present and the other way around. A historical perspective is thus never a given, but is often actively chosen as part of an analytical strategy.

A discipline like European ethnology, where one can study almost anything, is no longer held together by shared materials and knowledge, but, rather, through a set of skills and analytical approaches, and this means that the discipline has to constantly reinvent itself. And in this process, a bit of revisiting now and then is a good thing.

Note
1 I am grateful for Martine Segalen's and Monica Heintz' comments on the French situation.

References
Ahmed, S. 2006: Orientations: Toward a Queer Phenomenology. *GLG: A Journal of Lesbian and Gay Studies* 12:4, 543–574.
Bendix, R. 2012: From Volkskunde to the "Field of Many Names": Folklore Studies in German-Speaking Europe since 1945. In: R. Bendix & G. Hasan-Rokem (eds.), *A Companion to Folklore*. New York: Wiley Blackwell, pp. 364–390.
Bourdieu, P. 2007: *The Bachelors' Ball: The Crisis of Peasant Society in Bern*. Chicago: University of Chicago Press.
Bromberger, C. M. Segalen (eds.) 1996: Culture matérielle et modernité. Special issue. *Ethnologie française* 1996:1.
Buchowski, M. & V. Domininguez (eds.) 2012: Changing Flows in Anthropological Knowledge. Special issue. *Focaal* 63.
Hugger, P. 1994: Volkskunde in der Schweiz seit dem Zweiten Weltkrieg. *Österreichische Zeitschrift für Volkskunde* 97, 97–112.
Ingold, T. 2011: *Being Alive*. London: Routledge.
Kockel, U., M. Nic Craith & J. Frykman (eds.) 2012: *A Companion to the Anthropology of Europe*. London: Wiley-Blackwell.
Köstlin, K. & P. Niedermüller (eds.) 2002: *Die Wende als Wende? Orientierungen Europäischer Ethnologie nach 1989*. Wien: Inst. für Europäische Ethnologie.
Lennartsdotter, R. 2011: Notes on 'not being there': Ethnographic Excursions in Eighteenth-Century Stockholm. *Ethnologia Europaea* 41:1, 105–116.
Löfgren, O. 2014: Routinising Research: Academic Skills in Analogue and Digital Worlds. *International Journal of Social Research Methodology* 17:1, 73–86.
Lury, C. & N. Wakeford 2012: *Inventive Methods: The Happening of the Social*. London: Routledge.
Massey, D. 2005: *For Space*. London: Sage.
Mayer-Schönberger, V. & K. Cukier 2013: *Big Data: A Revolution that will Transform how we Live, Work and Think*. London: John Murray.
Morley, D. 2011: Communications and Transport: The Mobility of Information, People and Commodities. *Media, Culture & Society* 35:5, 743–759.
Pantzar, M. & E. Shove 2010: Temporal Rhythms as Outcomes of Social Practices. *Ethnologia Europaea* 40:1, 19–29.
Rudder, C. 2014: *Dataclysm: Who We Are (When We Think No One's Looking)*. New York: Random House.
Scharfe, M. 2012: Garen, gehen, gären: Zur Metaphorik des Umbruchs. In: K. Braun, C.-M. Dietrich & C. Schönholtz (eds.), *Umbruchzeiten: Epistemologie & Methodologie in Selbstreflexion*. Marburg: Förderverein der Marburger kulturwissenschaftlichen Forschung und Europäische Ethnologie e.V., pp. 10–18.
Segalen, M. 2005: *Vie d'un musée*. Paris: Stock.
Verhovsek, J. 2012: Die stille späte "(R)evolution": Auf Spurensuche nach dem "Umbruch" der Volkskunde in Österreich. In: K. Braun, C.-M. Dietrich & C. Schönholtz (eds.), *Umbruchzeiten: Epistemologie & Methodologie in Selbstreflexion*. Marburg: Förderverein der Marburger kulturwissenschaftlichen Forschung und Europäische Ethnologie e.V., pp. 79–100.

Orvar Löfgren is professor emeritus in European ethnology at Lund University, Sweden. The cultural analysis and ethnography of everyday life has been an ongoing focus in his research. Central research fields have been studies of national identity and transnational mobility, media and consumption.
(orvar.lofgren@kultur.lu.se)

FLUID CLASSICS
Ethnographic Challenges in Everyday Fields

Katharina Eisch-Angus

Ethnologia Europaea editor Marie Sandberg, in her correspondence preceding this issue, outlined an intriguing theme, to write and comment on the revisiting of "classic" ethnological research and methodology, as they might be "spurred by current challenges and questions in our scholarly field. To be sure, such visits can take many forms and shapes; be it as a way of counter-balancing recent aspirations, as drawing inspiration, as a learning experience, or in order to highlight or even abandon previous approaches and concepts."[1] On this stimulus, the authors of this volume draw, in many fascinating ways, from the approaches and material of mostly Swedish and Danish folklorists from the nineteenth century up to post-war times. To pick out some examples: They rediscover a relational rather than individualising understanding of the everyday and a knowledge of the complexity of cultural change in folklife studies (Damsholt & Jespersen), trace "classic" attempts for conciliating concepts of historical continuity with those of social, as well as scientific, change (Mellemgaard), reflect the concept of ethnography as emerging from the conversations in heterogeneous fields back onto public discussions that accompanied traditional folk research (Hastrup), and reveal the abundance of meaning in ethnological photo archives, which had been missed out by the field researchers themselves in their explanatory notes (Gustavsson).

From a German perspective it appears curious to see how Scandinavian colleagues draw this lively and affirmative, and still critical, continuity from folk-life studies into present-day European ethnology, instead of going through tedious rituals of problematising what and whom to accept as the "classics" of our discipline (and even more so of German-speaking *Volkskunde*). Yet, talking of "revisiting" suggests that we are visitors in a house which we have previously left, where we are not – or no more – at home. Beyond that, this house of past ethnology is largely painted to hold a rather wooden view of peasant and underclass life worlds, accentuating everyday inertness and resistance to change (for example in the way that Damsholt and Jespersen put it: "that the ethnological idea of everyday life's inherent inertness is a legacy of the ways in which everyday life was shaped as an object of study within political practices of improvement"). In this way we commonly assume our scientific forerunners to have worked within a rather conservative and immobile mindset, gathering data for the sake of constructing historical continuities, preserving dying cultures, or intervening into familiar everyday practice, each depending on the ideological agendas of their time. Nonetheless, all authors in this issue show both respect and creativity in their attempts to reveal the inspirational sides of folklife research by turning it upside down, viewing it from new angles and with different eyes – all based on our shared desire for more fluid, emergent ways to explore practice and meaning, and especially cultural change, within contemporary everyday fields.

However, even when traditional folklife literature does support this static image of "classic" folklore research, how can one be sure not to construct a picture of our "classics" that follows our wishes to create an opposite to our today's aspirations and that obscures yet another side of the past research of everyday life? Naturally, as ethnographers we know that we cannot look at what is our own without resuming a distanced position. Nevertheless, it is my impression that by constructing a dichotomy of "past" folk culture research and "present" everyday ethnography we again render ourselves homeless, by disconnecting ourselves from the diverse and border-crossing discursivity of our discipline, that reaches from our present stand-points, via the post-war generations of ethnographic critique, to ethnological and folklore research in its various strands before the First and the Second World Wars.

Based on these observations, my following remarks aim firstly towards loosening the juxtaposition between the "classic" and the "experimental" by exemplifying traditions of ethnological rethinking and methodological critique from the 1970s that have become "classics" in their own right. Secondly, the researchers of the past were (as we are) bound to describe their findings within the social and cultural frames of their time and are indebted to the paradigms and mindsets of their scientific environments. However, I want to argue that any understanding of everyday culture demands curiosity and a sense for the miscellaneous and the ambiguous within lived culture. They escape and contradict dominant scientific norms, whilst they charge ethnographic field research with specific qualities and challenges. Whatever the scientific results may be, folklorists and ethnographers must have a rapport with their everyday fields that allows them to engage in, and with them, against the grain of established science.

Thirdly, due to global economic and political transformation, we are subjected to rapid changes of our social and cultural worlds, which should be taken into account more distinctly as ethnographic challenges and as a new frame of reference for present ethnological rethinking and methodological reflection.

In this light I want, fourthly, to encourage not only any rethinking of ethnological traditions in their heterogeneous and discursive settings, but also suggest interdisciplinary revisits outside the box of European ethnology. These could include classics of cultural theory and methodological reflexivity that support creative processes of context- and subject-oriented, ethnographic understanding.[2]

Classics In-Between

Signe Mellemgaard, in her article on Bjarne Stoklund, emphasises the post-1968s and 1970s, with their rising social and societal consciousness, as a period of changing paradigms as well as intense reconsideration in European ethnology. To widen this scope a bit further, this is also the era of the discovery of "the subject" and the individual self, of the politicisation of the private, when traditional family and community ties were considered questionable and identities became fragmented: "Our aim is our way", to search, to engage in open-ended processes rather that in procedures with fixed results. Ideas of participation and empowerment started to dominate practical social efforts, seemingly stabile cultural systems got deconstructed. All of this had to find its echo in ethnological objectives and methodology that could grasp the everyday in its fluidity and subjectivity. Looking again at the debates in European ethnology from the 1970s into the 1990s, it appears that any reexamination of ethnographic classics was tightly linked to the need of reacting to the conditions and the changes in post-war societies and everyday cultures of the twentieth century. Beyond this, the necessity to face the involvements of the ethnographic and folklore sciences in nationalism, racism and, in the German and Austrian case, blood and soil Nazism, and the critique of the governmental and colonialist blind spots of the cultural and social anthropologies demanded a theoretical and methodological outreach towards social and political contexts of hegemony and ideology, which by no means could be kept within national and disciplinary in-groups.

If we look at the debates that were initiated at the later Institut für Empirische Kulturwissenschaft in the small university town of Tübingen from the early 1970s, Hermann Bausinger's rethinking of German *Volkskunde* resorted in a fundamental claim for contextualisation: The subjectivations and objectivations of the everyday, like material culture, everyday practices or narratives, should be carefully interpreted within the social and historical fabric of culture whilst rejecting any "narrowing fixation" (Bausinger 1980: 9) and having regard to the situational and processual conditions of a "smooth" research methodology (Bausinger 1980: 18).[3] Bausinger is deeply rooted in the discursive concerns of the 1970s and 1980s, just as Utz Jeggle with his early and persistent attention to subjectivity, emotion and memory in ethnographic research, and his calls for an empathic and self-critical reflexivity (Jeggle 1984).[4] At the same time, these (re-)affirmations of ethnographic sensitivity and curiosity in European ethnology are of unbroken – classic – relevance for today's ethnographic work. They are part of the same debates, for example, that were conducted within British cultural studies with Paul Willis, who encouraged cultural interpretation to be drawn from the social relations in ethnographic everyday fields and from the subjectivity of the researcher and the researched, from the contradictions and uncertainties of the research process, and from the ethnographer's skill "of being surprised" (Willis 1980: 90). Or think of American cultural anthropologist responses to postmodernism, like multi-sited ethnography or, in the writing culture debate, the consequential experimentation with the translation of multi-voiced everyday realities into ethnographic representation, all of which were taken up in European discussions and ethnographic practice from the 1990s. As I will point out below, the observations of "partial truths" (Clifford 1986) and "dispersed identity" (Marcus 1992: 315), of fragmented and flexibilised life-contexts that are ubiquitously interwoven with hard-to-grasp power relations have certainly not lost any of their relevance, nor have the questions of ethnographic understanding, translating and responding to the views and voices of everyday actors within today's changed life-world conditions.

All of these, and many other approaches, could be recognised as our inspirational base for a confident and creative restart of European ethnography into a new century, rooted in a self-reflexive ethnographic tradition of rethinking and adapting to changing cultural backgrounds. I say "could", as it seems that these flexible and dialogical, context- and subject-sensitive approaches to the everyday are (despite being, like especially participant observation, deeply engrained in our passed-down methodology) in the present disciplinary understanding widely left in a liminal grey-zone between an inflexible classic heritage and new responses, which are as future aspirations often introduced from outside the discipline (see Eisch 1999; Timm 2013).[5]

The Ambiguity and Multi-Perspectiveness of Everyday Culture

With their assumed difficulty to recognise, and to handle, their own diversity and critical potentials, past and present European ethnologists seem to share a defensive impulse to prove themselves as acceptable in the greater scientific world. Looking at our approaches and objectives towards everyday culture this seems hardly surprising. Ethnography as a science brings out what (as, for example, Zygmunt Bauman has impressively shown) the philosophy of modern science, in unity with progressive ideas of education and governing, attempt to eliminate – or would, at the very most, set aside safely enclosed within the arts and in literature (Bauman 1991):[6] That is to say the common and commonplace, the uncertain and ambivalent, the subjective and emotional. The everyday represents what falls between the clear-cut categories of rational cognition. Accordingly, ethnographers ask for opinions instead of reason, for subjective experience and biased memories, which they pick up in the streets and find expressed in gossip or fairy tales, urban legends or moral panics, and in the media. They enter the ambiguous worlds of superstition, or go along (critically deconstructing whatsoever) with everyday mythologies. They look with shining eyes at material objects that fall short of having any aesthetical significance or acceptable societal relevance, no matter if it is peasants' tools or industrial mass products: The ethnographic objectives of everyday culture populate the shady zones between the realms of hegemony and resilience, the "third spaces" of changing perspectives and oscillating meanings. "Normal science does not seek out the unpredictable," writes Signe Mellemgaard; "(...) in periods when normal science predominates, science is largely unconcerned with the general public and research is almost exclusively addressed to academics from within the same field. However, folklife research has always held the public's interest (...)." Contemporary ethnographers, just as folklorists, are tied into this irritating, ambivalent insignificance, they love these fields or they lose them by trying to screw them down, to fixate them, in normative scientific black and white categories. And what is worst: It is our own pre-scientific, fleeting and ordinary everyday lives that we are constantly thrown back at. There are no exotic worlds to be deciphered, no monographs to be written in (or against) Malinowski's classic tracks. Taking it strictly, how could European ethnology, as it moves about on the warped grounds of everyday life and far off from any lasting foundations, with ever-changing backgrounds and unreliably subjective personnel, ever produce anything classic?

I would like to take up Tine Damsholt's and Astrid Jespersen's observation "that there is an inherent dilemma or paradox entangled with the ethnological study of everyday life," but shift it from an "entanglement of investigation and intervention" towards an even more fundamental paradox of ethnography: Being distant researchers and observers on the one hand, ethnographers are, on the other hand, and quite un-scientifically, themselves parts of their own fields. Scientific reflexivity finds itself enmeshed into the immanent reflexivity of the everyday, as the ethnographic objects of investigation are subjects with their own awareness of the web of culture and its strands of meaning. It is the reflexive movement between observation and participation that is at the core of the ethnography of the everyday. Any ethnographic understanding (even when looking at material objects) is derived from this dialogue between the researcher and the researched other, with their emotions, experience and cultural symbolisms. It emerges from this movement between subjectivities, and is shaped through difference and heterogeneity, whilst being embedded into shared everyday contexts.

Instead of risking that the ethnographer's subjective bias, over-identification or fears, distort ethnographic research results, the Zürich school of ethnopsychoanalysis (with Fritz Morgenthaler, Paul Parin and Goldy Parin-Matthèy in its first generation) has, from the 1950s on, utilised the methods of psychoanalysis: the attitude of evenly suspended attention and of "listening with the third ear" – which seems so close to the sensitivity of participant observation – and the projective mechanism of transference and counter-transference, that allows images, scenes and stories to evolve and to be interpreted within an associative dialogue between the analyst/researcher and the patient/researched.

Especially Maya Nadig and Mario Erdheim have opened up this method for (European) ethnologists who are not trained in psychoanalysis (Nadig 1986; Nadig & Erdheim 1991). By no means does ethnopsychoanalysis impress any theoretical dogmas on our fields and interpretation, nor does it act therapeutically. Instead, notes and texts from observations and encounters in the field are read as expressions of their cultural fabric of meaning. They are interwoven with associations, emotions and irritations that are individual and subjective, and that are, just as inevitably, linked to varying aspects of the researched culture. They are brought out through the research dialogues of fieldwork, in an emergent process that is never complete, that depends on situative encounters as well as the subjectivities and different cultural backgrounds of all involved. However, they are never contingent, but follow the social and cultural codes of the everyday.

Over-Powered Fluidity

I want to point out this seemingly peripheral method because I believe that a subject-sensitive approach that follows fluid signification processes in everyday culture could be suitable to get a grip on the vast cultural changes that we witness in our present time under late capitalist and neoliberal conditions. An essential aspect of ethno-psychoanalytical approaches is their sensitivity to power structures that culture tends to blind out as taboos, but are held in anxieties or rituals and can be reexperienced and interpreted as they are mirrored within field research relationships. Increasingly, power cannot be described only in dichotomies of up and down, but it creeps into every private pocket of everyday life. Foucault, and subsequently the various branches of governmentality studies, have alerted us to intensified power regimes that exploit the individual subjectivities of the everyday by inscribing themselves into private relations and self-awareness, shaping notions of self-responsibility and morals whilst constantly switching roles and perspectives. However, a Foucaultian approach denies the individuals' voices and responses to be heard, and it does not lend itself to a bottom-up perspective that could give insight into the everyday milieus that are targeted by new power regimes.

I believe that these changes, which were noted already in the 1970s by Foucault and also Richard Sennett (Sennett 1974) and have become increasingly manifest from the late 1990s, provide a distinctive chance, as well as an important challenge, for ethnographic studies of the everyday. However, it feels like a puzzling occurrence that what European ethnologists recognise as the key principles and strengths, and especially the paradigms from the 1970s, seems to become compromised and turned against themselves. For example, as culturally and socially engaged researchers, we might wish for a wider visibility of the marginalised and their needs in society, and now find this positive attentiveness turned into ever more sophisticated public vigilance and control. Or, we work towards more ethical consciousness concerning our personal responsibilities and the empowerment of people and communities, and feed backhandedly into neoliberal regimes of self-government. We take pride in individual authenticity only to discover that self-realisation has become an ideology that has widely replaced social solidarity. In these ways, the recognition of the fluid contexts of everyday culture might well translate into the pressures of flexibility, whilst self-awareness and self-reflectivity (as Bourdieu has warned us) can tilt into a narcissistic, omnipotent ego, which haunts itself as well as others with the duty to constantly optimise his or her potentials (Bourdieu 1993). We all know these effects from our own post-Bologna university contexts, where we find ourselves caught in constant assessing, appraising, auditing, evaluating, reviewing and ranking of each other and thus, with best intentions of open and non-hierarchical cooperation, get inescapably entangled in the multiplication of academic power pressure and fears of failure, and the subjectivation of competition.

Reconnecting to Structure

Of course, in Bourdieu's, as well as in Nadig's and Erdheim's sense, all of this takes its effect also on the relationships with our fields (Bourdieu 1993; Nadig & Erdheim 1984). Therefore, a critical rethinking of our own position as ethnographers becomes even more pressing, in order to avoid to fall for the academic blind spots of our own power contexts once again, and to construct ourselves as superior researchers and authors simply by trying to perform within scientific norms and expectations.

I would like to argue for a collective recollection of the specific qualities of the ethnography of everyday lives that have been passed over from classic folklife and everyday research, and that have been repeatedly rediscussed and renegotiated within the history of our discipline. These potentials of ethnography result from an inevitable conflict between scientific norms and the inherent heterogeneity and ambiguity of everyday fields, which have led to a creative polarity in European ethnology: On the one hand we can draw from a flexible methodology that enables us to decode (and de-mythologise) the practices and symbolisms of everyday culture following situative and polyvalent contexts and changing social and economic backgrounds. In fieldwork we can create cultural understanding through the dialogic movement between reflexive distance and empathy (as it is expressed in the seemingly paradoxical methodology of participant observation). Whilst on the other hand, especially in these times of fluid or fragmented life worlds, cultural research needs the folklorists' ability to stabilise and root ethnographic knowledge, to ground it in the lived experience and collective memories of the everyday actors, and to locate it in tradition and history.

It cannot be a solution that we methodologically only stew in our own juice (and some of the old folklorists might have done a bit too much of that). Our ethnographic involvement into everyday contexts can bring forward a sensitivity for the significance of the marginal and subjective, and a critical view for changing life worlds. However, stating fragmentation on an everyday level needs a background idea of what belongs together, of contexts and interrelations – meaning a way of recognising structures, no matter in which fluid, interchangeable and processual ways they might be realised in the field. It seems that following postmodern critique and neoliberal turbulence, ethnographic studies have now difficulties to raise themselves onto analytical and reflective levels, at least without subsequently disconnecting their empathic and associative insights and conversational findings from interpretation.

Therefore, I add – maybe in the way of a postscript – another recommendation, to take a look into the classics of cultural theory which can, from outside of our discipline, supplement the potentials of ethnography in methodological and especially interpretative and analytical terms. I have already mentioned psychoanalysis that provides us with a long-standing (however, in cultural science and ethnology rather hidden) legacy of associative cultural reflection.

A very similar approach of emergent signification, following everyday sign contexts, is offered by cultural semiotics, and especially by the pragmatic concept of the infinite triadic process of semiosis as it was first described by Charles S. Peirce (1839–1914). Irene Portis-Winner has referred to Peirce's semiotic process of one sign defining another associatively in relation to its situative, practical and symbolical contexts of everyday perception and communication, as "an open construct that permits the widest kinds of interpretations" (Portis-Winner 2006: 347). Furthermore, the complex analytical body of grounded theory is built on Peirce's pragmatism. But, although we are familiar with the methodical mechanism of triangulation, present ethnography seems rarely to get itself into this fluid and context-sensitive way of analysis on a more theoretical base.

Quite complementary, creative conceptualisations of culture, mythology and memory are offered by the Tartu-Moscow School of Semiotics and especially by its founder Yuri M. Lotman (1922–1993), who is still to be discovered for European ethnology from behind the former Iron Curtain (see Lotman 1977, 1990; Schönle 2006). Drawing from Russian literature, but also from folk narratives and from the spatial or discursive sign processes of the everyday, Lotman offers an exceptional approach to the anthropology of borders (Eisch 1996). He correlates geographical and ideological or mythological borderlines, cultural peripheries as well as narrative plots as expressions of a dynamic anthropological mechanism to strive for order and closure by drawing borders and differential divisions, and to cross them towards dialogue and change. In this way Lotman offers a holistic analytical concept to understand, for example, practices or discourses along geographical borderlines, and to integrate them into a more overarching anthropological theory (see Fredrik Nilsson in this volume). Lotman's "semiosphere", as the all-including realm of cultural codes and "texts", is fundamentally heterogeneous and changeable, a concept that nonetheless allows for self-protecting or hegemonial needs to create continuity, history and memory. Within this theoretical body the border, as a metalinguistic term, offers itself as an ever ambiguous, peripheral third space where attempts for dialogue and translation, as well as for demarcation and distinction, are constantly creating new cultural languages and constellations.

In that way, culture cannot exist at all as long as it is not on the move – and ethnography has, as ever, the best potentials to move along with it.

Notes
1 E-mail by Marie Sandberg to the commentators of this issue of *Ethnologia Europaea*, August 17, 2014.
2 Many thanks to Marion Hamm and Jochen Bonz for ongoing discussion and shared text work that inspired many of the following considerations, as well as to the contributors to the symposium "Subjektorientiertes Deuten. Kontext und Praxis der ethnografischen Feld-

forschungssupervision" ("Subject-Oriented Interpretation. Context and Practice of Ethnographic Field Research Supervision") in Bremen, June 20–21, 2014.
3 German: "anschmiegsam".
4 Quite in accordance with Bjarne Stoklund (see Signe Mellemgaard in this volume) the Tübingen school would strictly argue for the historical contextualisation of contemporary cultural research, furthermore they would suggest to complement a historical perspective with the recognition of collective and biographical memory and the deconstruction of mythological imageries of history.
5 Elisabeth Timm has only recently pointed out how in the context of practice and emergence theory the ethnographic wheel seems to be reinvented, whilst subject-sensitive ethnographic reflexivity is overturned by high-handed novelty claims (Timm 2013).
6 Marion Hamm points out how within the cultural sciences as late as in the 1960s, and after decades of ethnological work on folklife culture, "Raymond Williams, one of the father figures of cultural studies, changed the notion of culture by inserting the everyday" (Hamm 2008: 7).

References

Bauman, Zygmunt 1991: *Modernity and Ambivalence*. Cambridge: Polity Press.
Bausinger, Hermann 1980: Zur Spezifik volkskundlicher Arbeit. *Zeitschrift für Volkskunde* 76:1, 1–21.
Bourdieu, Pierre 1993: Narzißtische Reflexivität und wissenschaftliche Reflexivität. In: Eberhard Berg & Martin Fuchs (eds.), *Kultur, soziale Praxis, Text: Die Krise der ethnografischen Repräsentation*. Frankfurt a.M.: Suhrkamp, pp. 365–374.
Clifford, James 1986: Introduction: Partial Truths. In: James Clifford & George E. Marcus (eds.), *Writing Culture: The Poetics and Politics of Ethnography*. Berkeley, Los Angeles; London: University of California Press, pp. 1–26.
Eisch, Katharina 1996: *Grenze: Eine Ethnographie des bayerisch-böhmischen Grenzraums*. München: Bayerische Akademie der Wissenschaften.
Eisch, Katharina 1999: Immer anfangen: Überlegungen zu Feldforschung und volkskundlicher Identität. *Schweizerisches Archiv für Volkskunde* 95:1, 61–72.
Hamm, Marion 2008: *Studying Practices around EuroMayDay: A Practice-Based Multisited Ethnography on Mediated Subjectivations*. http://www.protestmedia.net/cms/upload/Publikationen/08_hamm_talk2_subjectivity.pdf Accessed September 16, 2014.
Jeggle, Utz (ed.) 1984: *Feldforschung: Qualitative Methoden in der Kulturanalyse*. Tübingen: Tübinger Vereinigung für Volkskunde.
Lotman, Yuri M. 1977: *The Structure of the Artistic Text*. Ann Arbor, Michigan: University of Michigan.
Lotman, Yuri M. 1990: *Universe of the Mind: A Semiotic Theory of Culture*. London; New York: I.B. Tauris.
Marcus, George 1992: Past, Present and Emergent Identities: Requirements for Ethnographies of Late Twentieth-Century Modernity Worldwide. In: Scott Lash & Jonathan Friedman (eds.), *Modernity and Identity*. Oxford: Blackwell, pp. 309–330.
Nadig, Maya 1986: *Die verborgene Kultur der Frau: Ethnopsychoanalytische Gespräche mit Bäuerinnen in Mexiko*. Frankfurt a.M.: Fischer.
Nadig, Maya & Mario Erdheim 1984: Die Zerstörung der wissenschaftlichen Erfahrung durch das akademische Milieu: Ethnopsychoanalytische Überlegungen zur Aggressivität der Wissenschaft. In: *Der Spiegel des Fremden: Ethnopsychoanalytische Betrachtungen. Psychosozial* 23. Reinbek: Rowohlt, pp. 11–27.
Nadig, Maya & Mario Erdheim 1991: Ethnopsychoanalyse. In: *Herrschaft, Anpassung, Widerstand. Ethnopsychoanalyse* 2. Frankfurt a.M.: Brandes & Apsel, pp. 187–201.
Portis-Winner, Irene 2006: Eric Wolf: A Semiotic Exploration in Power. In: *Between Semiotics and Anthropology: Life Histories and other Methodological Issues. Sign System Studies* 34:2, 339–356.
Schönle, Andreas (ed.) 2006: *Lotman and Cultural Studies: Encounters and Extensions*. Madison, Wisconsin: The University of Wisconsin Press.
Sennett, Richard 1974: *The Fall of Public Man*. New York: Alfred A. Knopf.
Timm, Elisabeth 2013: Bodenloses Spurenlesen: Probleme der kulturanthropologischen Empirie unter den Bedingungen der Emergenztheorie. In: Timo Heimerdinger & Silke Meyer (eds.): *Äußerungen: Die Oberfläche als Gegenstand und Perspektive der Europäischen Ethnologie*. Beiträge der dgv-Hochschultagung „Äußerungen. Die Oberfläche als Gegenstand und Perspektive der Europäischen Ethnologie" vom 28. bis 30. September 2012 am Institut für Geschichtswissenschaften und Europäische Ethnologie der Universität Innsbruck. Vienna: Verein für Volkskunde, pp. 49–75.
Willis, Paul 1980: Notes on Method. In: Stuart Hall, Dorothy Hobson, Andrew Lowe & Paul Willis (eds.), *Culture, Media, Language*. London: Hutchinson, pp. 88–95.

Katharina Eisch-Angus is professor of cultural anthropology/European ethnology at Graz University, Austria. In her ethnographic research and freelance cultural work, with an emphasis on subject-oriented and semiotic methods, she has worked on themes of borders and difference, especially in Czech-German fields, of art and visual anthropology, and of transformations of industrial work culture. At present she is researching neoliberal changes towards a society of security in British everyday contexts.
(katharina.eisch-angus@uni-graz.at)

EXPERIMENTS IN A TIME OF OVER-ABUNDANT DISCIPLINARY HISTORY

Regina F. Bendix

There is a lot of past scholarship – not only but also in ethnology. New dissertations fill library shelves next to older works, a plethora of studies emerge from ongoing research, conference proceedings and ever more journals find their way into print and circulate in cyberspace. Listservs inform us regularly of calls for papers and of new publications and send us the table of contents of the latest journal issues, including this present one. The shere mass of it all can bring about a sense of oppression vis-à-vis all that came before and happens next to us, in our mother tongue and many other tongues, of which, perhaps, we are able to read, well, one or two at best. Billy Ehn and Orvar Löfgren have demonstrated how academic life, patterned by constant evaluation, comparison, and hence potentially despiriting or embittering competition, impacts the emotions of scholars (Ehn & Löfgren 2007). How is one to select? How is one to know, what of the past is relevant for the present? In the course of our training, we are generally exposed to selections of the past: theoretical paradigms and their methodological consequences form part of the disciplinary curriculum. The selection will be imprinted by our teachers and how far ranging or narrowly they interpret their role as intermediaries between a discipline's genesis and history and its present role in academy and society. Fellow students and our own adventuresomeness to read beyond the curriculum also shape our sense of discipline and intellectual belonging – whereby the former need not be congruent with the latter. An unruly and intrinsically interdisciplinary field such as ethnology with its focus on everyday life – synomymous with "potentially everything" – makes the interaction between past and present all the more difficult. To top it off, departmental contours, university reorganization, cuts and expansions further contribute to a need for alliances and opportunities or opportunism – depending on how one experiences the steady transformations – that hardly cater to a nurturing of disciplinary identity built on firm knowledge of its past.

The present collection of papers gives insight into this very selectivity and into alternative ways of handling the past creatively. They allow us to see what young and younger scholars in the ambit of Lund and Copenhagen have chosen from the disciplinary past, in what intellectual style they shape this encounter, and what goal they might strive for. The freshness of this "what," "how" and "to what end" may occasion something of a sting to European ethnologists committed to both properly unfolding the field in its national and European trajectories over more than two hundred years, and engaging with disciplinary history in the manner of historiography and supported with the considerable amount of scholarship available for such tasks. Grasping the discipline's growth entails major research in and of itself, as demonstrated in various lines of inquiry surrounding the ethnological and anthropological disciplines – and mentioned here, but briefly and superficially as a contrasting context into which to place the present papers. One might think of Giuseppe Cocchiara's classic tracing of the field in Europe at large (1952, English translation 1981), or of the sustained effort on the part of George W. Stocking regarding the history of anthropology, for which he was able to interest many others so that an entire series of edited works could emerge, covering topics from fieldwork (Stocking 1983), to museums and material culture (Stocking 1985), to the romantic tenets inherent to some anthropological beginnings (Stocking 1989), to mention just a few of the themes he encouraged research on. Similarly, cooperation and comparison – and a lot of legwork – is evident in the fourfold examination of social anthropological history offered at the opening of the Max Planck Institute for Social Anthropology in Halle (Barth et al. 2005), as well as in the historiographic endeavor edited by Henrika Kuklick (2008). Grappling with disciplinary history in our field invariably also leads one to the politics of ethnological knowledge production, and a sensitizing for the ideological vulnerability of the field, whether it be called ethnology or folklore or yet something else.[1] This has been thoroughly investigated particularly in Germany (e.g., Bausinger 1971; Brinkel 2012; Emmerich 1971), Ireland (e.g., Briody 2008; Ó Giolláin 2000), and Estonia (Kuutma 2005), with many case studies on selected aspects of ideological histories completed (e.g., Klein 2003) or under way elsewhere. Finally there is the history of disciplinary emergence in its complex interaction with socio-economic milieus and the serendipities of knowledge transfers brought about by persons and places, as pursued in a multi-part research endeavor lead by Wolfgang Kaschuba in Germany (e.g., Dietzsch, Kaschuba & Scholze-Irrlitz 2009; Kaschuba et al. 2009; Welz, Davidovic-Walter & Weber 2011), again just naming one example. All of these endeavors took and take time, and next to everything else that an academic professional has to undertake (see the first paragraph of this essay), the disciplinary past can easily turn into a foreign country that is not among the top ten places one hopes to still visit.

The present articles are, therefore, deliberately cast as a visit with aspects of European ethnology's past, and the kind of travel guides I just sketched above equally deliberately do not form part of the baggage. Trained and positioned differently amongst one another, these authors' travels also have highly divergent contours and outcomes, which hopefully will encourage others to consider past theories, archival deposits, individual oeuvres and lacunae in canonical topics as suitable sites for mental journeys.

Of the present articles, Signe Mellemgaard's portrait of Bjarne Stocklund comes closest to a more traditional historiographic engagement, with its focus on an individual scholar (such as, e.g., Zumwalt 1988, 1992) who pursued rupture and continuity, the familiar pairing of terms in twentieth-century social and cultural research. Ethnology all over Europe, as well as of course sociology, have addressed tradition and modernity, as well as tradition and innovation, critiquing a scholarly mindset focused on continuity alone (e.g., Bausinger & Brückner 1969). Yet even Mellemgaard's query contributes to the broader endeavor launched by these essays in as much as she, too, looks at the research and thinking practices that characterized Stoklund as an ethnologist. Also engaging with one protagonist from the past, but in completely presentist mode, Frida Hastrup's paper is at the farthest end of the experimental spectrum assembled in this issue. She reads and uses nineteenth-century Norwegian ethnologist Eilert Sundt's observations and thoughts on ethnographic work and the goals he formulated for this work, and extrapolates from it generalizable tenets on what ethnography is: putting Sundt's practices next to her own, and intermeshing that with field consultant and readers' participation "enables me to argue that ethnography is always about crafting and articulating different ideas, perspectives and practices in order to craft and articulate more ideas, perspectives and practices." Seeking to avoid any semblance of ethnography as representation, Hastrup writes from the purview of a globally mobile ethnologist, who experiences her work as a cooperative endeavor that "continually processes the world" and simultaneously participates in crafting a world to live in. Faded out are space and the particularities of historically circumscribed location, gender and status of the researcher, distance as well as the cumbersomeness of largely paper- and print-driven communication vis-à-vis the speed of communication in a digitally connected globe. The relevance of the "professional" disappears as he and she are shown to be but participants in world making. The specificities of Eilert Sundt's agency disappear in this effort to understand universals of ethnographic practice. Hastrup concludes that ethnography communicates "ways of living with the knowledge that alternative ways are (logically, if not always actually) possible," and maintains curiosity about these very alternatives. In this collapsing of time, place and circumstance, what disappears is the sense of purpose and responsibility a given disciplinary actor brings to the mix in a specific time and place. This may healthily lessen the self-import that inheres to disciplinary historiography, but it also lessens the sense of responsibility, purpose and meaning an individual is provided with or has to construct for her or his ethnographic doings within contextual specificities.

Karin Gustavsson's uncovering of fieldwork photographs and sketches opens vistas to a very different engagement with history, focused not on timeless disciplinary universals but rather seeking to witness the concrete ways of being in the field on the part of (then) young ethnologists measuring and photographing houses, leaving in their documentation very little evidence of the kind of interaction and co-creation of knowledge foregrounded by Hastrup. Illustration 2, "Having dinner together," with three properly suited men, even wearing ties, emphasizes the very distance between objects and makers. Giving space to the connection of builders and houses, rural hosts and urban academic guests is irrelevant for the task at hand, never mind whether it was felt and known in the experience of the measuring team: it was not part of the question to be answered. The picture transported me mentally to a photo showing the Swiss Volkskundler Richard Weiss and a group of his students posing with a cowherd in front of an alpine hut sometime in the early 1950s. The cowherd wears the attire suitably worn for working with livestock in high altitude, Weiss and his students wear suits and mid-hight shoes, which could not be less appropriate for the setting but mark the difference in milieu and purpose and allow one to imagine the peculiarities or rather, the normalicies, of ethnological study trips en groupe of that time. While the "thought collective's" assumptions about objectivity and photography have to be revised in Gustavsson's assessment, the suggestive power of photography is so present, that it has made it even on the cover of this issue of *Ethnologia Europaea*: a fieldworker wearing a student's cap – thus marking status in the field – jumping out of one of the measured houses bears testimony to the spirit present in this ethnological labor. Perhaps this was a rare snap shot, but it provides contours for an atmospheric contrast I glean between this Swedish practice of material culture research and stories I was told during my graduate training in folklore in the United States. There, one was introduced to stories about the lone researcher seeking traces of old houses, shying away neither from brambles nor the viles of poison ivy, and triumphing with evidence, carefully measured, photographed and drawn by himself, all attesting to the crafty mind of pioneer builders. Team effort and the assembly of an archive in Sweden smile at us out of such a photograh, while the scholarly loner in search of proof for his hypothesis is part of oral history in the USA. While the contributors to this issue may, in general, be weary of disciplinary history in and of itself, and comparison of this sort may lack appeal, Gustavsson's unearthing of disciplinary practice does open comparative horizons slightly akin to Johan Galtung's classic essay on intellectual styles (1981).

How else can one experiment with disciplinary pasts? Fredrik Nilsson starts with a set of historical source materials: reports on smugglers finding ways to transgress borders and evade border patrols provide seeds for a re-consideration of the parameters of present and past ethnological work on borders. Reports on smugglers having access to better and faster boats than the coast guard brings into focus speed as an elementary, largely overlooked component of border studies. In addition to the actual, measurable speed permitted by a given means of locomotion through land, water, or air, one immediately thinks of the felt speed or lack thereof by transgressors and pursuers, refugees and oppressors – dimensions that thicken the sensory and emotional understanding of the arbitrariness of borders. Anders Kristian Munk and Torben Elgaard Jensen develop their experiment out of the present: mapping endeavors in science and technology studies (STS) are brought into conversation with the folklife atlases of the early and mid-twentieth century. Here it is past ethnologists' critical engagement with the theoretical premise underlining their method that might stimulate STS researchers with regard to the premises underlying their work; out of the juxtaposition, ethnology might reconsider its departure from mapping and consider its use under new theoretical premises.

Tine Damsholt and Astrid Pernille Jespersen's experiment in uncovering disciplinarity in close encounters of the interdisciplinary kind struck home for me the most. For close to a decade, cultural and social anthropologists in Göttingen were involved in planning and carrying through an interdisciplinary project on cultural property with colleagues in economics, law, and subdisciplines of both. Even as the project draws to a close, principal investigators and perhaps even more so the junior scholars involved, recognize the power of disciplinary habits and the chasms that some conceptual and methodological differences cannot overcome without challenging disciplinary habits. Very often, we felt simply frustrated that "the others" still had not grasped, for example, our practice-based and dynamic concept of culture without realizing that for their methodological toolkit, a thickly contextualized and historized concept led to more variables than a potential model could accommodate. The interdisciplinary collaboration became an additional fieldsite. The ethnographers in the team, blessed by their discipline's capacity to find ethnographic interest in everything, used participant observation to better grasp what made the others tick; they pointed to events and discussions that illustrated blockades in understanding, and at least some of the other players participated in these cross-disciplinary reflections, some of us made interdisciplinarity the focus of an additional collaborative research and writing endeavor (Bendix, Bizer & Noyes, in preparation), and most firmed up their sense of what their own discipline could competently do while hesitating to formulate how this competence could benefit the interdisciplinary goal. Damsholt and Jespersen journeyed along this latter path but carried it to a potent conclusion. They felt irritated with the concepts and associated tasks allotted to them within an interdisciplinary project focused on innovation, but used this friction productively to examine the semantics of every day life – one of the concepts at issue in this project – in its permutations within ethnology's disciplinary past. The disciplinary self-understanding gained in their genealogical query helped them to turn about their contribution to the overall project so as to augment for the other participants how innovation needed to be reconceptualized so as to find accommodation within everyday life. While laborious in its rigor, Damsholt and Jespersen's focused engagement with ethnology's past is what one would want to recommend to all – not just ethnologists – who are headed into interdisciplinary undertakings. The insights, approaches, and concepts accumulated in a discipline's unfolding can be pruned to reveal their relevance in informing research about the present and contribute to the future.

Barbro Klein once gave the following advice: "I am thinking about a daily exercise that I do in my current work, one that often calms me down: I am part of a field but I am constantly open to other fields. I think this kind of positioning is essential for scholarly work" (Klein & Löfgren 2004: 108). The experiments assembled in this issue suggest an expansion to this advice, particularly if the (academic) world we live in and the mountains of ethnological historiography I sketched initially are causing stress and uncertainty: just as we can be open to other disciplines while being part of a particular field, we can be open to disciplinary history with the perspectives, interests and ethnological practices of the present.

Note
1 Due to the particular history of ethnology in Sweden and Denmark, work carrying the term folklore in its title may be automatically associated with research on verbal arts or even just narrative and therefore ex-

cluded from purview of a younger generation; in addition, the naming and renaming of the field in Sweden, from folklife to ethnology signalled departures from particular ways of inhabiting the discipline. During a workshop on naming the discipline in Göttingen, Orvar Löfgren noted that one way of handling the past and its national confines in Sweden was irony (Klein & Löfgren 2004: 96–97). The pragmatic handling of disciplinary names within one locale does lead to a narrowing of perception of what the field has and can contain and occasionally renders the notion of a European ethnology a misnomer, as for a long time one has practiced "ethnology in European countries." Even now, we tend to teach only excerpts of the disciplinary past of our national traditions and enmesh into our practice particularly those excerpts of international scholarship, particularly Anglo-American and French, that appear theoretically exciting. The excitement, in turn, is subject to an ecomony of notability that furthers the pragmatism of keeping focused. Every national or even local ethnological tradition interacts with international trends differently, making it even more difficult to web between the European ethnologies (Bendix 2004).

References

Barth, Fredrik, Andre Gingrich, Robert Parkin & Sydel Silverman 2005: *One Discipline, Four Ways: British, German, French, and American Anthropology*. The Halle Lectures. Chicago: University of Chicago Press.

Bausinger, Hermann 1971: *Volkskunde: Von der Altertumsforschung zur Kulturanalyse*. Berlin: Deutsche Buch-Gemeinschaft.

Bausinger, Hermann & Wolfgang Brückner (eds.) 1969: *Kontinuität? Geschichtlichkeit und Dauer als volkskundliches Problem*. Berlin: Schmidt.

Bendix, Regina 2004: Translating between European Ethnologies. In: A. Paládi-Kovacs et al. (eds.), *Times – Places – Passages: Ethnological Approaches to the New Millenium*. Budapest: Akademiai Kiado, pp. 371–380.

Bendix, Regina, Kilian Bizer & Dorothy Noyes, in preparation: Sustainable Interdisciplinarity: Social Research as Social Process.

Brinkel, Teresa 2012: *Volkskundliche Wissensproduktion in der DDR: Zur Geschichte eines Faches und seiner Abwicklung*. Münster: LIT-Verlag.

Briody, Michaél 2008: *The Irish Folklore Commission 1935–1970*. Studia Fennica Folkloristica 17. Helsinki: Finnish Literature Society.

Cocchiara, Giuseppe 1952: *La Storia del Folklore in Europa*. Turin: Einaudi. (English translation: *The History of Folklore in Europe*. Philadelphia: ISHI 1981.)

Dietzsch, Ina, Wolfgang Kaschuba & Leonore Scholze-Irrlitz (eds.) 2009: *Horizonte ethnographischen Wissens*. Köln: Böhlau.

Ehn, Billy & Orvar Löfgren 2007: Emotions in Academia. In: Helena Wulff (ed.), *The Emotions: A Cultural Reader*. New York: Berg, pp. 101–117.

Emmerich, Wolfgang 1971: *Zur Kritik der Volkstumsideologie*. Frankfurt a.M.: Suhrkamp.

Galtung, Johan 1981: Structure, Culture, and Intellectual Style: An Essay Comparing Saxonic, Teutotic, Gallic and Nipponic Approaches. *Social Science Information* 20:6, 817–856.

Kaschuba, Wolfgang et al. 2009: Volkskundliches Wissen und gesellschaftlicher Wissenstransfer: Zur Produktion kultureller Wissensformate im 20. Jahrhundert (DFG-Forschungsverbund). In: Thomas Hengartner et al. (eds.), *Bilder, Bücher, Bytes: Zur Medialität des Alltags*. Münster: Waxmann, pp. 183–199.

Klein, Barbro 2003: Silences, Cultural Historical Museums, and Jewish Life in Sweden. *Ethnologia Europaea* 33:2, 121–131.

Klein, Barbro & Orvar Löfgren 2004: Intermezzo: Workshop with Barbro Klein and Orvar Löfgren (transcript). In: Regina Bendix & Tatjana Eggeling (eds.), *Namen und was sie bedeuten: Beiträge zur Volkskunde in Niedersachsen 19*. Göttingen: Schmerse Verlag.

Kuklick, Henrika (ed.) 2008: *A New History of Anthropology*. Oxford: Blackwell.

Kuutma, Kristin (ed.) 2005: *Studies in Estonian Folkloristics and Ethnology: A Reader and Reflexive History*. Tartu: Tartu University Press.

Ó Giolláin, Diarmuid 2000: *Locating Irish Folklore: Tradition, Modernity, Identity*. Cork: University Press.

Stocking, George W. (ed.) 1983: *Observers Observed: Essays on Ethnographic Fieldwork*. History of Anthropology vol. 1. Madison: University of Wisconsin Press.

Stocking, George W. (ed.) 1985: *Objects and Others: Essays on Museums and Material Culture*. History of Anthropology vol. 3. Madison: University of Wisconsin Press.

Stocking, George W. (ed.) 1989: *Romantic Motives: Essays on Anthropological Sensibility*. History of Anthropology vol. 6. Madison: University of Wisconsin Press.

Welz, Gisela, Antonia Davidovic-Walter & Anke S. Weber (eds.) 2011: *Epistemische Orte: Gemeinde und Region als Forschungsformate*. Notizen 80. Frankfurt: Institut für Kulturanthropologie und Europäische Ethnologie.

Zumwalt, Rosemary L. 1988: *The Enigma of Arnold van Gennep (1873–1957): Master of French Folklore and Hermit of Bourg-la-Reine*. Helsinki: Suomalainen Tiedeakatemia.

Zumwalt, Rosemary L. 1992: *Wealth and Rebellion: Elsie Clews Parsons, Anthropologist and Folklorist*. Urbana: University of Illinois Press.

Regina F. Bendix has been co-editor of *Ethnologia Europaea* since 2007 and teaches cultural anthropology/European ethnology at Göttingen University, Germany.
(rbendix@gwdg.de)

Ethnologia Europaea
JOURNAL OF EUROPEAN ETHNOLOGY

Ethnologia Europaea is a lively and interdisciplinary, peer-reviewed journal with a focus on European cultures and societies. It carries material of great interest not only for European ethnologists and anthropologists but also for sociologists, social historians and scholars involved in cultural studies.

An impression of the areas covered by the journal is reflected in some of the thematic topics of the issues recently published: *Foodways Redux* (2013), *Imagined Families in Mobile Worlds* (2012), *Irregular Ethnographies* (2011), *Performing Nordic Spaces* (2010), *Sense of Community* (2009), *Europe* (2008), *Double Homes, Double Lives?* (2007).

For more information on purchase
and subscription visit
www.mtp.dk/ethnologia_europaea

Museum Tusculanum Press : : University of Copenhagen
Birketinget 6, 2300 Copenhagen S, Denmark
WWW.MTP.DK